The problem of disparities between different estimates of GDP is well known and widely discussed. Here, the authors describe a method for examining the discrepancies using a technique allocating them with reference to data reliability. The method enhances the reliability of the underlying data and leads to maximum-likelihood estimates. It is illustrated by application to the UK national accounts for the period 1920 to 1990. The book includes a full set of estimates for this period, including runs of industrial data for the period 1948 to 1990 which are longer than those available from any other source. The statistical technique allows estimates of standard errors of the data to be calculated and verified; these are presented both for data in levels and for changes in variables over 1, 2 and 5-year periods. A disc with the dataset in machine readable form is available separately.

STUDIES IN THE NATIONAL INCOME AND EXPENDITURE OF THE UNITED KINGDOM

a series published under the auspices of the

National Institute of Economic and Social Research, London

and

Department of Applied Economics, University of Cambridge

Founding editor

The late Sir Richard Stone

---

7 Reconciliation of national income and expenditure

Balanced estimates of national income for the United Kingdom, 1920–1990

STUDIES IN THE NATIONAL INCOME AND EXPENDITURE OF THE UNITED KINGDOM

The scope of the series is the measurement and analysis of the size, trend and interrelationships of the components of the British national income, output, expenditure, saving and asset formation. The investigations published in these *Studies* are confined to those undertaken at the National Institute of Economic and Social Research or at the Cambridge University Department of Applied Economics by members of their respective staffs and others working in direct collaboration with them.

The National Institute of Economic and Social Research and the Department of Applied Economics assume no responsibility for the views expressed in these *Studies*.

The titles in this series are:

1 *The Measurement of Consumers' Expenditure and Behaviour in the United Kingdom, 1920–1938*, vol. I, by RICHARD STONE, assisted by D. A. ROWE and by W. J. CORLETT, RENEE HURSTFIELD and MURIEL POTTER
2 *The Measurement of Consumers' Expenditure and Behaviour in the United Kingdom, 1920–1938*, vol. II, by RICHARD STONE and D. A. ROWE
3 *Consumers' Expenditure in the United Kingdom, 1900–1919*, by A. R. PREST, assisted by A. A. ADAMS
4 *Domestic Capital Formation in the United Kingdom, 1920–1938*, by C. H. FEINSTEIN using material provided by K. MAYWALD
5 *Wages and Salaries in the United Kingdom, 1920–1938*, by AGATHA L. CHAPMAN, assisted by ROSE KNIGHT
6 *National Income, Expenditure and Output of the United Kingdom, 1855–1965*, by C. H. FEINSTEIN
7 *Reconciliation of National Income and Expenditure: Balanced Estimates of National Income for the United Kingdom, 1920–1990*, by JAMES SEFTON and MARTIN WEALE

STUDIES IN THE NATIONAL INCOME AND EXPENDITURE OF THE UNITED KINGDOM

a series published under the auspices of the

National Institute of Economic and Social Research, London

and

Department of Applied Economics, University of Cambridge

Founding editor

The late Sir Richard Stone

---

7 Reconciliation of national income and expenditure

Balanced estimates of national income for the United Kingdom, 1920–1990

STUDIES IN THE NATIONAL INCOME AND EXPENDITURE OF THE UNITED KINGDOM

The scope of the series is the measurement and analysis of the size, trend and interrelationships of the components of the British national income, output, expenditure, saving and asset formation. The investigations published in these *Studies* are confined to those undertaken at the National Institute of Economic and Social Research or at the Cambridge University Department of Applied Economics by members of their respective staffs and others working in direct collaboration with them.

The National Institute of Economic and Social Research and the Department of Applied Economics assume no responsibility for the views expressed in these *Studies*.

The titles in this series are:

1 *The Measurement of Consumers' Expenditure and Behaviour in the United Kingdom, 1920–1938*, vol. I, by RICHARD STONE, assisted by D. A. ROWE and by W. J. CORLETT, RENEE HURSTFIELD and MURIEL POTTER
2 *The Measurement of Consumers' Expenditure and Behaviour in the United Kingdom, 1920–1938*, vol. II, by RICHARD STONE and D. A. ROWE
3 *Consumers' Expenditure in the United Kingdom, 1900–1919*, by A. R. PREST, assisted by A. A. ADAMS
4 *Domestic Capital Formation in the United Kingdom, 1920–1938*, by C. H. FEINSTEIN using material provided by K. MAYWALD
5 *Wages and Salaries in the United Kingdom, 1920–1938*, by AGATHA L. CHAPMAN, assisted by ROSE KNIGHT
6 *National Income, Expenditure and Output of the United Kingdom, 1855–1965*, by C. H. FEINSTEIN
7 *Reconciliation of National Income and Expenditure: Balanced Estimates of National Income for the United Kingdom, 1920–1990*, by JAMES SEFTON and MARTIN WEALE

Reconciliation of national income and expenditure

Balanced estimates of national income for the United Kingdom, 1920–1990

James Sefton and Martin Weale
National Institute of Economic and Social Research

CAMBRIDGE UNIVERSITY PRESS
Cambridge, New York, Melbourne, Madrid, Cape Town, Singapore, São Paulo, Delhi

Cambridge University Press
The Edinburgh Building, Cambridge CB2 8RU, UK

Published in the United States of America by Cambridge University Press, New York

www.cambridge.org
Information on this title: www.cambridge.org/9780521120074

First published 1995
This digitally printed version 2009

A catalogue record for this publication is available from the British Library

Library of Congress Cataloguing in Publication data

Sefton, James.
Reconciliation of national income and expenditure: balanced estimates of national income for the United Kingdom, 1920–1990 / James Sefton and Martin Weale.
p. cm. – (Studies in the national income and expenditure of the United Kingdom; 7)
Includes bibliographical references and index.
ISBN 0 521 49635 7
1. National income – Great Britain – Statistical methods. 2. Consumption (Economics) – Great Britain – Statistical methods. I. Weale, Martin, 1955– . II. Title. III. Series.
HC260. I5S44 1995
339.341–dc20 94–49047 CIP

ISBN 978-0-521-49635-3 hardback
ISBN 978-0-521-12007-4 paperback

Contents

Illustrations

Tables

Tables of balanced national accounts

Summary tables

Components of expenditure

Components of income

Sectoral current accounts

Sectoral capital accounts

Preface

This book is the seventh in a series which began in 1954 with Richard Stone's *The Measurement of Consumers' Expenditure and Behaviour in the United Kingdom, 1920–1938*. It follows Charles Feinstein's *National Income, Expenditure and Output of the United Kingdom, 1855–1965* which appeared in 1972. Despite the long interval since Feinstein's volume, we consider that this study is in very much the same intellectual tradition as the earlier volumes; we hope that it will prove a worthy companion. Richard Stone, the general editor of the earlier volumes, inspired this work and provided a great deal of encouragement in its early stages. We are profoundly sorry that he did not live to see it completed.

We are grateful to Charles Feinstein for allowing us to use his data source for the period 1920 to 1948 and to the Central Statistical Office for allowing us to publish results based on their data for the period 1946 to 1990. Both Charles Feinstein and Solomos Solomou also provided much helpful discussion. From the Central Statistical Office, Michael Baxter and Robin Lynch provided helpful comments on the manuscript and Shirley Carter was always ready to explain particular issues of national accounting.

The bulk of the work was carried out in the Department of Applied Economics with the kind support of the Economic and Social Research Council. We should, however, record our thanks to the National Institute of Economic and Social Research for tolerating the time that James Sefton has put into the study while working there.

The publishers of the *Journal of the Royal Statistical Society, Series A* and the *Journal of Applied Econometrics* have kindly given permission to publish material which first appeared in those journals.

Part one

The theory of data reconciliation

1 The reconciliation of national accounts

1.1 Introduction

There are, traditionally, three measures of GDP: expenditure, output and income. If these measures are calculated independently, they cannot be expected to be equal, because data are collected by surveys and other disparate sources which cannot be completely accurate. In practice the measures are reduced to two for each of constant and current prices. Factor incomes are not, at least in the United Kingdom, measured independently of the industries in which those incomes are earned. In constant prices output and expenditure are measured separately, but the income measure is calculated by applying the expenditure deflator to current price income, and it does not offer a third independent measure of output. Thus there are discrepancies between income and expenditure measured at current prices and output and expenditure measured at constant prices. This book discusses the question of how these different measures should be reconciled.

The first part of the book presents the statistical theory needed to solve the problem of reconciling inconsistent data. The second part explains how the methods can be applied to the UK national accounts for the period 1920 to 1990 and the third part presents new estimates for the same period, calculated by reconciling the inconsistent estimates provided by Feinstein (1972) for the period 1920 to 1948 and from the official sources from 1948 to 1990. Estimates of the standard deviations of the measurement errors associated with some of the key variables of interest are also presented.

Figure 1.1 shows the discrepancies between expenditure and income at current prices and expenditure and output measured at constant prices as a percentage of the expenditure measure.[1] There are no output measures

[1] Or, more accurately as $100\times\{\log(\text{Income or Output})-\log(\text{Expenditure})\}$.

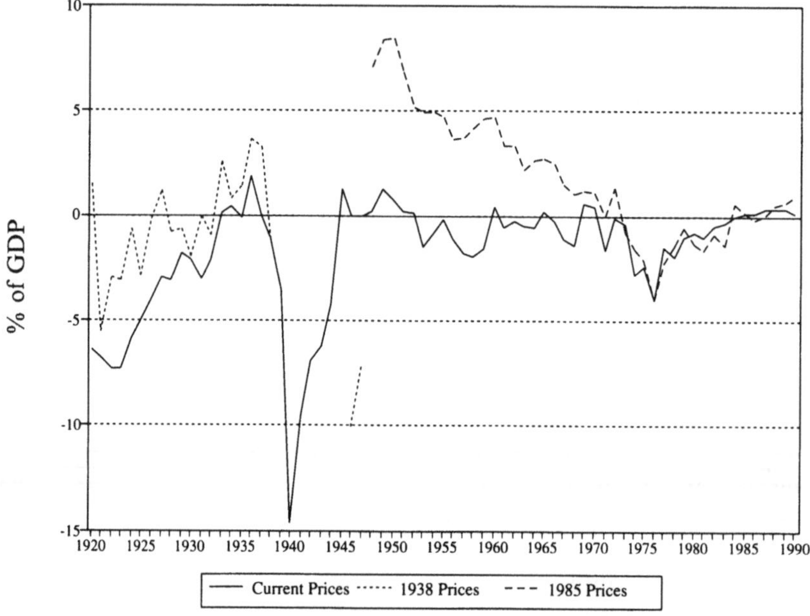

Fig. 1.1 The residual errors in constant and current price GDP

of GDP during the period 1939–45 and therefore no constant price residual can be calculated for this interval. It can be seen that the problems are more pronounced with constant than with current price data, but in neither case are they trivial. The constant price estimates are calculated to 1938 prices for the periods 1920 to 1938 and 1946 to 1947, with none being available for the war years. They are calculated to 1985 prices for the period 1948 to 1990. This means that in 1938 and in 1985 the discrepancies are the same in constant and current prices. In the period after 1948 there is a tendency for the two constant price measures to drift apart – a tendency which is absent from the current price data – while there seems to be a considerable amount of drift in both residuals before 1938. During the Second World War the two current price measures of GDP showed very substantial discrepancies.

The inconsistency between the expenditure and the income/output measure of GDP poses problems for the user of economic statistics. The aim of this book is threefold. First of all it presents the statistical theory of methods for resolving these discrepancies. Second, it treats UK national income as a case study for illustrating these methods and produces new estimates of UK national income and expenditure calculated using these methods. Third, it aims to make data users aware of the likely margins of error associated with the data which they use; to that end it presents estimates of standard errors of the data. The data presented in part three are also available on floppy disc (see Preface)

1.2 The average estimate of GDP

Godley and Gillion (1964) suggested resolving the inconsistency by taking an arithmetic average,[2] and for many years the mean of income and expenditure was the recommended measure of GDP at current prices. In constant prices the average of expenditure, income and output was used.

The method of averaging does not, on its own, allocate the discrepancy across the components of national income. If expenditure is above income, then averaging brings down aggregate expenditure, but it offers no indication as to how much of the adjustment should be allocated to consumption, investment, government consumption or trade flows.

There is another problem which arises from the interaction of constant and current price data. It may well be the case that in current prices expenditure is above income, while in constant prices it lies below output and deflated income. If the current price data are adjusted independently of the constant price data there may be large adjustments placed on the implicit deflator. One would be happy with a downward adjustment of current price expenditure if there were a similar adjustment in constant price expenditure. After all, many of the constant price data are simply measured by deflating the current price data. Account should be taken of this in the reconciliation process.

1.3 Allocation in recent estimates

Recently the presentation of official statistics has changed. The discrepancies are allocated in a manner which reflects, one way or another, the views of the statisticians concerned. While their method is nowhere described in detail, it is clear that it does not involve full use of the procedures explained below.

As far as the constant price measures are concerned, the output measure is regarded as defining movements of GDP in the short term, but in measuring output movements between base years (1948, 1958, 1963, 1970, 1975, 1980 and 1985) no weight at all is put on the output index, so that long-term movements in real GDP are estimated from the average of the income and expenditure data deflated by the expenditure

[2] We are grateful to David Savage for drawing their role to our attention.

GDP deflator. The methods by which the output index is elided into the deflated income/expenditure index are described in *Economic Trends*, No. 420 (CSO, 1988).

The current price data are treated slightly differently. The most recent estimates presented in the 1993 *Blue Book* (CSO, 1993a) show no residual at all between 1985 and 1990. This does not mean that the estimates are exact. The notes to the *Blue Book* explain that there were residuals of between £43m and £217m in 1985–8. These residuals were themselves derived after substantial use had been made of the 1989 and 1990 input–output tables (CSO, 1993a, pp. 144–5) to reconcile disparate sources. They have been allocated equally between income and expenditure, but no clues are given as to the components of income/expenditure to which the adjustments have been made. Thus this is, in aggregate, similar to averaging, with the errors allocated across the data in an undisclosed manner. In 1989 and 1990 no residuals are shown because the data are constructed from the input–ouput tables for those years; these tables are constructed to balance. The residuals remain in the pre-1985 data.

The averaging method is essentially arbitrary. The approach based on input–output tables relies on a great deal of disaggregated data and allows consideration of commodity balances as well as discrepancies between income and expenditure. In practice it may be similar to an application of the techniques described in this book, carried out in finer detail. However it is not applied to a long time-series in one go and so the mechanics of the adjustment process remain obscure.

As a separate exercise the CSO applies the techniques described in this book to a span of three years' data at a time. The results are described each November (e.g. CSO, 1993b), but the outcome does not appear in the standard national accounts, and the process of data revision means that, on each occasion, the coherent data set is only three years long.

1.4 Adjustment on the basis of data reliability

1.4.1 Least-squares/maximum-likelihood adjustment

Intuitively it makes a great deal of sense that those adjustments needed to create accounting balance should be borne in some inverse relation to the degree of confidence one has in the data. Any adjustments to expenditure data should be made disproportionately to variables like stockbuilding because it is known that this cannot be measured satisfactorily. The knowledge that the accounting constraints must be satisfied by the true data provides extra information which can be used to refine the accuracy of the data collected through conventional means.

The solutions to the problem of data inconsistency used hitherto can, of course, be seen in this context. If one believed that income and expenditure data were of equal reliability, then the arithmetic average would be the result produced by adjustment with reference to reliability. But the concept of reliability could be applied to the income/expenditure components and used to allocate the corrections across the series which make up the national accounts. This would lead to a fully consistent set of income/expenditure data.

Such a dataset may lead to important changes in the way economic variables are perceived. For example, in the period 1920 to 1924 a negative personal sector savings ratio is shown by Feinstein (1972). But at the same time the expenditure measure of GDP is well above the income measure. Since personal consumption is the largest component of expenditure and wage income the largest type of factor income, any reconciliation will almost certainly reduce consumption and raise personal income, thereby raising the savings ratio. Adjustments of this type, which do no more than reflect accounting identities, cannot be made unless the adjustments are allocated across the income/expenditure components.

The reliability with which changes in data are measured is of course closely related to that with which levels are measured. The link between the two depends on the degree of serial correlation in the measurement error. If there are large measurement errors in the output index, but they are strongly serially correlated, then it makes sense to put more weight on the output index in the short run than in the long run. But to give no weight to it in the long run, as is current practice, implies that it conveys no information at all about long-run movements in output; this seems inherently unlikely.

The idea of adjusting data with reference to reliability has to be given a precise meaning. The most usual way of doing this is to minimise the sums of the squared changes of the data, weighted by the variances of the measurement errors of the data: this gives balanced data which are a linear combination of the initial data. Thus, if the variance of expenditure were half that of income, two-thirds of the adjustment would be borne by income and one-third by expenditure. As is implicit in this example, it is the relative and not the absolute variances of the data which determine the allocation of the adjustments. This makes considerable sense since the residuals to be allocated are determined by the measurement process. The least-squares estimates which emerge from this process have the attraction that, if the original measurement errors are normally distributed, they are also maximum-likelihood estimators: this is a general property of least-squares estimators.

It is a property of estimators calculated by minimising the sum of squares that they are the linear estimators with the lowest variance (or best linear unbiased estimators). Not only can one calculate the variances of the reconciled data, but one can also be assured that they are lower than those which would be delivered by some other linear combination, such as the arithmetic average.

Obviously, this conclusion is dependent on starting with the correct data variances. If incorrect variances are supplied it is no longer possible to be sure that the reliability of the data is enhanced. Where nothing is known about data reliability, it might be sensible to start from an assumption of equal reliability, but it is still necessary to decide whether this means equal proportionate reliability or equal absolute reliability.

1.4.2 Covariances

The discussion so far has assumed that the measurement errors in one variable are independent of those in other variables. In such a case the variance matrix of the data is diagonal. However, it is not universally true that measurement errors are independent of each other. For example, some of the data used to measure government consumption (on the expenditure side) may also be used to measure output of public administration and defence on the income/output side. In such a case adjustments to government consumption also imply adjustments to public administration and defence output, and will be of relatively little use in reconciling discrepancies between income and expenditure. The covariances between different entries in the data are represented by diagonal elements in the variance matrix of the dataset.

At the level at which we have worked, there is not much evidence of problems of this type, although we have made allowances for the effect described above. However, there are two very important ways in which off-diagonal elements arise. The first is from the presence of constant and current price data. If the constant price data are calculated by deflating current price data, then there will be a covariance between the two equal to the variance of the current price data. The second arises from serial correlation. This means that the error in a variable in one period is correlated with that error in the same variable in a different period, so that an adjustment to a variable in one year would also imply an adjustment to the same variable in neighbouring years. Serial correlation can be taken account of by considering a long time-series of observations of the components of the national accounts simultaneously. The data can be stacked as a single data vector which has to satisfy accounting constraints for each year of the component data. The effect of serial correlation shows up in off-diagonal elements of the variance matrix of this multi-period dataset. The technique is then just the same as when data for a single observation are considered. It is only the size of the problem which is larger. This approach is used in part three of this book.

1.4.3 Validation of the variance matrix

The approach assumes that a data variance matrix can be inferred from available sources. The researcher is, nevertheless, not left completely at the mercy of those providing the data variance matrix. It is possible to carry out two tests to see whether the variance matrix is consistent with the data. From the variance matrix it is possible to calculate the variance matrix of the accounting residuals. This is simply a linear transformation of the data variance matrix. In the simplest case, in which there is only one accounting residual, the variance matrix is a scalar equal to the sum of the income and expenditure variances. One can then test the actual variance of the residual against the hypothesised variance calculated from the statisticians' estimates of data reliability, and adjust relevant parameters in order to ensure that well-defined criteria are satisfied.

1.4.4 Hypothesis testing

The structure offered by least-squares/maximum-likelihood adjustment provides opportunities for testing behavioural hypotheses. There is no doubt about the validity of the accounting restrictions; they must be true. But one may wish to test behavioural restrictions to see if they are true. The algebra of behavioural restrictions is just like that of accounting restrictions, but since the introduction of restrictions is achieved by maximum-likelihood estimation, successive restrictions can be tested by means of likelihood-ratio tests. One may, for example, wish to test whether the measurement error in the data is such that they would accept the hypothesis that imports equals exports. It is not enough simply to look at the measurement errors in imports and exports in order to assess this. A reduction in imports would require an increase in factor incomes or a reduction in domestic demand if the GDP identity is to be maintained. The test must therefore be carried out with reference to all the data in the accounts concerned, and not just with reference to external flows.

1.4.5 Unobserved components

It might be thought that, in the national accounts, there would be accounting constraints applying to the sectoral data as well as to the components of GDP. For example, the current account of the balance of payments, identified as the gap between exports and imports of goods and services (including property income), should be offset exactly by the capital flows identified in the financial accounts. This would suggest that the observed gap between the two is a residual like the residual in the GDP account.

Unfortunately this is not correct. Observed financial transactions do not cover all financial transactions. Large items such as flows of trade credit are not recorded and it is unlikely that it will ever be possible to record them in full sectoral detail (Begg and Weale, 1992). This means that the sectoral financial balances do not offer extra usable constraints. They must be calculated as residual items; the fact that balancing ensures that the GDP identity is satisfied means, nevertheless, that these residual balances will satisfy the constraint of adding to zero across all the sectors. More generally, one must be careful to distinguish genuine accounting residuals from figures which combine them with unobserved data.

1.4.6 Unknown variances

The discussion so far has focused on the need for some estimates of data reliability in order to make the least-squares adjustment possible. Is it possible to make the adjustments without knowledge of data reliability? The answer turns out to be yes. If the residuals are regressed on the data, then the regression coefficients converge asymptotically to the weights which would be used to allocate the residuals if the true error variance matrix were known. Furthermore, it is possible to carry out statistical tests on the weights to test, for example, the hypothesis that two different observations of the same variable should be given equal weight.

The analysis can be extended to the case where the measurement errors are proportional to some linear combination of the data. One would not expect the absolute standard deviation of money consumption to be the same now as it was in 1948, but it may well be a constant proportion of nominal GDP. Thus problems of heteroscedasticity can be avoided.

Nevertheless, this result is not as helpful as might be thought, at least with the sort of dataset we consider in part two. It turns out that, with the number of observations available, no degree of precision can be given to the estimated weights. This problem could have been resolved by making more assumptions about the underlying structure of the data. The methods suggested by Harvey (1989) would be suitable means of doing this. Instead, however, we have used assumptions about the data variance. These are derived from published information on data reliability and are then assessed using the tests of the data variances summarised above.

2 Basic issues in data reconciliation

2.1 Introduction

This chapter sets out the simple theory of the estimation of national accounts data from a number of disparate sources, building on the results which were first presented by Stone, Champernowne and Meade (1942) and Durbin and Fischer (1953). The method has since been applied by Byron (1978), van der Ploeg (1982), Barker, van der Ploeg and Weale (1984), and Dunn and Egginton (1990). Kenny (1989) presents the first official application to UK data.

The idea underlying the method of this chapter, and indeed the basis for the whole of this book, is that data are collected from a number of independent sources, in order to compile the component entries of the national accounts. These component entries are distinguished from a disorderly system of data, in that they should satisfy a number of accounting identities. Because the data are collected from disparate sources on the basis of sample surveys which may have an incomplete sampling frame, the accounting identities will not normally be satisfied in the raw data. This problem may be aggravated if transactions can be observed, but there is uncertainty as to the time period in which they took place.

The failure of the accounting identities to be satisfied means that there are a number of residuals typically observed in the accounts. In the UK national accounts these residuals are visible as the error between expenditure and income measures of GDP, and as a discrepancy in the measured financial saving of each institutional sector. Not too much attention should be paid to the latter because the measure of financial saving is not comprehensive. However, as figure 1.1 (p. 4) shows, the discrepancies between the measures of GDP can be substantial. Obviously more careful measurement is a way of improving the reliability of the statistics and so reducing the discrepancies; this book is not intended to argue against the benefits of more accurate data collection. But improved data collection is not the only way of dealing with the problem of the residual errors. We show that it can be complemented by statistical techniques which have the effect of allocating the residual errors and, in doing so, of enhancing the accuracy of the data.

2.2 Least-squares estimation

The basic result can be derived by the method of least-squares, as originally suggested by Stone, Champernowne and Meade (1942), or as a maximum-likelihood estimate (Weale, 1985). It is assumed that there is a data vector $\mathbf{x}$, which should satisfy the accounting constraints, $\mathbf{Ax}=\mathbf{s}$. In many cases $\mathbf{s}$ will be the zero vector. There are, however, some circumstances in which it may be non-zero. Perhaps the best-known of these is the situation in which the components of an input–output table are being adjusted to meet known marginal totals.[1] However, because of the problem of measurement errors, in fact $\mathbf{Ax}=\mathbf{r}$, where $\mathbf{r}$ is a vector of accounting residuals. It is also assumed that the observed data are distributed without bias around the true data $\mathbf{x}^*$ with known variance matrix $\mathbf{V}$, so that

$$\mathbf{x} = \mathbf{x}^* + \epsilon \tag{2.1}$$

with

$$E(\epsilon) = 0 \tag{2.2}$$

and

$$E(\epsilon\epsilon') = \mathbf{V}. \tag{2.3}$$

The least-squares problem is then one of finding a vector $\mathbf{x}^{**}$ which satisfies the accounting constraints, $\mathbf{Ax}^{**} = \mathbf{s}$, and is as close as possible to the observed data, $\mathbf{x}$. Closeness could be defined in a number of ways. Here we choose to define it as the sum of the squared deviation of each element of $\mathbf{x}^{**}$ from $\mathbf{x}$, weighted by the data reliability matrix, $\mathbf{V}$.

Proposition 1: *The best least-squares estimator*, $\mathbf{x}^{**}$ *of the data* $\mathbf{x}$ *which satisfies the accounting constraints* $\mathbf{Ax}^{**} = \mathbf{s}$ *is:*

[1] See Bacharach (1970) for an account of the *rAs* method of achieving the same end. The *rAs* method does not, however, meet any clear statistical criteria and is quite different from this method.

$$\mathbf{x}^{**} = [\mathbf{I} - \mathbf{VA}'(\mathbf{AVA}')^{-1}\mathbf{A}]\mathbf{x} + \mathbf{VA}'(\mathbf{AVA}')^{-1}\mathbf{s}. \tag{2.4}$$

Proof: The problem is that of minimising

$$(\mathbf{x}^{**} - \mathbf{x})'\mathbf{V}^{-1}(\mathbf{x}^{**} - \mathbf{x}) \tag{2.5}$$

subject to the constraint

$$\mathbf{Ax}^{**} = \mathbf{s}. \tag{2.6}$$

This can be set out as a Lagrangian

$$\text{Min } L = (\mathbf{x}^{**} - \mathbf{x})'\mathbf{V}^{-1}(\mathbf{x}^{**} - \mathbf{x}) - \lambda(\mathbf{Ax}^{**} - \mathbf{s}) \tag{2.7}$$

Differentiating with respect to $\mathbf{x}^{**}$

$$\frac{\partial L}{\partial \mathbf{x}^{**}} = 2\mathbf{V}^{-1}(\mathbf{x}^{**} - \mathbf{x}) - \mathbf{A}'\lambda \tag{2.8}$$

Setting this equal to zero we find

$$\mathbf{VA}'\lambda = \mathbf{2}(\mathbf{x}^{**} - \mathbf{x}). \tag{2.9}$$

Premultiplying by $\mathbf{A}$ and rearranging

$$\lambda = 2(\mathbf{AVA}')^{-1}\mathbf{A}(\mathbf{x}^{**} - \mathbf{x}) \tag{2.10}$$

and, since $\mathbf{Ax}^{**} = \mathbf{s}$,

$$\lambda = -2(\mathbf{AVA}')^{-1}(\mathbf{Ax} - \mathbf{s}). \tag{2.11}$$

Substituting this in (2.9), we find

$$\mathbf{x}^{**} = [\mathbf{I} - \mathbf{VA}'(\mathbf{AVA}')^{-1}\mathbf{A}]\mathbf{x} + \mathbf{VA}'(\mathbf{AVA}')^{-1}\mathbf{s}. \tag{2.12}$$

It can be seen that this estimator is unaffected by premultiplication of the variance matrix $\mathbf{V}$ by any scalar constant. This implies that the balancing process depends on relative but not on absolute data reliability.

It follows from (2.12), not very surprisingly, that this estimator is unbiased. Since $E(\mathbf{x}) = \mathbf{x}^*$ and $\mathbf{Ax}^* = \mathbf{s}$,

$$E(\mathbf{x}^{**}) = [\mathbf{I} - \mathbf{VA}'(\mathbf{AVA}')^{-1}\mathbf{A}]\mathbf{x}^* + \mathbf{VA}'(\mathbf{AVA}')^{-1}\mathbf{s} = \mathbf{x}^*. \tag{2.13}$$

Balancing of the data also leads to a reduction (or at least to no increase) in the data variance. This can be demonstrated by evaluating the variance matrix of the balanced data.

Proposition 2: *The variance of* $\mathbf{x}^{**}$, $\mathbf{V}^{**}$ *is*

$$\mathbf{V}^{**} = \mathbf{V} - \mathbf{VA}'(\mathbf{AVA}')^{-1}\mathbf{AV}. \tag{2.14}$$

Proof:

$$\begin{aligned}\mathbf{V}^{**} &= E(\mathbf{x}^{**} - E[\mathbf{x}^{**}])(\mathbf{x}^{**} - E[\mathbf{x}^{**}])' \\ &= (\mathbf{I} - \mathbf{VA}'[\mathbf{AVA}']^{-1}\mathbf{A})(\mathbf{x} - E[\mathbf{x}]) \\ &= (\mathbf{x} - E[\mathbf{x}])'(\mathbf{I} - \mathbf{A}'[\mathbf{AVA}']^{-1}\mathbf{AV}) \\ &= \mathbf{V} - \mathbf{VA}'[\mathbf{AVA}']^{-1}\mathbf{AV}, \end{aligned} \tag{2.15}$$

since $\mathbf{A}E[\mathbf{x}] = \mathbf{s}$, because the expected values of the observed data satisfy the accounting constraints.

Since $\mathbf{VA}'(\mathbf{AVA}')^{-1}\mathbf{AV}$ is a positive semi-definite matrix, it follows that the process of least-squares balancing has the effect of not making the data less accurate. In normal circumstances, when there are discrepancies in the original data, $\mathbf{VA}'(\mathbf{AVA}')^{-1}\mathbf{AV}$ will be positive definite, and balancing results in a gain in reliability.

2.2.1 The maximum-likelihood solution

Just as in ordinary regression, so too with data estimation, the maximum-likelihood estimator calculated on the assumption that the error vector, ϵ, is normally distributed, is the same as the least-squares estimator.[2] For, with this extra assumption, the likelihood function of the estimate is given as

$$L = T/(2\pi)^{\frac{1}{2}}|\mathbf{V}|e^{-(\mathbf{x}-\mathbf{x}^*)'\mathbf{V}^{-1}(\mathbf{x}-\mathbf{x}^*)/2}. \tag{2.16}$$

If one is to choose an estimator, $\mathbf{x}^{**}$ of $\mathbf{x}^*$ which maximises the likelihood, and therefore the log-likelihood, subject to the constraint that $\mathbf{Ax}^{**} = \mathbf{s}$, then, with $\mathbf{V}$ known, the problem is simply

$$\text{Min } -(\mathbf{x} - \mathbf{x}^{**})\mathbf{V}^{-1}(\mathbf{x} - \mathbf{x}^{**}), \tag{2.17}$$

given $\mathbf{Ax}^{**} = \mathbf{s}$, and this is exactly the same as the problem to be solved in calculating the least-squares solution. The two estimators are identical.

2.2.2 Step-by-step estimation

In any balancing exercise, the constraints are normally imposed simultaneously. Nevertheless, there may be good reasons why it is easier to

[2] This follows directly from the Cramer–Rao inequality (Cramer, 1946; Rao, 1945).

adopt a step-by-step approach, imposing the accounting constraints in two or more stages. It can be shown that, provided the variance matrix in use is updated to reflect the accounting constraints which have already been imposed, step-by-step balancing gives the same results as are found when all the restrictions are imposed in one go. The proof is presented in three stages, considering first the situation where the data are split into only two groups.

Proposition 3a: *If the restrictions are split into two groups so that* $\begin{bmatrix}\mathbf{A}_1\\ \mathbf{A}_2\end{bmatrix}\mathbf{x}^{**} = \begin{bmatrix}\mathbf{s}_1\\ \mathbf{s}_2\end{bmatrix}$, *then*

$$\begin{aligned}\mathbf{x}^{**} = [\mathbf{I} - \mathbf{V}_1\mathbf{A}_2'(\mathbf{A}_2\mathbf{V}_1\mathbf{A}_2')^{-1}\mathbf{A}_2]\{[\mathbf{I} - \mathbf{V}\mathbf{A}_1'(\mathbf{A}_1\mathbf{V}\mathbf{A}_1')^{-1}\mathbf{A}_1]\mathbf{x} \\ + \mathbf{V}\mathbf{A}_1'(\mathbf{A}_1\mathbf{V}\mathbf{A}_1')^{-1}\mathbf{s}_1\} + \mathbf{V}_1\mathbf{A}_2'(\mathbf{A}_2\mathbf{V}_1\mathbf{A}_2')^{-1}\mathbf{s}_2\end{aligned} \tag{2.18}$$

where

$$\mathbf{V}_1 = \mathbf{V}[\mathbf{I} - \mathbf{A}_1'(\mathbf{A}_1\mathbf{V}\mathbf{A}_1')^{-1}\mathbf{A}_1\mathbf{V}]. \tag{2.19}$$

Proof: It follows from proposition 1 that

$$\begin{aligned}\mathbf{x}^{**} = \left\{\mathbf{I} - \mathbf{V}[\mathbf{A}_1' \ \mathbf{A}_2']\begin{bmatrix}\mathbf{A}_1\mathbf{V}\mathbf{A}_1' & \mathbf{A}_1\mathbf{V}\mathbf{A}_2'\\ \mathbf{A}_2\mathbf{V}\mathbf{A}_1' & \mathbf{A}_2\mathbf{V}\mathbf{A}_2'\end{bmatrix}^{-1}\begin{bmatrix}\mathbf{A}_1\\ \mathbf{A}_2\end{bmatrix}\right\}\mathbf{x} \\ + \mathbf{V}[\mathbf{A}_1' \ \mathbf{A}_2']\begin{bmatrix}\mathbf{A}_1\mathbf{V}\mathbf{A}_1' & \mathbf{A}_1\mathbf{V}\mathbf{A}_2'\\ \mathbf{A}_2\mathbf{V}\mathbf{A}_1' & \mathbf{A}_2\mathbf{V}\mathbf{A}_2'\end{bmatrix}^{-1}\begin{bmatrix}\mathbf{s}_1\\ \mathbf{s}_2\end{bmatrix}.\end{aligned} \tag{2.20}$$

Now, Schur's matrix inversion formula states that

$$\begin{aligned}\begin{bmatrix}\mathbf{A} & \mathbf{B}\\ \mathbf{B}' & \mathbf{D}\end{bmatrix}^{-1} = \begin{bmatrix}\mathbf{A}^{-1} & -\mathbf{A}^{-1}\mathbf{B}\\ 0 & \mathbf{I}\end{bmatrix} \\ \begin{bmatrix}\mathbf{A} & 0\\ 0 & (\mathbf{D} - \mathbf{B}'\mathbf{A}^{-1}\mathbf{B})^{-1}\end{bmatrix}\begin{bmatrix}\mathbf{A}^{-1} & -\mathbf{A}^{-1}\mathbf{B}\\ 0 & \mathbf{I}\end{bmatrix}'.\end{aligned} \tag{2.21}$$

Here

$$\begin{aligned}\mathbf{D} - \mathbf{B}'\mathbf{A}^{-1}\mathbf{B} &= \mathbf{A}_2\mathbf{V}\mathbf{A}_2' - \mathbf{A}_2\mathbf{V}\mathbf{A}_1'(\mathbf{A}_1\mathbf{V}\mathbf{A}_1')^{-1}\mathbf{A}_1\mathbf{V}\mathbf{A}_2' \\ &= \mathbf{A}_2(\mathbf{V} - \mathbf{V}\mathbf{A}_1'[\mathbf{A}_1\mathbf{V}\mathbf{A}_1']^{-1}\mathbf{A}_1\mathbf{V})\mathbf{A}_2' \\ &= \mathbf{A}_2\mathbf{V}_1\mathbf{A}_2'.\end{aligned}$$

Substituting in and multiplying out

$$\mathbf{x}^{**} = \Bigg\{ \mathbf{I} - \mathbf{V}\left[\mathbf{A}_1'(\mathbf{A}_1\mathbf{V}\mathbf{A}_1')^{-1} \quad (\mathbf{I} - \mathbf{A}_1'[\mathbf{A}_1\mathbf{V}\mathbf{A}_1']^{-1}\mathbf{A}_1\mathbf{V})\mathbf{A}_2'\right]$$

$$\begin{bmatrix} \mathbf{A}_1\mathbf{V}\mathbf{A}_1' & \mathbf{0} \\ \mathbf{0} & (\mathbf{A}_2\mathbf{V}_1\mathbf{A}_2')^{-1} \end{bmatrix}$$

$$\left.\begin{bmatrix} (\mathbf{A}_1\mathbf{V}\mathbf{A}_1)^{-1}\mathbf{A}_1 \\ -\mathbf{A}_2(\mathbf{I} - \mathbf{V}\mathbf{A}_1'[\mathbf{A}_1\mathbf{V}\mathbf{A}_1']^{-1}\mathbf{A}_1) \end{bmatrix}\right\}\mathbf{x}$$

$$+\mathbf{V}\left[\mathbf{A}_1'(\mathbf{A}_1\mathbf{V}\mathbf{A}_1')^{-1} \quad (\mathbf{I} - \mathbf{A}_1'[\mathbf{A}_1\mathbf{V}\mathbf{A}_1']^{-1}\mathbf{A}_1\mathbf{V})\mathbf{A}_2'\right]$$

$$\begin{bmatrix} \mathbf{A}_1\mathbf{V}\mathbf{A}_1' & \mathbf{0} \\ \mathbf{0} & (\mathbf{A}_2\mathbf{V}_1\mathbf{A}_2')^{-1} \end{bmatrix}$$

$$\begin{bmatrix} (\mathbf{A}_1\mathbf{V}\mathbf{A}_1)^{-1}\mathbf{s}_1 \\ \mathbf{s}_2 - (\mathbf{A}_2\mathbf{V}\mathbf{A}_1'[\mathbf{A}_1\mathbf{V}\mathbf{A}_1']^{-1}\mathbf{s}_1) \end{bmatrix}$$

$$= \Bigg\{ [\mathbf{I} - \mathbf{V}\mathbf{A}_1'(\mathbf{A}_1\mathbf{V}\mathbf{A}_1')^{-1}\mathbf{A}_1]$$

$$-\mathbf{V}_1\mathbf{A}_2'(\mathbf{A}_2\mathbf{V}_1\mathbf{A}_2')^{-1}\mathbf{A}_2$$

$$\left.[\mathbf{I} - \mathbf{V}\mathbf{A}_1'(\mathbf{A}_1\mathbf{V}\mathbf{A}_1')^{-1}\mathbf{A}_1]\right\}\mathbf{x}$$

$$+[\mathbf{I} - \mathbf{V}_1\mathbf{A}_2'(\mathbf{A}_2\mathbf{V}_1\mathbf{A}_2')^{-1}\mathbf{A}_2]\mathbf{V}\mathbf{A}_1'(\mathbf{A}_1\mathbf{V}\mathbf{A}_1')^{-1}\mathbf{s}_1$$

$$+\mathbf{V}_1\mathbf{A}_2'(\mathbf{A}_2\mathbf{V}_1\mathbf{A}_2')^{-1}\mathbf{s}_2$$

$$= \Bigg\{ [\mathbf{I} - \mathbf{V}_1\mathbf{A}_2'(\mathbf{A}_2\mathbf{V}_1\mathbf{A}_2')^{-1}\mathbf{A}_2]$$

$$\{[\mathbf{I} - \mathbf{V}\mathbf{A}_1'(\mathbf{A}_1\mathbf{V}\mathbf{A}_1')^{-1}\mathbf{A}_1]\mathbf{x}$$

$$\left.+\mathbf{V}\mathbf{A}_1'(\mathbf{A}_1\mathbf{V}\mathbf{A}_1')^{-1}\mathbf{s}_1\}\right\}$$

$$+\mathbf{V}_1\mathbf{A}_2'(\mathbf{A}_2\mathbf{V}_1\mathbf{A}_2')^{-1}\mathbf{s}_2.$$

Proposition 3b: *Let x_1 be the best least square estimate of x^* satisfying $A_1x_1 = S_1$ given the variance matrix V and data x. Let x_2 be the best least square estimate of x^* satisfying $A_2x_2 = S_2$ given the variance matrix $V_1 = V - VA_1(A_1VA_1')^{-1}V$ and data x_1 then x_2 is also the best least square estimate of x^* satisfying $\begin{bmatrix} A_1 \\ A_2 \end{bmatrix} x_2 = \begin{bmatrix} S_1 \\ S_2 \end{bmatrix}$ given the variance matrix V and data x.*

Proof:

$$\begin{aligned} \mathbf{x_1} =& [\mathbf{I} - \mathbf{VA_1'}(\mathbf{A_1VA_1'})^{-1}\mathbf{A_1}]\mathbf{x} \\ & + \mathbf{VA_1'}(\mathbf{A_1VA_1'})^{-1}\mathbf{s_1} \end{aligned}$$

from proposition 1; $\text{var}(\mathbf{x_1}) = \mathbf{V_1}$ defined by (2.19) from proposition 2.

$$\begin{aligned} \mathbf{x_2} =& (\mathbf{I} - \mathbf{V_1A_2'}[\mathbf{A_2V_1A_2'}]^{-1}\mathbf{A_2})\mathbf{x_1} \\ & + \mathbf{V_1A_2'}(\mathbf{A_2V_1A_2'})^{-1}\mathbf{s_2} \\ =& [\mathbf{I} - \mathbf{V_1A_2'}(\mathbf{A_2V_1A_2'})^{-1}\mathbf{A_2}] \qquad (2.22) \\ & \{[\mathbf{I} - \mathbf{VA_1'}(\mathbf{A_1VA_1'})^{-1}\mathbf{A_1}]\mathbf{x} \\ & + \mathbf{VA_1'}(\mathbf{A_1VA_1'})^{-1}\mathbf{s_1}\} \\ & + \mathbf{V_1A_2'}(\mathbf{A_2V_1A_2'})^{-1}\mathbf{s_2} \\ =& \mathbf{x}^{**} \qquad (2.23) \end{aligned}$$

from (2.18) in proposition 3a.

Proposition 3c: *Consider the series of restrictions*

$$\begin{bmatrix} A_1 \\ A_2 \\ : \\ A_n \end{bmatrix} x = \begin{bmatrix} S_1 \\ S_2 \\ : \\ S_n \end{bmatrix} \qquad (2.24)$$

and define

$$\begin{aligned} \mathbf{x_j} =& (\mathbf{I} - \mathbf{V_{j-1}A_j'}[\mathbf{A_jV_{j-1}A_j'}]^{-1}\mathbf{A_j})\mathbf{x_{j-1}} \\ & + \mathbf{V_{j-1}A_j'}(\mathbf{A_jV_{j-1}A_j'})^{-1}\mathbf{s_j} \\ \mathbf{V_j} =& \mathbf{V_{j-1}} - \mathbf{V_{j-1}A_j'}[\mathbf{A_jV_{j-1}A_j'}]^{-1}\mathbf{A_j})\mathbf{V_{j-1}} \qquad (2.25) \end{aligned}$$

where $\mathbf{x_0} = \mathbf{x}$ *and* $\mathbf{V_0} = \mathbf{V}$. *Then* $\mathbf{x_n} = \mathbf{x}^{**}$.

Proof: Proposition 3b proves the result for $n = 2$. The first $n - 1$ restrictions can be grouped together. It follows immediately that $P(n-1) \Rightarrow P(n)$. But proposition 1 implies that $P(1)$ is true and hence by mathematical induction $P(n)$ is true.

2.3 Aggregation

Related to the question of estimation in stages is the issue of whether the results of a balancing exercise are sensitive to the level of aggregation at which the balancing is performed. It turns out that this is not the case, provided that the aggregation does not change the nature of the restrictions imposed.

Our balanced estimator $\mathbf{x}^{**}$ of the data vector $\mathbf{x}$ is

$$\mathbf{x}^{**} = \left[\mathbf{I} - \mathbf{VA}'(\mathbf{AVA}')^{-1}\mathbf{A}\right]\mathbf{x} + \mathbf{VA}'(\mathbf{AVA}')^{-1}\mathbf{s}. \tag{2.26}$$

Proposition 4: *A linear combination* $\mathbf{y} = \mathbf{Cx}^{**}$ *of the balanced data is equal to the vector found by balancing the same linear combination of the original data,* $\mathbf{Cx}$, *satisfying the accounting constraints* $\mathbf{By}^{**} = \mathbf{s}$ *using variance matrix* $\mathbf{U} = \mathbf{CVC}'$.

Proof: First of all note, $\mathbf{BC} = \mathbf{A}$. The balanced estimate of the aggregate vector is

$$\begin{aligned}
\mathbf{y}^{**} &= [\mathbf{I} - \mathbf{UB}'(\mathbf{UBU}')^{-1}\mathbf{B}]\mathbf{y} + \mathbf{UB}'(\mathbf{UBU}')^{-1}\mathbf{s} \\
&= \left[\mathbf{I} - \mathbf{CVC'B}'(\mathbf{BCVC'B}')^{-1}\mathbf{B}\right]\mathbf{y} \\
&\quad + \mathbf{CVC'B}'(\mathbf{BCVC'B}')^{-1}\mathbf{s} \\
&= \mathbf{C} - \mathbf{CVA}'(\mathbf{AVA}')^{-1}\mathbf{Ax} \\
&\quad + \mathbf{CVA}'(\mathbf{AVA}')^{-1}\mathbf{s} = \mathbf{Cx}^{**}
\end{aligned} \tag{2.27}$$

and is therefore the same as the aggregate of the balanced vector.

It can be seen that $\mathbf{BC} = \mathbf{A}$ is essential to the above proof. This will only hold if the aggregation matrix $\mathbf{C}$ does not aggregate so as to remove any of the accounting constraints. Otherwise aggregation changes the number of restrictions imposed; it is not surprising that this changes the balanced data.

2.4 Derived data

One particular point to be aware of is that some of the data in a set of national accounts may be derived. If personal sector saving is calculated as the gap between income and consumption, then knowledge of this identity cannot be used to improve the reliability of the underlying data. It is as though the savings estimate has an infinite variance, so that it adjusts to accommodate the constraints imposed by the rest of the accounting framework.

Such a situation can also arise if only part of an aggregate is identified. For example the UK and US national accounts provide estimates of financial saving, but these estimates do not cover all financial assets. Coverage of trade credit is only partial (Begg and Weale, 1992). This means that the accounting identities for the different sectors do not convey any further information.

Suppose that the data are divided into two groups (Barker, van der Ploeg and Weale, 1984): $\mathbf{x}_1$ represents the known data and $\mathbf{x}_2$ the derived data. The variance matrix of the known data is $\mathbf{V}_1$. The accounting constraints are

$$\mathbf{A}_1\mathbf{x}_1 + \mathbf{A}_2\mathbf{x}_2 = \mathbf{0}. \tag{2.28}$$

The problem now becomes

$$\text{Min}(\mathbf{x}_1^{**} - \mathbf{x}_1)'\mathbf{V}_1^{-1}(\mathbf{x}_1^{**} - \mathbf{x}_1) + \lambda(\mathbf{A}_1\mathbf{x}_1^{**} + \mathbf{A}_2\mathbf{x}_2^{**}). \tag{2.29}$$

The first-order conditions are

$$\begin{aligned} \mathbf{x}_1^{**} &= -\mathbf{V}_1\mathbf{A}_1'\lambda + \mathbf{x}_1 \\ \mathbf{A}_2'\lambda &= 0 \\ \mathbf{A}_1\mathbf{x}_1^{**} + \mathbf{A}_2\mathbf{x}_2^{**} &= 0 \end{aligned} \tag{2.30}$$

and the solution is given as

$$\begin{aligned} \mathbf{x}_1^{**} &= \mathbf{x}_1 - \mathbf{V}_1\mathbf{A}_1'(\mathbf{A}_1\mathbf{V}_1\mathbf{A}_1')^{-1}(\mathbf{A}_1\mathbf{x}_1 + \mathbf{A}_2\mathbf{x}_2^{**}) \\ \mathbf{x}_2^{**} &= -\,[\mathbf{A}_2'(\mathbf{A}_1\mathbf{V}_1\mathbf{A}_1')^{-1}\mathbf{A}_2]^{-1} \\ &\quad \mathbf{A}_2'(\mathbf{A}_1\mathbf{V}_1\mathbf{A}_1')^{-1}\mathbf{A}_2\mathbf{x}_2. \end{aligned} \tag{2.31}$$

The *ex-post* variances are

$$\begin{aligned} \mathbf{V}_{11}^{**} &= \mathbf{V}_1 - \mathbf{V}_1\mathbf{A}_1'(\mathbf{A}_1\mathbf{V}_1\mathbf{A}_1')^{-1}(\mathbf{A}_2\mathbf{V}_{12}^{**} + \mathbf{A}_1\mathbf{V}_1) \\ \mathbf{V}_{12}^{**} &= \mathbf{V}_{11}^{**} - \mathbf{A}_2'(\mathbf{A}_1\mathbf{V}_1\mathbf{A}_1')^{-1}\mathbf{A}_1\mathbf{V}_1 \\ \mathbf{V}_{22}^{**} &= [\mathbf{A}_2'(\mathbf{A}_1\mathbf{V}_1\mathbf{A}_1')^{-1}\mathbf{A}_2] \end{aligned}$$

where $\mathbf{V}_{11}^{**} = \mathrm{Var}(\mathbf{x}_1^{**})$, $\mathbf{V}_{12}^{**} = \mathrm{Cov}(\mathbf{x}_1^{**}, \mathbf{x}_2^{**})$ and $\mathbf{V}_{22}^{**} = \mathrm{Var}(\mathbf{x}_2)$.

Note that the solution can only be found if $\mathbf{A}_1\mathbf{V}_1\mathbf{A}_1'$ is invertible. For the identification of the unidentified items we require

$$\mathrm{rank}\{\mathbf{A}_2'(\mathbf{A}_1\mathbf{V}_1\mathbf{A}_1')^{-1}\mathbf{A}_2\} \leq \mathrm{dim}(\mathbf{x}_2) \tag{2.32}$$

and it follows that $\mathrm{dim}(\mathbf{x}_1)$ cannot be greater than the number of independent restrictions for the unidentified items to be extracted.

If there is one unidentified item per account, this implies that no balancing is possible. The accounting constraints are satisfied simply by calculating the unknown items as residuals.

This situation is in fact exploited in part two. The accounting structure dichotomises into two groups. There are the GDP identities in constant and current prices for which all the items are known. Beyond this there are the institutional/transfer accounts. Here each account contains a residual item. In the transfer accounts it is clear that some items are residual because there are no accounting discrepancies. Sectoral financial saving is residual because not all items are identified. In other words, the step-by-step approach of section 2.2.2 is applied with the accounting constraints imposed sequentially, and with the variance matrix being updated at each stage. However, once the GDP constraints have been imposed and the variance matrix updated, there are, at the next stage, as many independent unidentified items as there are new accounting constraints. No further balancing is possible since the latter can be satisfied simply by recalculating the residual items.

This means that the sectoral accounts can be calculated using the balanced GDP figures. There is no basis for changing any of the transfer estimates and the financial balances of the institutional sectors are calculated by subtraction. While it would be desirable to have independent estimates of transfers and financial saving, the absence of such estimates greatly facilitates the calculations.

2.5 Sensitivity analysis

Having calculated our data estimator, we are naturally concerned about the sensitivity of it to the underlying assumptions. What is the effect of a change in either the raw data or the data reliability on the estimated vector, $\mathbf{x}^{**}$?

2.5.1 A change in data

The effect of a change in data on the balanced estimator is worked out easily, because the balanced data are a linear function of the raw data.

Differentiating (2.13) shows that the effect of a change in the jth element of $\mathbf{x}$ on the ith element of $\mathbf{x}^{**}$ is given as

$$\frac{dx_i^{**}}{dx_j} = [\mathbf{I} - \mathbf{VA}'(\mathbf{AVA}')^{-1}\mathbf{A}], \tag{2.33}$$

so that changes in the raw data are allocated in the same way as the data themselves.

2.5.2 *A change in the reliability*

The effect of a change, $d\mathbf{V}$, in the variance matrix, $\mathbf{V}$ is slightly more complicated. Using the product rule,

$$d\mathbf{x}^{**} = d\mathbf{VA}'(\mathbf{AVA}')^{-1}(\mathbf{Ax} - \mathbf{s}) + \mathbf{VA}'d(\mathbf{AVA}')^{-1}(\mathbf{Ax} - \mathbf{s}). \tag{2.34}$$

Now,

$$d(\mathbf{AVA}')^{-1} = -(\mathbf{AVA}')^{-1}\mathbf{A}d\mathbf{VA}'(\mathbf{AVA}')^{-1} \tag{2.35}$$

and, using this result we may write

$$\begin{aligned} d\mathbf{x}^{**} &= d\mathbf{VA}'(\mathbf{AVA}')^{-1}(\mathbf{Ax} - \mathbf{s}) \\ &\quad - \mathbf{VA}'(\mathbf{AVA}')^{-1}\mathbf{A}d\mathbf{VA}'(\mathbf{AVA}')^{-1}(\mathbf{Ax} - \mathbf{s}) \\ &= [\mathbf{I} - \mathbf{VA}'(\mathbf{AVA}')^{-1}\mathbf{A}]d\mathbf{VA}'(\mathbf{AVA}')^{-1}(\mathbf{Ax} - \mathbf{s}). \end{aligned} \tag{2.36}$$

We can see that the effect of a change in the reliability is like a change in the raw data of

$$d\mathbf{x} = d\mathbf{VA}'(\mathbf{AVA}')^{-1}(\mathbf{Ax} - \mathbf{s}) \tag{2.37}$$

in that both are allocated across the balanced data by premultiplication by $\mathbf{I} - \mathbf{VA}'(\mathbf{AVA}')^{-1}\mathbf{A}$. This, incidentally, guarantees that the perturbed data will also satisfy the accounting constraints.

2.5.3 *Testing of linear hypotheses*

The other side of the issue of sensitivity of the results to initial data and of identifying the changes needed in order to ensure that the data satisfy certain constraints is the question of hypothesis testing. The data must satisfy the accounting constraints, but there may be other additional behavioural constraints which it is desirable to test. It is true that the variance matrix allows us to calculate confidence limits for each element of the data vector, but this does not allow for the fact that, in view of the accounting constraints, a change in one element implies changes in the other elements of the vector; this has to be taken into account in assessing whether the behavioural constraints are plausible or not.

The behavioural constraints can be denoted as the linear condition

$$\mathbf{Bx} = \mathbf{0}. \tag{2.38}$$

The result of section 2.2.2 implies that the answer can be found in one of two ways. One may use the least-squares solution for the joint restrictions, $\mathbf{Ax}_\mathbf{B}^{**} = \mathbf{0}$ and $\mathbf{Bx}_\mathbf{B}^{**} = \mathbf{0}$. Or the restrictions $\mathbf{Bx}_\mathbf{B}^{**} = \mathbf{0}$ can be applied to the balanced vector $\mathbf{x}^{**}$ using $\mathbf{V}^{**}$ as the relevant variance matrix.

The natural structure for investigating the plausibility of the behavioural constraints is offered by the maximum-likelihood framework of section 2.2.1 (see Weale, 1985). The value of the log-likelihood can be calculated, first of all just with the accounting constraints in place and, second, with both accounting and behavioural constraints in place. Twice the difference between the two is χ^2 distributed with the number of degrees of freedom equal to the number of extra restrictions imposed by the behavioural constraints.

If $\mathbf{x}^{**}$ is the least-squares/maximum-likelihood estimator which satisfies the accounting constraints, and $\mathbf{x}_\mathbf{B}^{**}$ is the maximum-likelihood estimator which satisfies the linear constraints, $\mathbf{Ax}_\mathbf{B}^{**}$ and $\mathbf{Bx}_\mathbf{B}^{**} = \mathbf{0}$, then the statistic

$$\begin{aligned} Z &= (\mathbf{x} - \mathbf{x}_\mathbf{B}^{**})'\mathbf{V}^{-1}(\mathbf{x} - \mathbf{x}_\mathbf{B}^{**}) \\ &\quad - (\mathbf{x} - \mathbf{x}^{**})'\mathbf{V}^{-1}(\mathbf{x} - \mathbf{x}^{**}) \\ &\sim \chi_q^2 \end{aligned} \tag{2.39}$$

where q is the rank of the matrix $\mathbf{B}$ and thus of the number of behavioural restrictions which are being tested.

The χ^2 test is of course a large sample test. It is worth noting that the small-sample adjustment described by Evans and Savin (1982) can be applied. If N is the number of variables in the $\mathbf{x}$-vector and p is the number of accounting restrictions (the rank of $\mathbf{A}$), then the F-statistic can be calculated as

$$F(q, N - P) = (e^{Z/N} - 1)(N - p)/q. \tag{2.40}$$

2.6 The Mahalanobis criterion

The other side of hypothesis testing is offered by the Mahalanobis criterion, which should be mentioned here. Since it is known that the accounting constraints must be true, the χ^2 statistic

$$Z = \sum_t (\mathbf{x}_t - \mathbf{x}_t^{**})\mathbf{V}^{-1}(\mathbf{x}_t - \mathbf{x}_t^{**}), \tag{2.41}$$

which defines the distance of the balanced data from the raw data, can be regarded as a measure of the accuracy with which **V** is measured. There are t observations with r restrictions per year. This means that there are tr degrees of freedom.

In fact the calculation of the Mahalanobis score can be simplified. Substituting for $\mathbf{x}^{**}$ in Z using (2.4) with $\mathbf{s}=0$,

$$Z' = \sum_t \mathbf{x}_t'\mathbf{A}'(\mathbf{AVA}')^{-1}\mathbf{AVV}^{-1}\mathbf{VA}'(\mathbf{AVA}')^{-1}\mathbf{Ax}_t \tag{2.42}$$

$$= \sum_t \mathbf{x}_t\mathbf{A}'(\mathbf{AVA}')^{-1}\mathbf{Ax}_t. \tag{2.43}$$

Thus the Mahalanobis score is simply the χ^2 statistic which would be calculated if the assumed variance matrix of the residuals $\mathbf{AVA}'$ were assessed against the residuals, $\mathbf{Ax}_t$ themselves.

The most likely value of the χ^2 statistic is $\chi^2_{tr}(50\%) = N$ since the likelihood function takes its maximum at the median value. One can therefore argue (see Stone, 1987; Baxter, 1992) that $Z\mathbf{V}/N$ offers a better estimate of the variance matrix than does **V** on its own. Scaling of the variance matrix does not, of course, change the balanced data estimates.

Stone (1987) notes, applying this to a single year, that it suggests a level of accuracy much higher than that believed by the national accountants and also one much higher than the subsequent experience of revisions suggests. One possible reason for this may be that there is strong serial correlation in the measurement errors, and that any application which is more than illustrative must recognise this. Certainly the observation, frequently made by statisticians, that changes are measured more reliably than levels, supports the view that there is serial correlation present.

2.7 Serial correlation

2.7.1 Common autocorrelation in the measurement errors

Simple results can only be obtained if the pattern of autocorrelation is common to all the variables. This section extends the earlier results for the case where there is common autocorrelation of order K in the residuals. It should be presumed to take the form specified in proposition 5.

Proposition 5: *If the vector of measurement errors follows the pattern*

$$\epsilon_t = \sum_{k=1}^{K} \rho_k \epsilon_{t-k} + \upsilon_t \tag{2.44}$$

with $E(\upsilon_t \upsilon_{t+k}) = \mathbf{U}, (k = 0), E(\upsilon_t \upsilon_{t+k}) = 0, (k \neq 0)$ *and* ρ_k *scalar then the least squares/maximum-likelihood estimator of* $\mathbf{x_t}$ *is*

$$\mathbf{x_t^{**}} = [\mathbf{I} - \mathbf{VA'}(\mathbf{AVA'})^{-1}\mathbf{A}]\mathbf{x_t}. \tag{2.45}$$

(The proposition and proof are set out with the restriction that $\mathbf{Ax_t} = 0$. This makes them less involved than if $\mathbf{Ax_t} = \mathbf{s_t}$ but does not affect the basic argument. The proposition does not require $\mathbf{s_t} = 0$ to be true.)

Proof: Consider $\mathbf{z_t} = \mathbf{x_t} - \sum_{\mathbf{k=1}}^{\mathbf{K}} \rho_\mathbf{k} \mathbf{x_{t-k}}$. $\mathbf{z}$ satisfies the accounting constraints, since

$$\mathbf{Az_t} = \mathbf{A}\left(\mathbf{x_t} - \sum_{\mathbf{k=1}}^{\mathbf{K}} \rho_\mathbf{k} \mathbf{x_{t-k}}\right) = \mathbf{Ax_t} - \sum_{\mathbf{k=1}}^{\mathbf{K}} \rho_\mathbf{k} \mathbf{Ax_{t-k}} = 0. \tag{2.46}$$

For the reasons given in section 2.2, a balanced estimator of $\mathbf{z_t}$, $\mathbf{z_t^{**}}$ is therefore

$$\mathbf{z_t^{**}} = [\mathbf{I} - \mathbf{UA'}(\mathbf{AUA'})^{-1}\mathbf{A}]\mathbf{z_t}. \tag{2.47}$$

Now, from the definition of $\mathbf{U}$ and $\mathbf{V}$,

$$\mathbf{V} = \mathbf{U} + \psi\mathbf{V} \quad \text{or} \quad \mathbf{U} = \frac{\mathbf{V}}{1-\psi} \tag{2.48}$$

where $\psi = \psi(\rho_1, ..., \rho_K)$ is calculated by evaluating the expected value of ϵ_t^2 with ϵ_t defined by (2.44), and hence

$$\begin{aligned} \mathbf{z_t^{**}} &= \left[\mathbf{I} - \frac{\mathbf{VA'}}{1-\psi}\left(\frac{\mathbf{AVA'}}{1-\psi}\right)^{-1}\mathbf{A}\right]\mathbf{z_t} \\ &= [\mathbf{I} - \mathbf{VA'}(\mathbf{AVA'})^{-1}\mathbf{A}]\mathbf{z_t}. \end{aligned} \tag{2.49}$$

Equation (2.49) will only hold true for any $\mathbf{x_t}$ making up $\mathbf{z_t}$ if

$$\mathbf{x_t^{**}} = [\mathbf{I} - \mathbf{VA'}(\mathbf{AVA'})^{-1}\mathbf{A}]\mathbf{x_t}, \tag{2.50}$$

showing that the least-squares/maximum-likelihood estimator (2.12) is unaffected by common autocorrelation.

2.7.2 General autocorrelation

In the more general case in which the pattern of serial correlation can take any form, the solution has to be found by stacking the data, observation vector by observation vector, to give a single large vector. This has to be adjusted to satisfy the accounting restrictions in each year. The variance–covariance matrix of the large vector has, on its diagonal, the variance matrices for the data in each individual year. The off-diagonal terms represent the correlations between the measurement errors in one year and those in another year and thus reflect the serial correlation in the measurement errors.

If $\mathbf{z}' = \mathbf{x}_1', \mathbf{x}_2' ..., \mathbf{x}_T'$,

$$\mathbf{W} = \begin{pmatrix} \mathbf{V}_{11} & \mathbf{V}_{12} & \cdots & \mathbf{V}_{1T} \\ \mathbf{V}_{21} & \mathbf{V}_{22} & \cdots & \mathbf{V}_{2T} \\ .. & .. & \cdots & .. \\ \mathbf{V}_{T1} & \mathbf{V}_{T2} & \cdots & \mathbf{V}_{TT} \end{pmatrix} \tag{2.51}$$

$$\mathbf{D} = \begin{pmatrix} \mathbf{A} & 0 & \cdots & 0 \\ 0 & \mathbf{A} & \cdots & 0 \\ 0 & 0 & \cdots & 0 \\ 0 & 0 & \cdots & \mathbf{A} \end{pmatrix} \tag{2.52}$$

then the vector of balanced data is given as

$$\mathbf{z}^{**} = \left[\mathbf{I} - \mathbf{W}\mathbf{D}'(\mathbf{D}\mathbf{W}\mathbf{D}')^{-1}\mathbf{D}\right]\mathbf{z}. \tag{2.53}$$

This is the estimation method used in part two of this book. Obviously, the Mahalanobis criterion can be applied to $\mathbf{z}'\mathbf{D}'(\mathbf{D}\mathbf{W}\mathbf{D}')^{-1}\mathbf{D}\mathbf{z}$ with the number of the degrees of freedom being the total number of restrictions in $\mathbf{D}$.

2.8 Constant and current price data

Special mention should be made of the issues raised by the reconciliation of constant and current price data. Only the more recent studies of problems of data reconciliation have looked at this (Weale, 1988, Solomou and Weale, 1991, 1993), with the earlier ones looking solely at current price data.

Care needs to be taken with constant price data for two reasons. First of all, there may well be a correlation between the constant price data and their current price equivalent. If an adjustment is made to current price consumption, but no change is made to constant price consumption, then there is an implicit change in the price of consumption goods. If this price is believed to be measured reasonably accurately, then a change in current price consumption should be broadly reflected in a change in constant price consumption.

The basic non-linear identity underlying this is

$$Value = Volume \times Price.$$

None of these variables is measured independently. Usually either value and volume data are measured, with prices being implicit, or value and price data are measured with volumes being derived; there may, however, be some cases in which value data are calculated from observed volumes and prices. It should be noted that there do not seem to be any examples in which all three are measured giving rise to an inconsistency.

There may be information on the extent to which volume data are calculated by deflation rather than by direct observation (CSO, 1985) and if one can say that a fraction k of volume data are measured by direct observation, with the remainder $1 - k$ being measured by deflation, then the covariance between the value and the volume data is

$$(1 - k) \times \textit{Variance of the value data.}$$

The off-diagonal elements of the data variance–covariance matrix can be calculated in this way. However, if one works at a reasonable level of disaggregation, it may be the case that k is either 1 or 0 (see part two).

The second point arises from the fact that constant price data are always in the prices of some base-year.[3] Any change in the base-year data, arising from their balancing, must lead to a change in all the constant price data based on that year. In other words, there is covariance between constant price data away from the base-year and the current price data of the base-year equal to the variance of the current price base-year data. This has to be reflected in the covariance matrix of the data. This too is discussed at greater length in part two.

2.9 Illustration

2.9.1 The Central Statistical Office exercise

The application of these methods by statistical offices is relatively rare despite the enthusiasm shown by some official statisticians (see Kenny, 1991). Official statistics sometimes show the discrepancies, as in the United Kingdom until recently, or the United States. Alternatively the residuals are allocated on a basis which may correspond approximately

[3] This point was missed by Weale (1988) and Solomou and Weale (1991).

to least-squares balancing, with the residuals being allocated to those components which are believed to be least reliable. The most recent national accounts for the UK have followed this procedure and the manner in which it was done means that it is not possible to identify where the residuals have been added.

There have, nevertheless, been a number of applications of least-squares. The first example is provided by Arkhipoff (1969) for the Cameroons. Byron (1978) showed how the method could be used to estimate a social accounting matrix for Malaysia. His study was particularly important in that it presented an algorithm for the calculation of the least-squares solution without the need to calculate $(\mathbf{AVA}')^{-1}$. This made it possible to balance a social accounting matrix with a large number of accounting constraints. Barker, van der Ploeg and Weale (1984) applied Byron's method to the reconciliation of a 297×297 social accounting matrix of the United Kingdom for 1975. Antonello (1990) has calculated an Italian input–output table on the same basis.

Kenny (1989) presents the results of a study by the Central Statistical Office looking at the least-squares balancing of UK national accounts in current prices. That study, which looked separately at the years 1985, 1986 and 1987, provides the material for the illustrations which are discussed here. Kenny took the estimates for 1987 available at the time of his study, and asked those responsible for the various items to provide information on biases which they thought might be present, but which were too speculative to be included in the official estimates. These bias corrections were then added on, to give the estimates shown in table 2.1.[4] Ninety per cent confidence intervals were also provided by those collecting the data: the error ranges, denoted as unreliabilities, shown in table 2.1 represent half those ninety per cent confidence ranges and might therefore be taken to represent $1.64 \times$ the standard deviation of each item.

There are a number of accounting constraints in this dataset. First of all, net transfers should sum to zero. There is in fact a discrepancy of −£0.8bn in this sum. Second, taxes on capital should (and do) sum to zero. Third, the net acquisition of financial assets in the economy should sum to zero once the overseas sector is taken into account, and there is a discrepancy of −£0.8bn. These discrepancies are introduced in the bias corrections; the published national accounts do not show any inconsistencies in these data.

It then follows that the receipts of each sector (personal, industrial and

[4] The disaggregate detail of financial assets in Kenny's article has been consolidated solely for reasons of convenience.

commercial, financial, public and overseas, with the financial sector disaggregated to monetary and other financial in the capital accounts) should equal its payments; income from employment is a receipt of the personal sector and imports are a receipt of and exports a payment by the overseas sector. These identities offer five further constraints. As the table shows, there are substantial errors in the raw data which lead to marked discrepancies in these sectoral accounts.

The accounting constraints described above have made no reference to the GDP identity, which the balanced data should obviously satisfy. The reason for this is that once all the above identities are satisfied, then the GDP identity will also be satisfied as it is linearly dependent on those eight accounting constraints described above.

As expected, the balancing process results in the largest adjustments being made to the least reliable data. Industrial profits change by £2.76bn and there are very substantial changes to the sectoral net acquisition of financial assets, with the net acquisition of financial assets by the personal sector rising by £12.6bn and a balance of payments deficit (positive net acquisition of financial assets by the overseas sector) of £3.9bn turning into a surplus of £1.235bn. However, a high unreliability does not guarantee a large adjustment, as the figure for the net transfers of the financial companies shows; the reason for this is that a large adjustment to this figure would not greatly facilitate meeting the accounting identities.

The table also shows the unreliabilities (0.5×90 per cent confidence intervals) of the balanced data. It can be seen that there are useful reductions in unreliability achieved through balancing, with the biggest reductions generally being associated with the largest changes in the data. Such improvements could otherwise only be achieved by a careful reassessment of the methods of data collection.

Two further columns are shown. Kenny presents results with an additional constraint that the balanced figure of GDP should equal the average of the income and the expenditure estimates, denoted as GDP(A). There is no rationale for this to be true, but nevertheless it may be something acceptable to the data, and it can be imposed as described in section 2.2.2 and then tested using the χ^2 test of section 2.5.3. These data are shown in column (b). A second linear restriction is also imposed. Noting that the balance of payments changes sign between the raw and the balanced data, it seems reasonable to consider the restriction that the balance of payments deficit (= net acquisition of financial assets by the overseas sector) is zero. The resulting data are shown in column (c). This second restriction can also be tested before it is imposed. Both restrictions are accepted with $\chi_1^2 = 1.8$ for GDP=GDP(A), $\chi_1^2 = 1.4$ for zero balance of payments and $\chi_2^2 = 2.3$ for the hypotheses taken jointly. It can be seen that the bulk of this adjustment is met by an adjustment to net transfers received by the overseas sector. The shift of £0.8bn compares with an error range (= 1.64 × the standard deviation) of £4.2bn; although other adjustments have to be made to maintain the adding-up properties of the data, it is not very surprising that the restriction on the balance of payments is accepted. The imposition of these further restrictions would lead to a further reduction in the unreliabilities associated with the data. However, the 'enhancement' of the national accounts by the imposition of such restrictions has little to recommend it.

Table 2.1 *Balanced national accounts: the United Kingdom, 1987*

	Raw data	Reliability		Balanced data		
		before balancing	after balancing	a	b	c
Income from employment	227.4	3.7	3.1	228.8	228.9	228.5
Gross profits and other trading income						
Personal	34.4	1.4	1.4	34.6	34.6	34.6
Ind. cos	68.9	3.2	2.6	65.1	65.2	65.0
Fin. cos	−4.4	2.8	2.3	−6.3	−6.3	−6.5
Public	6.4	0.3	0.3	6.3	6.3	6.3
Other factor income						
Personal	18.7	1.3	1.3	18.9	18.9	18.8
Ind. cos	−1.3	0.8	0.8	−1.5	−1.5	−1.5
Fin. cos	0.4	0.1	0.1	0.4	0.4	0.4
Public	6.3	0.3	0.3	6.2	6.2	6.2
Factor cost adjustment	62.2	0.2	0.2	62.2	62.2	62.2
Net transfers						
Personal	−4.7	2.3	2.1	−2.8	−2.6	−2.6
Ind. cos	−27.2	2.7	2.3	−28.0	−27.8	−27.7
Fin. cos	18.0	4.2	2.8	18.2	18.6	18.8
Public	15.8	0.2	0.2	15.8	15.8	15.8
Overseas	−2.5	4.2	2.9	−3.2	−4.0	−4.2
Consumption						
Personal	−260.1	3.4	2.9	−259.0	−258.9	−258.3
Public	−85.8	0.4	0.4	−85.9	−85.9	−85.9
Exports	−106.1	1.6	1.5	−106.9	−107.0	−107.0
Imports	111.9	1.5	1.4	111.2	111.1	111.1
Gross capital formation						
Personal	−21.0	1.3	1.3	−20.8	−20.8	−20.7
Ind. cos	−32.8	2.0	1.9	−34.3	−34.2	−34.0

Table 2.1 (*cont.*)

	Raw data	Reliability before balancing	Reliability after balancing	Balanced data a	Balanced data b	Balanced data c
Mon. sec.	−1.3	0.1	0.1	−1.3	−1.3	−1.3
Oth. fin. cos.	−7.0	0.5	0.5	−7.1	−7.1	−7.0
Public	−10.6	0.4	0.4	−10.7	−10.7	−10.7
Taxes on capital						
Personal	−0.3	0.1	0.1	−0.3	−0.3	−0.3
Ind. cos	−0.4	0.1	0.1	−0.4	−0.4	−0.4
Mon. sec.	0.0	0.0	0.0	0.0	0.0	0.0
Oth. fin. cos.	−0.3	0.0	0.0	−0.3	−0.3	−0.3
Public	1.0	0.1	0.1	1.0	1.0	1.0
Net acquisition of financial assets						
Personal	−11.9	6.7	3.4	0.7	0.3	0.2
Ind. cos.	5.3	5.8	3.2	−0.9	−1.3	−1.2
Mon. sec	−6.0	1.7	1.6	−6.2	−6.2	−6.2
Oth. fin. sec	3.7	4.3	3.1	2.6	2.2	2.2
Public	5.7	1.1	0.6	5.1	5.1	5.1
Overseas	3.9	6.8	3.2	−1.2	0.0	0.0

a – Accounting constraints only
b – Accounting constraints and $GDP = GDP(A)$
c – Accounting constraints, $GDP = GDP(A)$ and $NAFA_{Rest\ of\ World} = 0$

2.9.2 *The sensitivity of balanced data*

Table 2.2 shows the effects of a 10 per cent increase in variance of each data item on the balanced value of three aggregates of interest: the balance of trade, the gross domestic product and the level of personal saving. The first three columns show the sensitivity calculated from the approximation of section 2.5.2, while the second group of three columns show the same result calculated exactly by changing the variances, one at a time, and then rebalancing the data. It can be seen that the approximate figures are very close to the exact ones, suggesting that the repeated calculations needed to produce the exact figures are unnecessary. For example, a 10 per cent increase in the variance of income from employment leads to the estimate of the balance of trade falling by £0.053bn, to GDP falling by £0.029bn and to personal saving rising by £0.204bn if the linear approximation is used. The last figure changes to £0.235bn if the exact figure is calculated, while the other figures are barely changed.

Table 2.2 *The effect of a 10 per cent increase in variance on selected aggregates*

	Calculated using the linear approximation			Calculated exactly		
	Balance of trade	GDP	Personal saving	Balance of trade	GDP	Personal saving
Income from employment	−0.053	−0.029	0.204	−0.052	−0.028	0.235
Gross profits and other trading income						
Personal	−0.008	−0.004	0.029	−0.007	−0.004	0.034
Ind. cos	−0.045	−0.116	−0.148	−0.045	−0.117	−0.171
Fin. cos	−0.036	−0.059	−0.112	−0.035	−0.058	−0.130
Public	0.000	−0.003	−0.001	0.000	−0.003	−0.002
Other factor income						
Personal	−0.006	−0.004	0.025	−0.006	−0.003	0.029
Ind. cos	−0.003	−0.007	−0.009	−0.003	−0.007	−0.011
Fin. cos	0.000	0.000	0.000	0.000	0.000	0.000
Public	0.000	−0.003	−0.001	0.000	−0.003	−0.002
Net transfers						
Personal	0.000	−0.016	−0.016	0.000	−0.019	−0.017
Fin. cos	−0.002	0.030	−0.035	−0.002	0.027	−0.038
Public	0.000	−0.001	0.000	0.000	−0.001	0.000
Overseas	−0.001	−0.050	−0.093	−0.001	−0.044	−0.112
Factor cost adjustment	0.000	−0.001	−0.001	0.000	−0.001	−0.001
Income from employment	−0.053	−0.029	0.204	−0.052	−0.028	0.235
Consumption						
Personal	−0.044	−0.242	0.173	−0.044	−0.249	0.198
Public	−0.001	0.017	−0.002	−0.001	0.017	−0.003
Exports	0.119	0.117	−0.045	0.117	0.115	−0.053
Imports	0.105	0.103	−0.039	0.103	0.101	−0.047
Gross capital formation						
Personal	−0.006	−0.037	−0.008	−0.006	−0.036	−0.004
Ind. cos	−0.018	0.241	−0.058	−0.018	0.249	−0.067
Mon. sec.	0.000	0.001	0.000	0.000	0.000	0.000
Oth. fin. cos	−0.001	0.010	−0.004	−0.001	0.010	−0.004
Public	−0.001	0.017	−0.002	−0.001	0.017	−0.003
Taxes on capital						
Personal	0.000	0.000	0.000	0.000	0.000	0.000
Ind. cos	0.000	0.000	0.000	0.000	0.000	0.000
Mon. sec.	0.000	0.000	0.000	0.000	0.000	0.000
Oth. fin. cos	0.000	0.000	0.000	0.000	0.000	0.000
Public	0.000	0.000	0.000	0.000	0.000	0.000

Table 2.2 (*Cont.*)

	Calculated using the linear approximation			Calculated exactly		
	Balance of trade	GDP	Personal saving	Balance of trade	GDP	Personal saving
Net acquisition of financial assets						
Personal	0.115	0.279	−0.567	0.113	0.283	−0.659
Ind. cos	0.066	−0.101	0.231	0.065	−0.105	0.265
Mon. sec.	0.005	0.003	0.020	0.005	0.003	0.023
Oth. fin. sec.	0.034	0.016	0.131	0.034	0.017	0.149
Public	0.002	−0.026	0.008	0.002	−0.027	0.009
Overseas	−0.222	−0.169	0.177	−0.220	−0.171	0.212
Memorandum: balanced estimate using original reliabilities						
	1.235	352.48	19.629			

This suggests that the derivatives are helpful for studying the sensitivity of balanced data to assumptions about reliability. It also indicates that, at least in this particular example, aggregates of interest are not very sensitive to moderate changes in data reliability.

2.10 Conclusion

Least-squares reconciliation of national accounts normally uses given values for data reliability. This chapter has set out the theory of reconciliation in this case and has dealt with some important extensions to the methodology. The effects of step-by-step adjustment and of aggregation have been discussed and the Mahalanobis criterion for assessing variance estimates has been presented.

One of the most important issues is that of the sensitivity of the results to the assumptions which are made. This chapter has set out the linear approximation needed to assess the sensitivity of the results to the variance matrix in use. It has also offered a framework for testing the validity of linear hypotheses about the data. An important conclusion which follows is that, at least in the example discussed, the results are not very sensitive to the data variances used.

Nevertheless, there may be some occasions when reliance on given assumptions about data reliability is unsatisfactory. The next chapter therefore looks at the solution to the problem when nothing is known *ex ante* about data reliability.

3 Reconciliation without knowledge of data reliabilities

3.1 Introduction

In the previous chapter we considered the problem of estimation of data of known reliability. The methods we described are reasonably straightforward even if the calculations involved might sometimes be rather complicated. In this chapter we present an estimator for use with a sequence of observations when the data variances are not known. It is calculated from the time-series variances and covariances of the inconsistent observations. The estimator converges asymptotically to the Stone, Champernowne and Meade estimator which can be calculated in the case where reliabilities are known. As such it may be helpful in combining estimates from different sources, or in estimating data to meet known linear restrictions.

It may seem strange that the variance of the measurement error can be inferred from the time-series variances. An immediate reaction might be that genuinely volatile data will be treated as unreliable. However, the reason that the time-series variance can be utilised is that the accounting constraint can be used to purge the genuine volatility, leaving only the noise. In the national accounts, there are two partially independent measures of the same variable (GNP or GDP). Since they measure the same thing, greater volatility in one must indicate less reliability; it cannot indicate greater genuine volatility, at least if the measurement errors are independent of the true data.

The technique provides a means of identifying sufficient information about the data unreliability to make balancing possible. It is used, in section 3.11 to estimate quarterly US GNP and in section 3.12 to provide some of the information needed to calibrate the subsequent reconciliation of UK GDP.

3.2 The problem specified

The problem to be considered is that of estimating a vector of p data items from observed estimates which are measured subject to error. As a consequence of measurement error, non-zero elements are found in those linear combinations of the elements of the data vector, which should equal zero.

In order to consider possible data estimators, it is first necessary to make some assumption about the nature of the measurement error, which leads these discrepancies. If, in a sequence of T observations, $\mathbf{x}_t^*$ is the true value taken by a vector of data and $\mathbf{x}_t$ is its measured value, then the standard assumption, which we adopt, is

Assumption 1: $\mathbf{x}_t, \mathbf{x}_t^*$ *and* ϵ_t *are vectors of dimension* p,

$$\mathbf{x}_t = \mathbf{x}_t^* + \epsilon_t \tag{3.1}$$

and

$$E(\mathbf{x}_t^* \epsilon_t') = 0 \tag{3.2}$$

The random component of the data, ϵ_t, is orthogonal to the true data, $\mathbf{x}_t^*$. This structure will be found if, for example, data are collected by means of surveys, and the results of these surveys are open to reporting and sampling errors. When the error is of this type the data variance about its time-series mean will exceed the true variance. On the other hand, assumption 1 will not hold if guesses are used instead of estimates.[1]

In order to find an asymptotic maximum-likelihood estimator of national income, it is necessary to make further assumptions about the structure of the errors.

Assumption 2: $\mathbf{V}$ *is a matrix of dimension* $p \times p$. ϵ_t *is independently identically normally distributed with mean* 0 *and variance* $\mathbf{V}$.

$$\epsilon_t \sim \mathrm{N}(0, \mathbf{V}). \tag{3.3}$$

The assumption of normality is common to almost all derivation of maximum-likelihood estimators. Serial independence is assumed in the derivation of the estimator, although, as is demonstrated in section 3.8, the estimator is also valid when all components of the error term, ϵ_t, have the same pattern of serial correlation.

[1] We are grateful to James Meade for pointing this out.

The nature of the linear restrictions must now be formally specified.

Assumption 3: $\mathbf{A}$ *is a* $k \times p$ *matrix. The true data,* $\mathbf{x}_t^*$ *satisfy the* k *accounting constraints,* $\mathbf{A}\mathbf{x}_t^* = \mathbf{0}$.

Any estimator should also satisfy these constraints.

It was established in chapter 2 that, with the log-likelihood function

$$C - T\log|\mathbf{V}| - \frac{1}{2}\sum_{t=1}^{T}(\mathbf{x}_t - \mathbf{x}_t^*)'\mathbf{V}^{-1}(\mathbf{x}_t - \mathbf{x}_t^*) \tag{3.4}$$

maximisation subject to the constraint $\mathbf{A}\mathbf{x}_t^* = \mathbf{0}$ will yield an estimate of $\mathbf{x}_t^*$,

$$\mathbf{x}_t^{**} = [\mathbf{I} - \mathbf{V}\mathbf{A}'(\mathbf{A}\mathbf{V}\mathbf{A})^{-1}\mathbf{A}]\mathbf{x}_t. \tag{3.5}$$

Here we consider the problem of finding an estimator of $\mathbf{x}_t^{**}$ in the case where $\mathbf{V}$ is unknown.

3.3 Unknown variance and a data estimator

The basic result proved in this chapter is that the data-covariance matrix, $\mathbf{W}$, may be used in place of $\mathbf{V}$ to give an estimator of $\mathbf{V}\mathbf{A}'$ which converges asymptotically to $\mathbf{V}\mathbf{A}'$.[2]

Proposition 1: *If* $\mathbf{W}$, *a* $p \times p$ *matrix, is the covariance matrix of the data*

$$\mathbf{W} = \sum_{t=1}^{T}(\mathbf{x}_t - \bar{x})(\mathbf{x}_t - \bar{x})'/T \textit{ and } \bar{x} = \sum_{t=1}^{T}\mathbf{x}_t/T,$$

then it follows that

$$\operatorname{plim} \mathbf{W}\mathbf{A}(\mathbf{A}\mathbf{W}\mathbf{A}')^{-1} = \mathbf{V}\mathbf{A}(\mathbf{A}\mathbf{V}\mathbf{A}')^{-1}. \tag{3.6}$$

Proof: $\mathbf{W}\mathbf{A}' = \sum_{t=1}^{T}(\mathbf{x}_t - \bar{\mathbf{x}})(\mathbf{x}_t - \bar{\mathbf{x}})'\mathbf{A}'/T.$

Further,

2 White (1980) offers an example arising in a different situation in which a variance–covariance matrix cannot be estimated but the information which is needed from the variance–covariance matrix can be estimated.

$$\mathbf{WA}' = \sum_{t=1}^{T}(\mathbf{x}_t^* + \epsilon_t - \bar{x})(\mathbf{x}_t^* + \epsilon_t - \bar{x})'\mathbf{A}'/T$$
$$= \sum_{t=1}^{T}(\mathbf{x}_t^* + \epsilon_t - \bar{x}^* - \bar{\epsilon})(\epsilon_t - \bar{\epsilon})'\mathbf{A}'/T \tag{3.7}$$

where $\bar{\epsilon} = \bar{x} - \bar{x}^*$, since

$$\mathbf{x}_t^{*\prime}\mathbf{A}' = (\mathbf{A}\mathbf{x}_t^*)' = \mathbf{0}. \tag{3.8}$$

It then follows that

$$E(\mathbf{WA}') = \mathbf{VA}' - \mathbf{VA}'/T \tag{3.9}$$

since $E[(\mathbf{x}_t^* - \bar{x}^*)\epsilon_t'] = \mathbf{0}$, $E[(\mathbf{x}_t^* - \bar{x}^*)\bar{\epsilon}'] = \mathbf{0}$ (assumption 1) and

$$E\left(\sum_{t=1}^{T}\epsilon_t\bar{\epsilon}'\right)\mathbf{A}'/T = \mathbf{VA}'/T. \tag{3.10}$$

Furthermore the variance of $\mathbf{W}$ is of order $1/T$ (Kendall, 1980), and, taking the limit in probability, it therefore follows that

$$plim\ \mathbf{WA}' = \mathbf{VA}' \tag{3.11}$$

The covariance matrix of the residuals allows us to derive an estimator of $\mathbf{WA}'$, which converges in probability to $\mathbf{VA}'$.

This implies that the covariance matrix of the data, $\mathbf{W}$, may be used in place of $\mathbf{V}$ for the calculation of asymptotic maximum-likelihood estimates of the true data, $\mathbf{x}_t^*$. The reason for this is that the data variance reflects both the true data and the measurement error. However, the true data satisfy the accounting constraint and are filtered out on postmultiplying by $\mathbf{A}'$. Only the noise remains and so the above result is found.[3]

The above result leads to the immediate conclusion that

$$\mathbf{x}_t^{**} = \text{plim}\ [\mathbf{I} - \mathbf{WA}'(\mathbf{AWA}')^{-1}\mathbf{A}]\mathbf{x}_t. \tag{3.12}$$

This converges asymptotically to the estimator calculated with known error variance, but it can be calculated without knowledge of the variance of the measurement error.

[3] This was not realised by Britton and Savage (1984), who assert that one has to assume that the measurement errors in different estimates are independent of each other in order to make any progress.

3.4 A simple algebraic example

The ideas underlying the matrix algebra of the previous section may be clarified by means of a simple algebraic example, in which there are two different estimates, x_{1t} and x_{2t} of the same variable, $\mathbf{x_t}$. This situation would arise if, for example, there were separate expenditure and income estimates of GNP. The two estimates should be the same, but they are not because they are estimated in different ways, and the method of section 3.3 can therefore be used.

We write $x_{1t} = x_t^* + \epsilon_{1t}$, $x_{2t} = x_t^* + \epsilon_{2t}$ and the linear constraint matrix is simply $\mathbf{A} = (1, -1)$. It now follows, continuing with the notation of the previous section, that

$$\mathbf{WA'} = (1/\mathrm{T}) \sum_{t=1}^{T} \begin{bmatrix} \mathrm{x}_t^* - \bar{x}^* + \epsilon_{1t} - \bar{\epsilon}_1 \\ \mathrm{x}_t^* - \bar{x}^* + \epsilon_{2t} - \bar{\epsilon}_2 \end{bmatrix} (\epsilon_{1t} - \bar{\epsilon}_1 - \epsilon_{2t} + \bar{\epsilon}_2) \quad (3.13)$$

and

$$\mathbf{AWA'} = (1/\mathrm{T}) \sum_{t=1}^{T} (\epsilon_{1t} - \bar{\epsilon}_1 - \epsilon_{2t} + \bar{\epsilon}_2)^2$$

where $\bar{\epsilon}_i$ is the mean value of each error term, so that $\bar{x}_i = \bar{x}^* + \bar{\epsilon}_i$. Taking the limit in probability it may be shown, using assumptions 1 and 2, that

$$\text{plim } \mathbf{WA'} = \begin{bmatrix} \sigma_1^2 - \sigma_{12} \\ \sigma_2^2 - \sigma_{12} \end{bmatrix} (T-1)/T \quad (3.14)$$

and

$$\text{plim } \mathbf{AWA'} = [\sigma_1^2 + \sigma_2^2 - 2\sigma_{12}](T-1)/T$$

where

$$\text{var}(\epsilon_{1t}) = \sigma_1^2, \text{var}(\epsilon_{2t}) = \sigma_2^2 \quad \text{and} \quad \text{cov}(\epsilon_{1t}, \epsilon_{2t}) = \sigma_{12}.$$

It then follows that

$$\begin{bmatrix} x_{1t}^{**} \\ x_{2t}^{**} \end{bmatrix} = (\mathbf{I} - \mathbf{WA'}[\mathbf{AWA'}]^{-1}\mathbf{A}) \begin{bmatrix} \mathbf{x_{1t}} \\ \mathbf{x_{2t}} \end{bmatrix} \quad (3.15)$$

$$= \begin{bmatrix} x_{1t} \\ x_{2t} \end{bmatrix} - \frac{1}{\sigma_1^2 + \sigma_2^2 - 2\sigma_{12}} \begin{bmatrix} \sigma_1^2 - \sigma_{12} & \sigma_{12} - \sigma_1^2 \\ \sigma_{12} - \sigma_2^2 & \sigma_2^2 - \sigma_{12} \end{bmatrix} \begin{bmatrix} x_{1t} \\ x_{2t} \end{bmatrix}.$$

The balanced values of x_{1t} and x_{2t} are equal and given as

$$x_t^{**} = [x_{1t}(\sigma_2^2 - \sigma_{12}) + x_{2t}(\sigma_1^2 - \sigma_{12})]/(\sigma_1^2 + \sigma_2^2 - 2\sigma_{12}). \qquad (3.16)$$

This 'balanced' estimator is that given in any standard statistics textbook (e.g. Mood and Graybill, 1963), for combining two different estimates of the same variable on the basis of their reliabilities. The key distinction here is that no prior knowledge of data reliabilities is assumed to be available. Instead it has been proved that, provided assumptions 1 to 3 hold, it is possible to infer the data reliability from the data variance. The estimator converges in large samples to that which would be used if the data variances were known and did not have to be inferred.

3.5 An interpretation in terms of ordinary least squares

The residuals are allocated on the basis of the data covariance, with the accounting constraints filtering out the true data and leaving only the covariances of the measurement errors. However, coefficients by which the accounting residuals $\mathbf{Ax_t}$ are allocated can be given an interpretation in terms of ordinary least squares.

We denote the accounting residuals as $\mathbf{Z} = \mathbf{AX}$ where $\mathbf{X}$ is the matrix of data observations $\mathbf{x_1}, \ldots, \mathbf{x_n}$, and consider the regression of the ith row of $\mathbf{X}$, $\mathbf{X_i}$ on $\mathbf{Z}$. All the variables are considered measured relative to their means, because this does not alter the regression coefficients which are found, but simply avoids the need for constants. The row vector of regression coefficients is then

$$\hat{\beta}_i = \mathbf{X_i Z'}(\mathbf{ZZ'})^{-1} \qquad (3.17)$$

which looks slightly different from usual simply because $\mathbf{X}$ and $\mathbf{Z}$ are specified to show time along the rows rather than down the columns. If the regressions on the rows of $\mathbf{X}$ are stacked,

$$\hat{\mathbf{B}} = \mathbf{XZ'}(\mathbf{ZZ'})^{-1} \qquad (3.18)$$

gives the matrix of regression coefficients.

Now $\mathbf{ZZ'} = \mathbf{AWA'}$ and $\mathbf{XZ'} = \mathbf{WA'}$ since $\mathbf{Z} = \mathbf{AX}$ and all the variables are measured relative to their means, so that $\mathbf{B} = \mathbf{WA'}(\mathbf{AWA'})^{-1}$ and the estimator given by (3.12) is

$$\mathbf{x_t^{**}} = \text{plim}\ (\mathbf{I} - \mathbf{BA})\mathbf{x_t} = \text{plim}\ (\mathbf{x_t} - \mathbf{Bz_t}) \qquad (3.19)$$

with $\mathbf{z_t}$ being the tth column of $\mathbf{Z}$. In other words the accounting residuals $\mathbf{z_t}$ are allocated to the observed data, $\mathbf{x_t}$ by means of the ordinary least squares regression coefficients **B**. The estimates of the balanced data are, in effect, the residuals of regression equations trying to explain $\mathbf{X}_i$ by means of **Z**. The balanced data are then the components of the observed data which cannot be explained by the measurement error even when the measurement error does as well as it can. Given assumption 1 that the true data are independent of the errors this is an intuitively appealing way of interpreting the results.

3.6 The properties of the estimated weights

The previous section points to a means of testing whether some particular weighting structure is valid. For example, in the United Kingdom the simple average of the two measures of GDP is published. With constant price data an income estimate is calculated by deflating the current price income estimate by the implicit expenditure deflator. An average estimate is then produced by taking the mean of the output estimate, the expenditure estimate and the deflated income estimate. This would be justifiable if the three series were of equal reliability, but cannot be the most efficient estimate if that is not the case. Thus the question arises of testing whether a set of weights estimated by the method of section 3.3 above is significantly different from some set of weights in conventional use.

In fact a test can be constructed without too much difficulty. It is not immediately obvious that the regression coefficients identified in section 3.5 will be t-distributed, but it turns out to be the case when there is only one restriction or when the number of restrictions is one fewer than the number of variables. One can therefore test hypotheses on the weighting matrix using the conventional t and F-tests. Even when these conditions are not met the test has approximate validity. The results are described in detail by Satchell, Smith and Weale (1992).

3.7 Common autocorrelation in the measurement errors

We demonstrated in chapter 2 that the least-squares/maximum-likelihood estimator was unaffected by the presence of a common pattern of serial correlation in the data. The proof of proposition 1 in section 3.3 is also entirely unaffected by common autocorrelation in ϵ_t and therefore the calculation of the estimator proceeds just as before, giving

$$\tilde{\mathbf{x}}_t = \text{plim}\left(\mathbf{I} - \mathbf{W}\mathbf{A}'[\mathbf{A}\mathbf{W}\mathbf{A}']^{-1}\mathbf{A}\right)\mathbf{x}_t. \tag{3.20}$$

3.8 General serial correlation

The methods set out above can be extended to test for and estimate the effects of general serial correlation in the measurement errors, at least if the serial correlation is assumed to have a moving average rather than an autoregressive structure. As in chapter 2, we stack the data into one big vector. We then have to find a way of estimating the variance–covariance matrix of this vector.

We replace assumption 1 by the assumption that the measurement errors are serially correlated

$$E(\epsilon_i \epsilon_{i+j}) = \mathbf{V_j} \tag{3.21}$$

so that $\mathbf{V_0}$ is the data variance matrix estimated by the methods above and $\mathbf{V_k}, k \neq 0$ represents the autocorrelation between $\mathbf{x_t}$ and $\mathbf{x_{t\pm k}}$. The pattern of serial correlation is assumed to be homoscedastic.

It is necessary to evaluate

$$\begin{pmatrix} \mathbf{V_0} & \mathbf{V_1} & .. & \mathbf{V_N} \\ \mathbf{V_1} & \mathbf{V_0} & .. & \mathbf{V_{N-1}} \\ \mathbf{V_N} & \mathbf{V_{N-1}} & .. & \mathbf{V_0} \end{pmatrix} \begin{pmatrix} \mathbf{A}' & 0 & .. & 0 \\ 0 & \mathbf{A}' & .. & 0 \\ .. & .. & .. & .. \\ 0 & 0 & .. & \mathbf{A}' \end{pmatrix}$$

$$= \begin{pmatrix} \mathbf{V_0A}' & \mathbf{V_1A}' & .. & \mathbf{V_NA}' \\ \mathbf{V_1A}' & \mathbf{V_0A}' & .. & \mathbf{V_NA}' \\ .. & .. & .. & .. \\ \mathbf{V_NA}' & \mathbf{V_{N-1}A}' & .. & \mathbf{V_1A}' \end{pmatrix} \tag{3.22}$$

and we therefore need estimators of the matrices $\mathbf{V_0A}'...\mathbf{V_NA}'$.

Section 3.3 gives an estimator of $\mathbf{V_0A}'$, and in principle the other matrices can be calculated in the same way.

Proposition 4: *If* $\mathbf{W_k}$ *is the covariance matrix between the data in period t and the residuals in period t + k,*

$$\mathbf{W_k} = \sum_{t=1}^{T-k} (\mathbf{x_t} - \bar{x})(\mathbf{x_{t+k}} - \bar{x})'/T$$

then

$$\text{plim } \mathbf{W_kA}' = \mathbf{V_kA}'. \tag{3.23}$$

Proof: As the proof of proposition 1.

There is, however, one problem with this approach. The number of observations over which the covariance can be estimated declines as the value of k increases. By the time k has reached N, there is only one observation, and it could reasonably be questioned whether a result which relies on a large sample is of a great deal of use. However, if one is prepared to accept the notion that the serial correlation may arrive from a moving average process, it becomes sensible to consider ways of testing for the significance of processes of various orders.

With the true data being independent of the measurement error and also with the measurement errors being normally distributed about zero mean, it follows that the matrix

$$\begin{pmatrix} \mathbf{W}_k & \mathbf{W}_k\mathbf{A}' \\ \mathbf{A}\mathbf{W}_k' & \mathbf{A}\mathbf{W}_k\mathbf{A}' \end{pmatrix} \tag{3.24}$$

is Wishart distributed. It is therefore, in principle, possible to test the hypothesis that $\mathbf{W}_k\mathbf{A}'=0$. Nevertheless, such a test is by no means straightforward except in the simplest of cases.

When there is only one accounting restriction, then the distribution of the correlation coefficient (Kendall and Stuart, 1993, p. 278) may be of some help. $\mathbf{W}_k\mathbf{A}'$ is then a row vector with the number of elements equal to the number of data variables. The test for zero correlation is also a test for zero covariance, and one can at least test individually (if not jointly) the hypothesis that the elements of $\mathbf{W}_k\mathbf{A}'$ are zero.

3.9 Heteroscedasticity

The method of section 3.3 can be applied without difficulty to a set of national accounts if the measurement errors are homoscedastic. But in fact the national income aggregates tend to grow over time and it is more than likely that the standard deviations of the components of national income and expenditure grow in much the same way. If the covariance matrix of the data changes over time the method of section 3.3 cannot be used because the covariance matrix cannot be estimated from the data. If the standard deviations of the measurement errors are assumed to be proportional to GDP (or to any scalar linear combination of the true data g_t^*), then knowledge of GDP would make it possible to evaluate the balanced data from the covariance matrix of the data vector measured as a fraction of GDP. Since the true data comprise an interdependent set of data, there will be two ways of deriving $g_t^*, g_t^* = \mathbf{c}_1'\mathbf{x}_t^* = \mathbf{c}_2'\mathbf{x}_t^*$. On the other hand GDP has to be estimated from the balanced data and is not known *a priori* for use as a scaling variable. It is demonstrated here that a consistent estimator can still be found, when there is only one linear restriction to be imposed on the data.

The error structure is now

$$\mathbf{x_t} = \mathbf{x_t^*} + g_t^* \epsilon_\mathbf{t} \qquad \mathbf{E}(\epsilon_\mathbf{t}\epsilon_\mathbf{t}') = \mathbf{V}. \tag{3.25}$$

We can calculate a consistent estimator of the value of g_t^{**} which would emerge from the balancing exercise if the variance matrix were known. The accounting identity means that, for any scalar linear combination, g_t^*, there are two estimates of GDP, g_1 and g_2. If the standard deviations of all the components are proportional to g_t^* it then follows that the standard deviations of the two estimates of g_t^* are also proportional to g_t^*,

$$g_{it} = g_{it}^*(1 + u_{it}), \; E(u_{it}u_{it}') = \mathbf{CVC}' \tag{3.26}$$

where $u_{it} = \mathbf{c}_i\epsilon_\mathbf{t}$. This in turn implies that, to a first-order approximation,

$$\log g_{it} = \log g_t^* + u_{it} \tag{3.27}$$

where u_{it} is homoscedastic. The method of section 3.3 can then be applied to the logarithms of the two estimates of national income. If there is only one linear restriction, the result of chapter 2, section 2.3, then implies that, to our first-order approximation, the result will be the same as if g_t^* had been estimated by balancing the components and then aggregating them up. When there is more than one linear restriction on the data the value of g_t^{**} is different from that which would be found if the variance matrix were known. With more than one linear restriction to be satisfied, the method set out here for dealing with heteroscedasticity cannot deliver the same answer as would be found if the error variance matrix were known.

Having evaluated g_t^{**} as the balanced estimate of g_t^* in this way, we can divide each data vector $\mathbf{x_t}$ by g_t^{**}, giving $\mathbf{y_t} = \mathbf{x_t}/g_t^{**}$ and then apply the method of section 3.3 to the vector $\mathbf{y_t}$. This method is good to a first-order approximation, with the approximation being necessary because the balanced estimate, g_t^{**} is not equal to the true value, g_t^*.

Put $g_t^{**} = g_t^*(1 + u_t^{**})$. Then the covariance matrix which is used to construct the balanced estimates is, with $\mathbf{w_t^*} = \mathbf{x_t^*}/g_t^*$, denoting the true values of the vector elements as fractions of GDP,

$$\mathbf{WA}' = \mathbf{E}\left(\mathbf{w}_t^* \frac{\mathbf{g}_t^*}{\mathbf{g}_t^{**}} + \epsilon_t \frac{\mathbf{g}_t^*}{\mathbf{g}_t^{**}} - \frac{1}{\mathbf{T}}\sum\left[\mathbf{w}_t^* \frac{\mathbf{g}_t^*}{\mathbf{g}_t^{**}} + \epsilon_t \frac{\mathbf{g}_t^*}{\mathbf{g}_t^{**}}\right]\right)$$
$$\left(\epsilon_t \frac{g_t^*}{g_t^{**}} - \frac{1}{T}\sum \epsilon_t \frac{g_t^*}{g_t^{**}}\right)' \mathbf{A}'$$
$$= E\left(\mathbf{w}_t^*(1-u_t^{**}) + \epsilon_t(1-u_t^{**}) - \frac{1}{T}\sum[\mathbf{w}_t^*(1-u_t^{**}) + \epsilon_t(1-u_t^{**})]\right)$$
$$\left(\epsilon_t(1-u_t^{**}) - \frac{1}{T}\sum \epsilon_t(1-u_t^{**})\right)' \mathbf{A}', \tag{3.28}$$

Now the proportionate difference between g_t^{**} and g_t^*, u_t^{**}, is not independent of ϵ_t, the vector of errors in $\mathbf{x}_t/g_t^*$ and, therefore, although

$$E\left(\mathbf{w}_t^* - \frac{1}{T}\sum \mathbf{w}_t^*(\epsilon_t - \frac{1}{T}\sum \epsilon_t)\right)' = 0 \tag{3.29}$$

it is not the case that

$$E\left(\mathbf{w}_t^*(1-u_t^{**}) - \frac{1}{T}\sum \mathbf{w}_t^*(1-u_t^{**})\right)$$
$$\left(\epsilon_t(1-u_t^{**}) - \frac{1}{T}\sum \epsilon_t(1-u_t^{**})\right)' \tag{3.30}$$

is zero even if third and fourth order terms are neglected.

Multiplying out $\mathbf{WA}'$, yields

$$\begin{aligned}\mathbf{WA}' = E\Big\{ & \mathbf{w}_t^*(1-u_t^{**})^2\epsilon_t' - \mathbf{w}_t^*(1-u_t^{**})\sum(1-u_t^{**})\epsilon_t'/T \\ & + (1-u_t^{**})^2\epsilon_t\epsilon_t' - \epsilon_t(1-u_t^{**})\sum\epsilon_t'(1-u_t^{**})/T \\ & - \frac{1}{T}\left(\sum \mathbf{w}_t^*[1-u_t^{**}]\right)(1-u_t^{**})\epsilon_t' \\ & + \frac{1}{T^2}\left(\sum \mathbf{w}_t^*[1-u_t^{**}]\right)\left(\sum(1-u_t^{**})\epsilon_t'\right) \\ & - \frac{1}{T}\left(\sum \epsilon_t(1-u_t^{**})\right)(1-u_t^{**})\epsilon_t' \\ & + \frac{1}{T^2}\left(\sum \epsilon_t(1-u_t^{**})\right)\left(\sum \epsilon_t'[1-u_t^{**}]\right)\Big\}\mathbf{A}'\end{aligned} \tag{3.31}$$

Multiplying out and neglecting third and fourth order terms:

$$\mathbf{WA}' = E\Big\{[1-\frac{1}{T}]\epsilon\epsilon' + (\frac{1}{T}\sum \mathbf{w}_t^* - 2\mathbf{w}_t^*)u_t^{**}\epsilon_t'$$
$$+\left(\frac{\mathbf{w}_t^* u_t^{**}}{T} - \frac{\sum \mathbf{w}_t^* u_t^{**}}{T^2}\right)\sum \epsilon_t'$$
$$+\left(\frac{\mathbf{w}_t^*}{T} - \frac{\sum \mathbf{w}_t^*}{T^2}\right)\sum u_t^{**}\epsilon_t' + \frac{1}{T}\left(\sum \mathbf{w}_t^* u_t^{**}\right)\epsilon_t'\Big\}\mathbf{A}'. \qquad (3.32)$$

Since $\mathbf{w}_t^*$ is independent of the measurement errors, and $u_t^{**} = \mathbf{c}_1\epsilon_t$ this expression simplifies to

$$\mathbf{QA}' = \left(\mathbf{I} - \mathbf{w}_t^*\mathbf{c}_1\right)^{-1}\mathbf{WA}' = \left(1 - \frac{1}{\mathrm{T}}\right)\mathbf{E}\left(\epsilon_t\epsilon_t'\right)\mathbf{A}' \qquad (3.33)$$

so that, in large samples

$$\mathbf{QA}'(\mathbf{AQA}')^{-1} \text{ converges to } \mathbf{VA}'(\mathbf{AVA}')^{-1}.$$

This then yields balanced estimates of $\mathbf{w}_t^{**}$ as

$$\mathbf{w}_t^{**} = (\mathbf{I} - \mathbf{VA}'(\mathbf{AVA}')^{-1}\mathbf{A})\mathbf{w}_t. \qquad (3.34)$$

Multiplying through by g_t^{**}, which is the same as would be found had it been calculated from balanced estimates, $\mathbf{x}_t^{**}$, this then yields

$$\mathbf{x}_t^{**} = (\mathbf{I} - \mathbf{VA}'(\mathbf{AVA}')^{-1}\mathbf{A})\mathbf{x}_t. \qquad (3.35)$$

The estimate $\mathbf{x}_t^{**}$ is the same as would be found if the variance matrix $\mathbf{V}$ were known, since the fact that the variances are $g_t^{*2}\mathbf{V}$ rather than simply $\mathbf{V}$ does not affect the balancing. This method deals with the problem of heteroscedasticity when there is only one accounting restriction to be imposed on the data.

3.10 Factor analysis and data extraction

In this section we compare our method of data reconciliation with an alternative approach. This involves the use of factor analysis and is thus a simple example of the approach suggested by Stock and Watson (1989). They proposed a method for extracting coincident and leading indicators from series of macroeconomic data based on dynamic factor analysis as described by Engle and Watson (1981). Their approach is compared with that of section 3.3 by simplifying their model to the static case.

Stock and Watson suggest that there is a vector of variables $\mathbf{x}_t$ related to a single indicator variable x_t^* in the following way.

$$\mathbf{x_t} = \boldsymbol{\beta} + \boldsymbol{\gamma}(L)x_t^* + \mathbf{u_t} \tag{3.36}$$

$$\mathbf{D}(L)\mathbf{u_t} = \boldsymbol{\varepsilon_t} \tag{3.37}$$

$$\phi(L)x_t^* = \delta + \eta_t \tag{3.38}$$

where $\boldsymbol{\gamma}(L)$, $\mathbf{D}(L)$ and $\phi(L)$ are polynomials of lag operators and $\boldsymbol{\varepsilon_t} \sim N(0, \mathrm{I})$, $\eta_t \sim N(0, 1)$. Stock and Watson assume that $x_t^*, \mathbf{u_t}$ are mutually uncorrelated and achieve this by making $\mathbf{D}$ (L) diagonal and η_t, $\boldsymbol{\varepsilon_t}$ mutually and serially uncorrelated. In other words, like our model, they assume that the disturbance terms which enter into the measured data are independent of the underlying variable. But they also assume that the disturbance terms which enter into the observed data are independent of each other, even though they may be serially dependent on themselves. This assumption is usual in factor analysis but was not made in section 3.2.

We can simplify their model by the extra restrictions, $\boldsymbol{\beta} = 0$, $\boldsymbol{\gamma}(L) = \mathrm{I}$ and $\mathbf{D}(L) = \mathbf{R}$.[4] This removes the dynamic structure from their model and simplifies a 'dynamic factor' model to one of conventional factor extraction. However, we do not assume that the two measurement errors are uncorrelated. They may not be, and the assumption is not required by our approach. We can now take the example of section 3.4 and calculate the latent variable which would be extracted by means of factor analysis. This can be compared with the balanced estimate of section 3.4.

In fact the analysis is very straightforward. With the possibly mistaken assumption that the error matrix is diagonal, the variance matrix is broken into two components

$$\operatorname{var}(\mathrm{x_{1t}}, \mathrm{x_{2t}}) = \mathbf{W} = \begin{pmatrix} \Sigma^2 + \sigma_1^2 & \Sigma^2 + \sigma_{12} \\ \Sigma^2 + \sigma_{12} & \Sigma^2 + \sigma_2^2 \end{pmatrix} \tag{3.39}$$

$$= \begin{pmatrix} \Sigma^2 + \sigma_{12} & \Sigma^2 + \sigma_{12} \\ \Sigma^2 + \sigma_{12} & \Sigma^2 + \sigma_{12} \end{pmatrix} + \begin{pmatrix} \sigma_1^2 - \sigma_{12} & 0 \\ 0 & \sigma_2^2 - \sigma_{12} \end{pmatrix}.$$

It should be noted that any covariance between the two error terms finds its way into the component of the covariance explained by the common factor.

There are a number of methods of identifying the common factor; with only a single factor the two described by Lawley and Mitchell (1971) are equivalent, and they both show the factor as being calculated from the

[4] In fact, in the static model with two variables and one factor, the restriction $\beta = 0$ is needed as an identifying restriction. The technique cannot identify bias. Even then, the model is not fully identified. Kendall (1980), p. 50, suggests that normally one would make some assumption about σ_1^2/σ_2^2 but in this case $\gamma = 1$ is the obvious extra restriction needed for the model to make statistical sense.

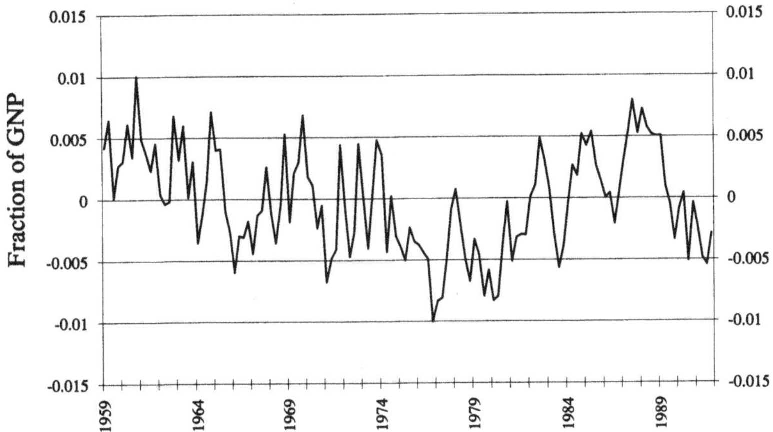

Figure 3.1 The statistical discrepancy in United States GNP

inverse of the component of variance not explained by the common factor as

$$z_t = \frac{(\sigma_1^2 - \sigma_{12})(\sigma_2^2 - \sigma_{12})}{\sigma_1^2 + \sigma_2^2 - 2\sigma_{12}} (1 \quad 1) \begin{pmatrix} \sigma_1^2 - \sigma_{12} & 0 \\ 0 & \sigma_2^2 - \sigma_{12} \end{pmatrix}^{-1}. \qquad (3.40)$$

It can be seen that this delivers the balanced value shown in section 3.4, equation (3.16) so that in this case the two methods produce identical results. This happens despite the fact that the measurement errors in the two series are assumed incorrectly to be uncorrelated.

3.11 Example 1: US quarterly data

The United States national accounts (US Bureau of Economic Analysis, 1989) present estimates of net national product calculated from the expenditure estimate of GNP. Deduction of the factor cost adjustment should lead to national income as calculated from the income/output side of the national accounts. In fact, as can be seen from table 1.10 of *The National Income and Product Accounts of the United States, 1959–89*, there is a discrepancy between the two.

Figure 3.1 shows this discrepancy and its quarter-on-quarter change measured as a proportion of GNP[5] with the data extended to 1991. There are seventeen occasions when it has exceeded 0.5 per cent of GNP. Figure 3.2 shows the change in the discrepancy. From this, we can see

[5] I.e. as log (GNP – statistical discrepancy).

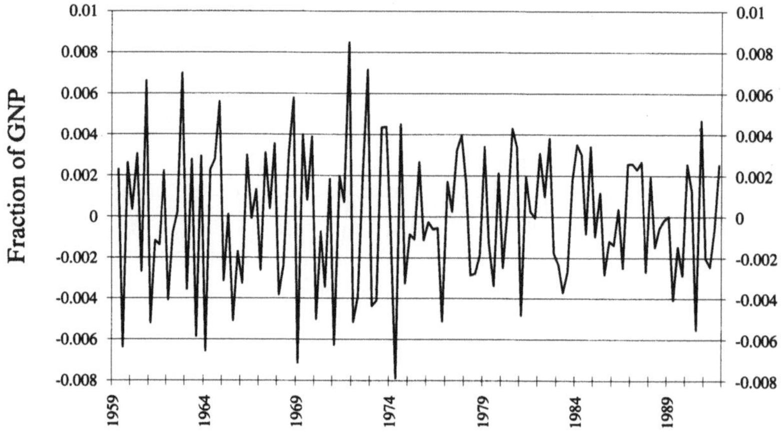

Figure 3.2 The change in the statistical discrepancy in United States GNP

that there are eighteen occasions when the change in the statistical discrepancy has exceeded 0.5 per cent of GNP, with the implication that the growth rates of the expenditure and income/output estimates of GNP differ by at least 0.5 per cent at an annual rate.

The method of section 3.3 can be illustrated by application to the two inconsistent estimates of US GNP. The results of section 3.3 suggest that we should calculate the covariance matrix between the statistical discrepancy and the two estimates of GNP implicit in the data. The ratio of these two covariances then indicates the proportions in which the discrepancy should be allocated between the two estimates of GNP. However, two steps must be undertaken before the data are in a suitable form for the calculations to be carried out.

First of all, data in levels must be expected to be heteroscedastic. As GNP has increased, one would expect the errors to increase in absolute size. Figure 3.1 suggests that the variance of the residual measured in proportionate terms may be reasonably stable. Since the logarithms of the two estimates should be equal, just as the estimates themselves should be equal, this suggests that heteroscedasticity should be avoided by working with the data in logarithmic form.

A second problem arises from the fact that GNP measured in constant prices is generally believed to be a random walk or to follow some process which is not very different from a random walk (Campbell and Mankiw, 1987). On the other hand, the residual as shown in figure 3.1 appears to be stationary (DF $= -5.0$). In such a situation more precise estimates are likely to be found if the calculations are performed by

Table 3.1 *The allocation of the US quarterly residual*

Observed data	Regression coefficient	R^2
DEXP	0.7961	0.073
DINC	−0.2039 (0.86)	0.006

Notes: DEXPΔ log (expenditure measure of GNP);
DINCΔ log (income measure of GNP);
DRES = DEX − DINC.
The regression is carried out using quarterly data in constant prices from 1959q2 to 1991q4.

considering the covariance between the change in the logarithmic residual and the changes in the two logarithmic estimates of GNP. The accounting constraint is not disturbed, because the changes in the two estimates should be equal. $\mathbf{A}\mathbf{x}_t^* = 0$ for all t implies $\Delta A x_t^* = 0$. If the original measurement errors giving rise to the residual were close to white noise, then the differencing process will introduce powerful negative serial correlation into the differences of the measurement errors. But in section 3.5 it was demonstrated that this did not affect the validity of the basic result of section 3.3, and our analysis is therefore not affected by this negative serial correlation. With the differenced data there is little evidence of a structural break in the mid 1950s.

The most convenient way of finding the results is to use a regression package. As described in section 3.5, the data are simply regressed on the residual so as to find the weights needed to allocate the residual. The results of this exercise are shown in table 3.1

The regression coefficient therefore implies that 80 per cent of the residual should be deducted from the expenditure estimate, with 20 per cent being added to the income estimate. The coefficient of 0.8 is statistically different from zero, and the results therefore reject the current US approach of attributing the whole of the residual to the income estimate.

The correlation coefficients between the current estimates of DEXP and DINC and current and lagged values of DRES are given in table 3.2. The 95 per cent confidence limit for the correlation coefficient is ±0.18, so that the correlation between the change in the expenditure measure and the residual lagged one period is just statistically significant. This implies that we have to set up the variance–covariance matrix for the full 131 observations, with the effects of serial correlation represented by

Table 3.2 *Correlation coefficients between current data and lagged residuals: US quarterly data*

	DEXP	DINC
DRES	0.32	−0.04
$DRES_{-1}$	−0.18	−0.10
$DRES_{-2}$	0.12	0.13
$DRES_{-3}$	−0.16	−0.05
$DRES_{-4}$	0.06	−0.06

suitable off-diagonal elements. However, the problem can be avoided. We started with the suggestion that the use of first differences ought to introduce moving-average error processes, since the residuals appeared to be stationary in levels. We can accept the joint hypothesis that the coefficients associated with the lagged residuals are equal but opposite to those associated with the residuals themselves.[6] This then implies that the conditions of chapter 2, section 2.7.1 hold, so that the serial correlation has no effect on the outcome.

3.12 Example 2: UK annual data

The method is also applied to UK annual data for the period 1948 to 1990. This differs from the US situation because there are two different estimates of both constant price and current price GDP,[7] with the implication that the joint adjustment of the four series can be considered.

Once again, in order to avoid the problem of heteroscedasticity and non-stationarity, we work in terms of logarithmic first differences[8] and use ordinary least squares regression to estimate the allocation of the residual errors (see tables 3.3 and 3.4).

The exercise is not very satisfactory. The regressions for the constant price data suggest that 31 per cent of the adjustment should be put on the expenditure data and 69 per cent on the output data. The current price residual has a small effect on both series. On the other hand, the current price regression suggests that more than the full adjustment should be made to the income data. If the increase in income exceeds the increase in

6 $F(2,262) = 2.53$.

7 The United States does not produce an output measure of GDP, but simply deflates both income and expenditure estimates by the GDP deflator. Obviously this means that nothing extra is gained by considering the constant price data as well as the current price data.

8 It is questionable whether the first difference of current price income is stationary, since inflation is usually regarded as an I(1) variable. However, with forty-two observations de Jong *et al.* (1992) argue that it is not really possible to test the hypothesis of stationarity.

Table 3.3 *The allocation of UK accounting residuals* (*i*), *1948–1990*

Observed data	Weight		R^2
	DRES	DRES85	
DEXP85	−0.10094	0.30646	0.0166
	(−0.27)	(0.78)	
DINC85	−0.10094	−0.69354	0.1269
	(−0.27)	(1.77)	
DEXP	−0.0654	1.3062	0.0665
	(1.35)	(1.57)	
DINC	−1.065	1.3062	0.0823
	(0.083)	(1.57)	

DEXP Δ log(expenditure measure of GDP in current prices);
DINC Δ log(income measure of GDP in current prices);
DEXP85 Δ log(expenditure measure of GDP in constant prices);
DINC85 Δ log(output measure of GDP in 1985 prices);
DRES = DINC−DEXP;
DRES85 = DINC85−DEXP85.

Table 3.4 *The allocation of UK accounting residuals* (*ii*), *1948–1990*

Observed data	Weight		R^2
	DRES	DRES85	
DEXP85		0.24458	
		(0.77)	
DINC85		−0.75542	0.1269
		(2.4)	
DEXP	0.64706		0.0665
	(0.99)		
DINC	0.35294		0.0823
	(0.053)		

Note: See note to table 3.3.

expenditure, the income growth figure should be reduced by 1.065 × the gap. The expenditure figure has to be reduced by 0.065 × the gap in order to reconcile the two. There is also a large response to the constant price residual. However, none of the weights appears to be statistically significant.

If the covariances between the constant and current price data are assumed to be zero, then slightly more plausible results are found. However, the only firm conclusion which can be drawn from this is that the error in the constant price data should not be attributed entirely to the expenditure estimate (requiring a zero coefficient in the regression on DINC85). And the underlying restriction that the constant and current price data are independent is rather unlikely, given that constant price expenditure data are for the most part calculated by deflating current price data.

The results demonstrate a problem which arises with these methods of data reconciliation. It is generally found that a large number of observations are needed in order to produce results which have any useful degree of precision: we have not found the method to be helpful for looking at annual data. Accordingly, for the production of balanced estimates of UK national income in the subsequent chapters we revert to working from statisticians' estimates of data reliability. However, the framework we use does require an estimate of the allocation of the gap between constant price expenditure and output in the long run. The statisticians have little to say on this, and we have therefore relied on the above regressions to ensure that about 70 per cent of the adjustment is made to output and about 30 per cent to expenditure.[9]

3.13 Conclusion

This chapter has demonstrated a way of combining different estimates of the same variable in the absence of knowledge about their reliabilities. The estimator has the property that it converges to the maximum-likelihood estimator which would be calculated if the variances of the measurement errors were known.

An application to the US national accounts suggests that 80 per cent of the discrepancy between expenditure and income–output estimates of GNP should be deducted from the expenditure account, with the remaining 20 per cent added to the estimate derived from the income/output side. The implication is that the income/output estimate of constant price GNP is considerably more reliable than the expenditure estimate. The presentation adopted in the US national accounts, which suggests that the whole of the error should be attributed to the income/output estimate, is misleading.

[9] This is consistent with the statisticians' view that the output measure is a good indicator of changes in real GDP in the short run, but a poor measure in the long run.

However, when the method is applied to annual data for the UK, the results are too poorly determined to be of great help in allocating the residuals. The subsequent chapters therefore describe an approach based on available information and inference about the structure of measurement error.

Part two

Application to UK national accounts

4 Patterns of autocorrelation

4.1 Introduction

This part of the book describes the practical issues which have to be resolved in order to apply the methods of chapter 2 to the UK national accounts. The first step is specification of the pattern likely to be observed in the measurement errors. This chapter deals with that issue. Chapters 5 and 6 describe how a coherent set of UK national accounts for the period 1920 to 1990 has been produced and how the error pattern has been quantified. Chapter 7 explains how the adjustments to the production account are linked to the income/outlay and capital accounts. Chapter 8 describes some of the consequences of the balancing exercise. The new dataset itself is presented in part 3.

In chapter 2 we drew attention to the possibility of serial correlation in the measurement errors. Those involved in constructing estimates of national income often argue that changes in aggregates from one period to the next are measured more reliably than are the aggregates themselves (CSO, 1985, p. 21; Feinstein, 1972, p. 22) with the clear implication that there is positive autocorrelation between the measurement error in one period and that in another period. Any attempt to remove the discrepancies from the national accounts which fails to take account of this autocorrelation is not using all that is known about the structure of measurement errors and is therefore less than fully satisfactory. The problem is likely to be more important for historical data than for current data for two reasons. First of all, the residuals are typically larger and second, because the estimates are produced *ex post* rather than contemporaneously, greater reliance is likely to be placed on methods of data construction which lead to autocorrelation of measurement errors. In this chapter we discuss the pattern of serial correlation which is likely to be found in estimates of national accounts. This pattern can be used to construct the general variance–covariance matrix of section 2.7.2. After selection of suitable parameters the balanced time-series of data described by equation (2.49) can be produced. The parametrisation is discussed in chapters 5 and 6.

4.2 The effect of autocorrelation on measurement error

In section 4.1 it was noted that references to the reliability of both historical and contemporary national accounting aggregates frequently point out that changes from one year to the next are measured more accurately than the data themselves. If the measurement errors were uncorrelated this would not be the case; the variance of the difference between two observations would equal the sum of the variances of the two observations. It is the presence of positive autocorrelation in the measurement errors which confers this property. A simple example can demonstrate this.

Suppose that data are constructed by extrapolating away from a benchmark using an indicator variable (see section 4.3.1), a method of data construction widely applied to both historic and current data. Working with proportionate or percentage errors (which assumes that the errors are in fact multiplicative), then if ϵ_N is the percentage error in the benchmark variable in year N, v_N is the percentage error in the indicator variable in year N and v_t is the percentage error in the indicator variable in year t, the total error for period t is

$$u_t = \epsilon_N + v_t - v_N \tag{4.1}$$

and its variance is, with ϵ_N independent of v_t and v_N given as

$$E(u_t^2) = E(\epsilon_N^2) + E(v_t^2) + E(v_N^2) - 2E(v_t v_N). \tag{4.2}$$

It is likely that the measurement error in the indicator variable v_t follows an autocorrelated process.

A simple example demonstrates this. The number of cars produced may be used as an indicator of the constant price value added in the car industry; in the short term changes in the number of cars produced are likely to be a fairly good indicator of changes in the constant price value added of the car industry. In the longer term quality changes and changes in product mix will almost certainly make the indicator less good.

We may then specify the autocorrelation process followed by v_t as

$$v_t = \rho v_{t-1} + w_t. \tag{4.3}$$

If $E(w_t^2) = \sigma_w^2$, then the variance of v_t, $E(v_t^2)$ is given by the asymptotic formula, $E(v_t^2) = \sigma_v^2 = \sigma_w^2/(1 - \rho^2)$. It then follows that

$$E(u_t^2) = \sigma_{\epsilon_N}^2 + 2\sigma_v^2(1 - \rho^{2|t-N|}) \tag{4.4}$$

and it can be seen that, in the simple case in which $\rho = 0$, there is a step increase in the variance outside the benchmark observation from $E(\epsilon_N^2) = \sigma_{\epsilon_N}^2$ to $\sigma_{\epsilon_N}^2 + 2\sigma_v^2$. If ρ is positive, this upper value is approached asymptotically rather than in one step. For given initial and asymptotic variances, the higher the degree of autocorrelation, the lower the variances in the intervening periods.

The error in the change in the variable from one period to the next is given, in percentage terms as

$$u_t - u_{t-1} = v_t - v_{t-1} = (\rho - 1)v_{t-1} + w_t \tag{4.5}$$

so that

$$\begin{aligned} E(v_t - v_{t-1})^2 &= (\rho - 1)^2 E(v_{t-1}^2) + \sigma_w^2 \\ &= \sigma_w^2\left(1 + \frac{[\rho - 1]^2}{1 - \rho^2}\right) = 2\sigma_w^2/(1 + \rho). \end{aligned} \tag{4.6}$$

Depending on the various parameter values, this variance may well be below $E(u_t^2)$. In particular, for a given value of $\sigma_v^2 = \sigma_w^2/(1 - \rho^2)$ a high value of ρ will reduce the variance of the growth rate relative to that of the level.

Interpolation (section 4.3.2) creates a different, and much more complicated, pattern of autocorrelation. Nevertheless, it remains the case that it results in measurement errors varying with the time from the benchmark years and in which changes are measured more reliably than levels. The presence of autocorrelation also, of course, means that adjustments to data for one period imply adjustments to data in other periods. This may have an important impact on the results of any data reconciliation exercise.

For these two reasons, the presence of autocorrelation in measurement error cannot be neglected. The subsequent sections describe the way in which the data of our study are constructed and the autocorrelation to which this is likely to give rise.

4.3 Patterns of autocorrelation and covariance

4.3.1 Extrapolation

If data are extrapolated from a single reference point, the error structure is simple. The relation between the indicator variable, i_t, and the true value, b_t^*, is given as

$$i_t = kb_t^*(1 + v_t) \tag{4.7}$$

where v_t is an error term with expected value of zero. This corresponds exactly to the assumption made about the error process of the indicator described in section 4.1 above. If the reference or benchmark year is N, then

$$b_t = b_N(i_t/i_N) \tag{4.8}$$

offers an extrapolated estimate of b_t^*. If $b_N = b_N^*(1 + \epsilon_N)$, with ϵ_N being a percentage error term in b_N and $E(\epsilon_N) = 0$, then, to a first-order approximation, as in equation (4.1),

$$u_t = \frac{b_t}{b_t^*} - 1 = \epsilon_N + v_t - v_N \tag{4.9}$$

where u_t is the proportionate error in b_t, $b_t = b_t^*(1 + u_t)$. It is now possible to calculate the autocorrelation between u_t and u_{t+k}. This is shown in a more general form which allows for the possibility that u_t is calculated with reference to benchmark N_1 while u_{t+k} is calculated with reference to benchmark N_2. Such a situation can arise in some cases (section 4.3.3) below, and there is no loss of generality since, with only one benchmark point, $N_1 = N_2$. The autocorrelation is

$$\begin{aligned} E(u_t u_{t+k}) &= E(\epsilon_{N_1}\epsilon_{N_2}) + E(v_t v_{t+k}) - E(v_{t+k} v_{N_1}) \\ &\quad - E(v_t v_{N_2}) + E(v_{N_1} v_{N_2}) \\ &= \sigma^2_{\epsilon_{N_1},\epsilon_{N_2}} + \frac{\sigma_w^2}{1 - \rho^2}(\rho^k + \rho^{|N_1 - N_2|} - \rho^{|t+k-N_1|} - \rho^{|t-N_2|}) \end{aligned} \tag{4.10}$$

on the assumption that the two sources of error ϵ_N and v_t are independent of each other. This expression should be interpreted bearing in mind that $E(\epsilon_{N_1}\epsilon_{N_2}) = \sigma^2_{\epsilon_{N_1},\epsilon_{N_2}} = 0$ unless $N_1 = N_2$. Approximating the true data by the observations, we may then write

$$\text{cov}\,(b_t, b_{t+k}) = b_t b_{t+k} E(u_t u_{t+k}) \tag{4.11}$$

as the covariance between the measured values of b_t and b_{t+k}.

4.3.2 *Interpolation between benchmarks*

Frequent use is made of interpolation in data construction. This can be described in the following way. A trend line is drawn between the two successive observations of the benchmark variable, b_{N_1} and b_{N_2} and the variable used for interpolation, i_{N_1} and i_{N_2}, for observations in benchmark years N_1 and N_2. The ratio of the indicator variable i_t to the trend value, $[(N_2 - t)i_{N_1} + (t - N_1)i_{N_2}]/(N_2 - N_1)$ is then applied to the trend value of the benchmark $[(N_2 - t)b_{N_1} + (t - N_1)b_{N_2}]/(N_2 - N_1)$ so that the interpolated value is given as

$$b_t = \frac{i_t[(N_2 - t)b_{N_1} + (t - N_1)b_{N_2}]}{[(N_2 - t)i_{N_1} + (t - N_1)i_{N_2}]}. \tag{4.12}$$

The true values of the benchmarked data are denoted by b^* and it is once again assumed that

$$b_N = b_N^*(1 + \epsilon_N) \tag{4.13}$$

in a benchmark year, while the indicator is related to the true data as

$$i_t = kb_t^*(1 + v_t). \tag{4.14}$$

We may then write the estimated data as

$$b_t = b_t^*(1 + v_t)\left[\frac{(N_2 - t)b_{N_1}^*(1 + 1\epsilon_{N_1}) + (t - N_1)b_{N_2}^*(1 + \epsilon_{N_2})}{(N_2 - t)b_{N_1}^*(1 + v_{N_1}) + (t - N_1)b_{N_2}^*(1 + v_{N_2})}\right]. \tag{4.15}$$

To a first-order approximation we may then replace $b_{N_1}^*, b_{N_2}^*$ by b_{N_1}, b_{N_2} and calculate the proportionate error in b_t,

$$\begin{aligned} u_t &= \frac{b_t}{b_t^*} - 1 \\ &= v_t + r_t([N_2 - t]b_{N_2}\epsilon_{N_1} + [t - N_1]b_{N_1}\epsilon_{N_2} - [N_2 - t]b_{N_1}v_{N_1} + \\ &\quad [t - N_1]b_{N_2}v_{N_2}) \end{aligned} \tag{4.16}$$

where

$$r_t = \frac{1}{(N_2 - t)b_{N_1} + (t - N_1)b_{N_2}}. \tag{4.17}$$

From (4.16) it is a straightforward, if involved, matter to work out the autocorrelation between the measurement errors in estimates of b_t and b_{t+k} where t lies between N_1 and N_2 and $t + k$ lies between N_3 and N_4.

$$
\begin{aligned}
E(u_t u_{t+k}) &= E(v_t v_{t+k}) - r_t b_{N_1}(N_2 - t)E(v_{N_1} v_{t+k}) \\
&- r_t b_{N_2}(t - N_1)E(v_{N_2} v_{t+k}) - r_{t+k} b_{N_3}(N_4 - t - k)E(v_{N_3} v_t) \\
&- r_{t+k} b_{N_4}(t + k - N_3)E(v_{N_4} v_t) \\
&+ r_t r_{t+k}\{b_{N_1} b_{N_3}[N_2 - t][N_4 - t - k]E(\epsilon_{N_1}\epsilon_{N_3} + v_{N_1} v_{N_3}) \\
&+ [t - N_1][t + k - N_3]b_{N_2} b_{N_4} E(\epsilon_{N_2}\epsilon_{N_4} + v_{N_2} v_{N_4}) \\
&+ [N_2 - t][t + k - N_3]b_{N_1} b_{N_4} E(\epsilon_{N_1}\epsilon_{N_4} + v_{N_1} v_{N_4}) \\
&+ [t - N_1][N_4 - t - k]b_{N_2} b_{N_3} E(\epsilon_{N_2}\epsilon_{N_3} + v_{N_2} v_{N_3})\} \\
&= \sigma_v^2\{\rho^k - r_t b_{N_1}(N_2 - t)\rho^{|t+k-N_1|} - r_t b_{N_2}(t - N_1)\rho^{|t+k-N_2|} \\
&- r_{t+k} b_{N_3}(N_4 - t - k)\rho^{|N_3 - t|} - r_{t+k} b_{N_4}(t + k - N_3)\rho^{|t-N_4|}\} \\
&+ r_t r_{t+k}(b_{N_1} b_{N_3}[N_2 - t][N_4 - t - k][\sigma^2_{\epsilon_{N_1},\epsilon_{N_3}} + \sigma_v^2\rho^{|N_1 - N_3|}] \\
&+ [t - N_1][t + k - N_3]b_{N_2} b_{N_4}[\sigma^2_{\epsilon_{N_2},\epsilon_{N_4}} + \sigma_v^2\rho^{|N_2 - N_4|}] \\
&+ [N_2 - t][t + k - N_3]b_{N_1} b_{N_4}[\sigma^2_{\epsilon_{N_1},\epsilon_{N_4}} + \sigma_v^2\rho^{|N_1 - N_4|}] \\
&+ [t - N_1][N_4 - t - k]b_{N_2} b_{N_3}[\sigma^2_{\epsilon_{N_2},\epsilon_{N_3}} + \sigma_v^2\rho^{|N_2 - N_3|}]) \quad (4.18)
\end{aligned}
$$

on the reasonable assumption that the v_N and ϵ_N are uncorrelated. It may also be assumed that the measurement errors in the benchmarks, $\epsilon_{N_1}, \epsilon_{N_2}, \epsilon_{N_3}$ and ϵ_{N_4} are uncorrelated, so that the terms in the final two lines of expression (4.18) only make a contribution to the covariance when the interpolation periods coincide or are consecutive.

4.3.3 Autocorrelation between interpolated and extrapolated data

The benchmarks used in interpolation will not, typically, fall at the ends of the data period and it may in practice be the case that benchmarking does not extend to a time outside the data period of interest. For example, if the interwar data are considered in isolation (and this makes a great deal of sense because the wars led to major data discontinuities), then the earliest benchmark year is 1924, with the latest 1935 for many data series of interest. The implication is that the estimates before 1924 or after 1935 are constructed by extrapolation rather than interpolation. The autocorrelation in the measurement error between an interpolated estimate and an extrapolated estimate is given by a combination of the error specifications of the previous two sections. Suppose that t lies between N_1 and N_2 so that b_t is calculated by interpolation, while $t + k$ lies above N_3 so that b_{t+k} is constructed by extrapolation. The autocorrelation of the measurement errors is then given as

$$
\begin{aligned}
E(u_t u_{t+k}) &= E(v_t v_{t+k}) - E(v_{N_3} v_t) \\
&\quad + E(\epsilon_{N_3}\epsilon_{N_1}) r_t b_{N_1}(N_2 - t) + E(\epsilon_{N_3}\epsilon_{N_2}) r_t b_{N_2}(t - N_1) \\
&\quad + E(v_{N_3} v_{N_1}) r_t b_{N_1}(N_2 - t) + E(v_{N_3} v_{N_2}) r_t b_{N_2}(t - N_1) \\
&\quad - E(v_{N_1} v_{t+k}) r_t b_{N_1}(N_2 - t) - E(v_{N_2} v_{t+k}) r_t b_{N_2}(t - N_1) \\
&= [G_w^2/(1-\rho^2)]\Big\{\rho^k - \rho^{|t-N_3|} \\
&\quad + \rho^{|N_3-N_1|} r_t b_{N_1}(N_2 - t) + \rho^{|N_3-N_2|} r_t b_{N_2}(t - N_1) \\
&\quad - \rho^{|t+k-N_1|} r_t b_{N_1}(N_2 - t) - \rho^{|t+k-N_2|} r_t b_{N_2}(t - N_1)\Big\} \\
&\quad + \sigma^2_{\epsilon_{N_3},\epsilon_{N_1}} r_t b_{N_1}(N_2 - t) + \sigma^2_{\epsilon_{N_3},\epsilon_{N_2}} r_t b_{N_2}(t - N_1). \qquad (4.19)
\end{aligned}
$$

Once again the autocorrelation between different benchmark errors (ϵ_N) may be assumed to be zero, so that the terms in $\epsilon_{N_1}\epsilon_{N_3}$ and $\epsilon_{N_2}\epsilon_{N_3}$ only enter if N_3 coincides with either N_1 or N_2. It cannot coincide with both.

Finally, if the series is extrapolated at both ends, then the autocorrelation will be given by equation (4.10), where N_1 and N_2 represent the observations from which extrapolation takes place.

Whichever method is appropriate for calculating the covariance between u_t and u_{t+k}, the final covariance between the observed data is given by equation (4.11).

4.3.4 Covariance between constant and current price data

There is inevitably covariance between constant and current price data. If the constant price data are constructed by deflating the current price data by means of a deflator which is calculated separately, then the covariance between the two will equal the variance of the current price data, and the covariance between the constant price data in one period and the current price data in another period will equal the covariance between the current price data in the two different periods. If only a fraction of the volume data, x per cent, are constructed in this way, then the relevant variances and covariances will be multiplied by x^2 (where x is assumed constant although, over long periods it will not be). This was described by Weale (1988) and Solomou and Weale (1991) but, at the disaggregate level considered here, is not a problem. The constant price series can be regarded as constructed either by means of deflation or by using volume indicators with reference to the year of the price base.

However, wage estimates are calculated from estimates of employment and wage rates, while output estimates are calculated from estimates of employment. To the extent that the estimates of employment are incorrect, there will be covariance between the output and wage data, while to the extent that they are poor indicators of the change in output, there will not be. Since only relatively small parts of the series which we consider are measured from employment indicators, and since a large part of the output error will arise from the inappropriate use of the employment data, we have neglected this.

There are, however, two aspects of the current price/constant price relationship which were not dealt with by Weale (1988) and Solomou and Weale (1991). The first arises when the constant price data are constructed by means of volume indices applied to current price base-year data. This means that any error in the base-year data is reflected in all the constant price data; it generates a specific pattern of autocorrelation.

The variance of output in the constant price series for the base-year must be the same as the variance shown in the current price series, because the numbers are exactly the same. The covariance between the two must equal the variance. If $\sigma^2_{val,base}$ is the variance for the base-year (taken from information on current price data), while $\sigma^2_{vol,t}$ is the variance implied from the information about output reliabilities provided by statisticians and interpreted by means of the formulae of sections 4.3.1 and 4.3.2, then the variances actually used must be adjusted to

$$\sigma^2_{vol,t} + \sigma^2_{val,base} - \sigma^2_{vol,base}. \tag{4.20}$$

Since the base-year adjustment is present in all the variances, the same adjustment, $\sigma^2_{val,base} - \sigma^2_{vol,base}$, must be made to the estimates of the covariance between the errors in output in years t and $t+k$. The implication of this, of course, is that any percentage change made to the base-year current price data is reflected in all the constant price data for the same variable, because constant price data are always measured relative to base.

The position is complicated further by the presence of autocorrelation in the current price series. Observation $t+k$ in the current price series will have a covariance with the base-year observation in the current price series. Because the base-year error in the current price series is added in to all the constant price data, the covariance between the constant price estimate for t and the current price estimate for $t+k$ will equal the covariance between the current price estimate for $t+k$ and that for the base-year.

To the extent that constant price series are constructed by deflation, the issue is more straightforward but still requires some account to be taken of autocorrelation. The variances in the constant price series are the sum of those in the current price data and those in the price series.

The covariance between the constant and current price data is then the same as that in the current price data, and the covariance in the constant price data is the sum of that arising from the current price series and from the construction of the price index itself. It is easier to measure short-term price changes than long-term price changes. The errors in the price series are likely to be strongly autocorrelated. By definition the measurement error in prices is zero in the base-year. Strong autocorrelation implies that this source of error rises gradually to its asymptotic maximum, while weak covariance would imply a more sudden rise to the asymptotic maximum[1].

There is, however, one important difference between the sort of autocorrelation which arises here and that which was found in section 4.1. There the variance of v_t, the autocorrelated component of the measurement error, was constant, $\sigma_w^2/(1-\rho^2)$. In the case of deflators, the errors in the price index in the base-year are zero. They cumulate as one moves away from the base. If the proportionate error in the price series, π_t follows the following pattern

$$\begin{aligned} \pi_t &= \rho_p \pi_{t-1} + w_t \quad t > \textit{base-year} \\ \pi_t &= \rho_p \pi_{t+1} + w_t \quad t < \textit{base-year} \\ \pi_{base} &= 0 \end{aligned}$$

then the covariance between errors in a deflated constant price series is given as

$$\begin{aligned} E(u_t u_{t+k}) &= \textit{covariance from current price data} \\ &+ \rho^k \frac{\sigma_w^2}{1-\rho^2}(1-\rho^{2|t+1-base|})(-1<\rho<1) \end{aligned} \tag{4.21}$$

if $t+k>t>base$ or $t<t+k<base$ and

$$E(u_t u_{t+k}) = \textit{covariance from current price data} \tag{4.22}$$

if $t<base<t+k$. With a unit root in the measurement error ($\rho=1$)

$$E(u_t u_{t+k}) = \textit{covariance from current price data} + t\sigma_w^2 \tag{4.23}$$

if $t+k>t>base$ or $t<t+k<base$ and

$$E(u_t u_{t+k}) = \textit{covariance from current price data} \tag{4.24}$$

if $t<base<t+k$.

[1] The example considered by Weale (1988) assumed that there was no covariance at all, and that therefore prices relative to base were measured with the same reliability for years distant from the base as for those years close to the base.

4.3.5 Unit roots in constant price data

In the current price data the assumption that the error processes are stationary makes reasonable sense. Otherwise the errors would be expected to worsen with the passage of time, and there is no obvious reason why that should be the case.

With constant price data the situation is rather different. If the error patterns were stationary, it would follow that the annual average growth rate could be computed with a measurement error which would fall asymptotically to zero. This seems inherently unlikely. While it is reasonable to expect that the standard error with which the annual average growth rate is measured declines over time, it should not be expected to decline to zero. The problems of measuring volume and price changes over long periods are well known and are referred to briefly in section 4.2. We think it sensible to include a small unit root error process in the error attributed to each volume series. The parametrisation of these unit root processes is discussed in chapters 5 and 6.

4.3.6 Covariance across accounts

One important point which must be taken into consideration in the calculation of balanced estimates of national income is the question of covariance between entries on the two sides of the accounts. This can be expected to arise if the same data are used to make both entries. For example, the imputed income from ownership of dwellings is a component of housing costs and is entered there both as income and as expenditure. Consumers' expenditure on domestic service is measured by employment and wage rates in domestic service and is a component of the output of the 'miscellaneous services' industry. Expenditure on public administration and defence is a part of public consumption. Measurement errors in any of these expenditure side variables will lead to equal errors in the output/income side variables, and any adjustment to one must lead to an equal adjustment in the relevant component on the other. Such an adjustment therefore cannot be used to allocate any residual error.

In this situation it is typically not the case that exactly the same number appears on both sides of the account. Rather an element on one side of the account includes as a component the entry on the other side of the account. The covariance between the two entries is then equal to the variance in the component. For example the covariance between spending on domestic service and output of miscellaneous services is equal to the variance of spending on domestic service. Since these data appear in both constant and current prices, the correction must be made to both. A covariance also exists between the constant price figure for spending on domestic service and the current price wage component of the value added of the miscellaneous services industry. This is equal to the covariance between the constant and current price estimates of domestic services expenditure. A similar covariance exists between current price domestic service consumption and constant price miscellaneous service output.

The examples above present situations in which the covariance between the two sides of the account is equal to the variance of the component concerned. A similar but more complicated situation arises when consumption data are calculated from the supply side. The variance of the consumption data is equal to the sums of the variances of the output, import and export data plus an allowance for errors in distributive margins, and the covariance between consumption and supply is equal to the variance of the supply estimate concerned.

Nevertheless, the fact is that, even if common sources are used, the consumption and output data tend to be constructed by different people making different assumptions. In view of this we have neglected cross-account variance from this source.

4.4 Conclusions

This chapter has set out the patterns of measurement error which are likely to arise in the construction of constant and current price components of national income. The practice of benchmarking leads to a situation in which the data in benchmark years are more reliable than those in other years and with errors in benchmark data permeating the other observations. Constant price data are likely to show some covariance with the related current price data, and the method by which they are constructed from a base-year is again likely to lead to a specific pattern of serial correlation.

The next step in the estimation of balanced estimates of national income is an assessment of the actual data reliabilities reported by researchers and official sources. This forms the basis for the parametrisation of the variance pattern described here.

5 The data and their reliability, 1920–1948

5.1 Data sources

The data covering the period 1920 to 1945 are those provided by Feinstein (1972) with only minor modifications. Feinstein, in turn, brought together estimates of the components of national income provided by a number of different authors for the period 1920 to 1938, while many of the data for 1939–45 are those provided by the *Statistical Digest of the War*. The main sources on which Feinstein draws are, for consumers' expenditure, Stone (1954) and Stone and Rowe (1966), for gross capital formation, Feinstein (1965), for wages and salaries Chapman (1953), for industrial output Lomax (1959) with the remainder of the data being the product of much painstaking research from a variety of official and other sources. Some of the official series, available from the Central Statistical Office, begin in 1946 and others in 1948. These, in current prices, are used in preference to Feinstein's figures for 1946–7 where they differ. Feinstein's disaggregation of investment and consumption is scaled to satisfy the newer aggregate estimates.

We have made three modifications to Feinstein's figures. First of all, he adds on an unallocated component to Chapman's figures for wages and salaries of 2 per cent of the total to cover the employment of juveniles. There are also unallocated components of employers' contributions and directors' fees. We have allocated all these by industry in the same proportions as the wage and salary figures reported by Chapman.

Second, Feinstein's profit data are gross of stock appreciation (inventory valuation adjustment). We have allocated this across industries in proportion to the 1938 level of stocks identified by Feinstein.

Third, Feinstein reports an unallocated component of profit for the years 1920 to 1925. This arose from payments net of repayments of excess profits duty and corporation profits tax and has been allocated in the same proportions as identified trading profits.

For the period up to 1948 we have used the same classification as Feinstein. From 1948 to 1990 we have worked to the 1980 Standard Industrial Classification. However, we have reallocated subcategories so as to produce industrial groupings which are as close as possible to those used by Feinstein. Thus, although there is a break in classification in 1948 we have kept it to a minimum. The reclassification post 1948 is discussed in chapter 6.

One aspect of the data is that less detail is available for the wartime years than for either the interwar or postwar period.[1] There are no estimates of industrial output between 1939 and 1945, so that there is no output estimate available for this period. Wages and profits are not distinguished by industry of origin but only by sector of receipt. The categories of consumers' expenditure and fixed capital formation are broader and no decomposition of public expenditure is available.

We have dealt with this by carrying out the balancing exercise in three stages. First of all we have balanced the interwar years (to 1938 prices) and the postwar years (to 1985 prices) quite independently. We then balanced the current GDP figures for 1938–48 with the additional constraints that the 1938 and 1948 figures should agree with the results of the two independent exercises. In addition, the constant price data in 1938 prices were balanced for 1946, 1947 and 1948. This allowed a link with the constant price data for the period 1948 to 1990 measured in 1985 prices. Such an approach seemed to be the best feasible means of coping with the loss of detail in the war years, while nevertheless maintaining a high level of detail for the periods 1920 to 1938 and 1948 to 1990.[2]

The rest of this chapter describes the data reliability for the period 1920 to 1948, with chapter 6 providing information on data sources and reliability for 1948–90. Chapter 7 explains how we have filled in the sectoral accounts, and chapter 8 offers a brief summary of the results presented in the Appendix.

5.2 Data reliability, 1920–1938

5.2.1 Reliability codes

The data sources tend to use reliability codings A, B, C and D, but the various authors place different interpretations on these codes. The error

1 There is some extra detail available in 1946 and 1947. However, we found it convenient to treat 1948 as our break point. The reader who requires more detail for 1946 and 1947 is referred to Feinstein (1972) and to the relevant *Blue Books*.

2 The alternative of balancing the entire dataset for 1920–90 in one go would have exceeded the limits of the computers available to us.

Table 5.1 *Reliability ranges used by Feinstein (1972) (by percentage)*

Reliability	Lower limit	Upper limit	Standard error	
			Lower limit	Upper limit
A	0.0	5.0	0.0	3.0
B	5.0	15	3.0	9.1
C	15	25	9.1	15.2
D	25	40	15.2	24.4

codes used by Feinstein (1972) are summarised in table 5.1. Feinstein suggests that these represent 0.5 × 90 per cent confidence intervals or 1.64 standard errors, and the standard errors of table 5.1 are calculated on that basis.

In the cases of wages and salaries, capital formation and consumers' expenditure, the primary sources have used different coding arrangements. These are explained where relevant and the standard errors are calculated from the relevant interpretations of the reliability codes, with the classification of table 5.1 being used unless indicated otherwise. Where standard errors are believed to be constant over time we have taken them to be the midpoints of the ranges found by dividing Feinstein's intervals by 1.64 or from the other information as appropriate.

As will be clear from chapter 4, many of the data are assumed to be measured with errors which are serially correlated with patterns described in section 4.3.2 when the data are extrapolated from a single base-year or in sections 4.3.3 and 4.3.4 when interpolation between reference points is involved.

Where extrapolation or interpolation is involved, we have assumed that the standard error rises from the bottom of the relevant range (or in the case of A-rated data 1.2 per cent corresponding to 2 per cent on Feinstein's scale) in the benchmark year asymptotically to the top of the range. Once the serial correlation parameter, ρ, is specified, the model is fully defined and it is then possible to work out the reliability with which year-on-year changes in variables are measured as percentages of the data themselves.

The error structure set out in chapter 4 was one with an error in the benchmark year of ϵ_N and an error in the indicator variable of v_t. The basic error structure is assumed to be multiplicative, so that overall proportionate errors can be calculated by adding and subtracting percentage standard errors. u_t is the overall percentage error in the data thus derived.

Table 5.2 *Reliability ranges (by percentage)*

Reliability	Lower limit	Upper limit	σ_w	$\sigma_{\Delta v}$
A	1.2	3.0	1.2	1.2
B	3.0	9.1	3.6	3.8
C	9.1	15.2	5.2	5.4
D	15.2	24.4	8.1	8.5

The two equations which defined the error model in chapter 4 (equations (4.1) and (4.3)) are

$$u_t = \epsilon_N + v_t - v_N \tag{5.1}$$

$$v_t = \rho v_{t-1} + w_t. \tag{5.2}$$

With the asymptotic standard error given by $E(u_\infty^2)$, we can derive, from equations (4.4) and (4.5)

$$\sigma_w^2 = \{E(u_\infty^2) - \sigma_\epsilon^2\}(1 - \rho^2)/2 \tag{5.3}$$

so that specification of the benchmark year variance σ_ϵ^2, the asymptotic variance, $E(u_\infty^2)$ and ρ allow σ_w^2 and thus σ_w to be calculated. The variance associated with a year-on-year change in the data is then given from equation (4.6) as

$$\sigma_{\Delta v}^2 = E(v_t - v_{t-1})^2 = 2\frac{\sigma_w^2}{1 + \rho}. \tag{5.4}$$

Table 5.2 shows the values of σ_w and $\sigma_{\Delta v}$ which are implied by Feinstein's reliabilities in table 5.1 with $\rho = 0.8$

It can be seen that, although differences are typically measured more reliably than levels, the margins of error remain considerable. Obviously, similar figures can be calculated for other values of ρ and for the reliability ranges quoted by other sources.

The calculated standard errors become rather more complex when interpolation is involved and no great purpose would be served by presenting analytically the reliabilities associated with year-on-year changes which ensue. There is, however, one particular point which should be mentioned. Often the data may be interpolated between two points which are given different reliability ranges. In that case the intermediate years between the two benchmarks would have two different values of $E(u_\infty)^2$ and σ_w^2 associated with them. In such circumstances we have used the geometric mean of the two values.

The overall effects of interpolation and extrapolation are visible in the standard errors shown in tables 5.8 and 5.9 on pages 89–91.

5.2.2 *Wages and salaries*

There are three main methods of data construction for these aggregates.

(i) Estimates based on employment figures in the 1931 Census. Employment figures are extrapolated forwards and backwards on the basis of unemployment insurance data. These are then multiplied by estimates of average wage rates. This leads to the error process of section 4.3.1.

(ii) Estimates calculated from the censuses of production in 1924, 1930 and 1935 and interpolated on the basis of estimated employment and earnings figures in the intervening years. This leads to the error process of section 4.3.2.

(iii) Accurate data from official returns. These have a small measurement error with no autocorrelation.

Despite the fact that the data estimated by methods (ii) and (iii) appear to be reasonably symmetric around the midpoint of our data series, Chapman suggests that the later data are more accurate than the earlier estimates, and our assessment of measurement errors should reflect this.

The classification by industry is as follows. With method (i) it is assumed that the 1931 data have the standard error associated with the bottom of the range quoted for 1938. This gives a value for $E(\epsilon_{1931}\epsilon_{1931})^{1/2}$ of 2.5 per cent for B-rated data, 5 per cent for C-rated data and 12.5 per cent for D-rated data. A value of 1 per cent has been used for A-rated data. The value of σ_w^2 associated with equations (4.4), section 4.3.1, and (4.16), section 4.3.2, is calculated using (5.3).

In some industries the 1920 data are regarded as less reliable than the 1938 data. In this case we have taken the asymptotic standard error to be the midpoint of the relevant range for 1920, and relied on the longer period of extrapolation to deliver a larger standard error to the 1920 data than to the 1938 data.

The same principles have been used for data calculated by method (ii). It is assumed that extrapolation would raise the error asymptotically from the bottom to the top of the relevant range, and this allows us to calculate values for σ_ϵ^2 and σ_w^2 as set out above. Of course, the use of interpolation means that actually each standard error remains close to the bottom of the relevant ranges (see table 5.3).

Table 5.3 *Reliabilities: wages and salaries*

Industry	Method	Reliability 1920	Reliability 1938	Standard error
Agriculture etc.	(i)	C	C	See below
Mining	Mainly (iii)	B	A	5% 1920–26, 2.5% 1927–38
Manufacturing	(ii)	C	B	See below
Building	(ii)	C	B	See below
Utilities	(ii)	C	B	See below
Transport	Railways (iii), others (i)	C	C	Method (iii) used. 8.6%
Communication	(iii)	A	A	1.3%
Distribution	(i)	D	C	See below
Banking and finance	(i)	D	C	See below
PAD	(iii)	B	A	1920–26 3.8%, 1927–38 1.3%
Other services	(i)	D	C	See below
The error ranges* quoted by Chapman are		A	0–5%	
		B	5–10%	
		C	10–25%	
		D	⩾25%	

Note: *These are twice standard errors. An upper limit of 40% has been assumed for D.

The benchmark years are 1924, 1930 and 1935. We have assumed that in 1930 and 1935 the reliabilities are described by the ranges quoted by Chapman for 1938, while the 1920 ranges are assumed to relate to the data calculated from the 1924 benchmark. With two different values for σ_w and $E(u_\infty^2)$ the geometric mean is used, as discussed in section 5.2.1. The value of ρ which we have used is 0.6.[3]

For method (iii) no autocorrelation is assumed. For an industry like mining, the data are described as having an A reliability in 1938 and a B reliability in 1920. We have assumed that the change takes place in 1927 and that the standard error falls from the middle of the B range to the upper limit of the A range.

[3] See section 5.3.

5.2.3 Profits

Profits data are compiled in the same way for all industrial groups. Between 1920 and 1926 inaccurate but annual data were used. Between 1927 and 1938 the method of interpolation was used, with benchmarks in 1927, 1932, 1936, 1937 and 1938. The pattern of autocorrelation thus corresponds to method (ii) for wages and salaries and is described by the formulae of section 4.3.2. As in the case of wages and salaries, it is assumed that in the benchmark years the errors are at the bottom of the range, and the process of autocorrelation would take them asymptotically to the top of the range. The autocorrelation parameter is again assumed to be 0.6. No autocorrelation is assumed for the years 1920 to 1926, and these estimates are also assumed to be uncorrelated with the later ones.

The suggested error ranges are B for 1927–38 and C for 1920–26 on Feinstein's definition. However, we have raised the standard errors associated with the data for the period 1927–38, because the use of B classification led to a standard error of total profit or operating surplus in some of the interwar years which was lower than that in some of the postwar years. This seemed inherently unlikely, and we have therefore, instead of the range specified in table 5.2, assumed that the standard error rose asymptotically from 8 per cent to 12.5 per cent for the profits of each industry. The value of ρ we have used is again 0.6.

5.2.4 Output

There are three types of output indicator used. The agricultural data are derived by double deflation, with price indices being used for both outputs and inputs. Except for the link introduced in the choice of reference year, these data are likely to be independent of the value added data. Autocorrelation will be present to the extent that the price indices 'go off'; changes in quality mean that it is easier to measure price changes over short periods than over long periods. The industrial output indices are those constructed by Lomax (1959), while volume indicators are used for the service sectors, combined by 1938 weights.

Lomax's series are constructed using the benchmarking principle (section 4.3.2, chapter 4) method (ii) based on the censuses of 1924, 1930, 1933, 1934 and 1935. These indices can be assumed to be uncorrelated with the profits data (which were not constructed from census data), but may be correlated with the wages data (which were). Indicator information is used to interpolate between the census years, in a method very similar to that of section 5.2.2, method (ii) for wages and salaries.

Correlation between the wages and salaries and output data will exist only to the extent that employment was used as the indicator variable in both cases; as explained in section 4.3.2, this has been neglected.

The assumption made, once again, is that in the census years the standard error is at the bottom of its range, but that errors in the indicator variables would take the standard error asymptotically to the top of its range. There is, in addition, assumed to be an element of autocorrelation arising from the use of deflated value rather than pure volume estimates. However, Lomax offers no clue as to the extent to which he has done this and we have assumed that the output series are constructed entirely from volume indicators.

Utilities' output may be assumed to be measured accurately without serial correlation except for that arising from the base-year of the price series.

For the services data, it is assumed that the method of section 4.3.1 is used. It is assumed that the pattern of autocorrelation is such that the standard error rises from the bottom of the range to approach the top of the range asymptotically. The volume indicator of service output is typically employment, and this is extrapolated from the 1931 census on the basis of unemployment data; 1931 therefore provides the benchmark year from which extrapolation takes place.

No specific reliability indicators are given. The standard errors for the components of manufacturing are given lower limits of 4 per cent and upper limits of 9.1 per cent. These have been assessed so that, when added up, they give the aggregate manufacturing series a reliability consistent with B on Feinstein's rating. Mining and the utilities are given A ratings. Public administration and defence is given an optimistic midpoint A rising to midpoint B reliability so as to offset the fact that the same data are used in the calculation of public consumption.[4] The serial correlation parameters are set to 0.8.[5]

In addition to the variances which these calculations give we have to add on the sum of the variances of wages and profit in 1938 as calculated in sections 4.3.1 and 4.3.2 to all the volume variances and to deduct the 1938 volume variance. This net adjustment must also be added to the covariances of the measurement errors between all the years of our sample. The reason for this is that a shift in the base-year value added data must imply a shift in all the constant price output data (see section 4.3.4). The adjustment ensures, of course, that the industrial output at

[4] This does, unfortunately, mean that our estimates of the standard error of GDP are slightly too low.

[5] See section 5.3.

constant prices is, in the base-year, equal to the value added in each industry.

These error patterns on their own would imply that the errors in the output data are stationary. As noted in section 4.3.5, this seems unlikely. We have added an additional unit-root process into the error pattern, with the standard error of the unit-root process being 0.66 per cent p.a.

5.2.5 *Gross fixed capital formation*

Current prices

The estimates of capital formation were compiled almost entirely as differences in estimated capital stocks, adjusted for depreciation. This should not lead to autocorrelation because the data are derived from firms' balance sheets, which will themselves be compiled by adding on the flow of new investment to the stock of capital inherited from the previous year. The measurement errors are of type (iii) of section 5.2.2. Feinstein describes the data sources in careful detail for at least two classes of asset in each of twenty industries. To work in this detail would seem to be unwarranted given that much less information is used for variables such as wages and salaries which are much more important components of the accounts.

In this study investment is classified by type of asset, and it is perhaps only putting a slightly optimistic gloss on Feinstein's account to believe that the current price data can be represented as having serially uncorrelated errors. This means that estimates of the variance can be compiled simply by adding up the variances provided by Feinstein (1965), p. 237. Standard errors have been calculated from his reliabilities, interpreting A to mean 1.8 per cent, B 5.5 per cent, C 10 per cent and D 16.8 per cent.[6] Weighting these together by the average expenditure on each type of asset in the period 1920 to 1938, the standard errors of table 5.4 for the aggregate categories result.

Constant price data

The constant price data are produced by deflating the current price data by rather arbitrary deflators (Feinstein, 1965, p. 24). There do not seem to be any important cases in which pure volume data are used. This means that the percentage error in the volume series is equal to the sum

[6] Feinstein (1965) gives error ranges *A*, 0–7 per cent, *B*, 7–15 per cent, *C*, 15–25 per cent, *D*, > 25 per cent, which are taken as twice standard errors. These ranges differ from the ranges quoted by Feinstein (1972) and shown in table 5.3. The mid-range values have been chosen for A, B and C data.

Table 5.4 *Capital formation reliabilities (% standard errors)*

Type of asset	Reliability
Plant and machinery	1.7
Ships	10.0
Other vehicles	4.3
Dwellings	5.5
Other buildings and works	1.4

of the percentage error in the value series and the percentage measurement error in the price index. This error is obviously zero in the base-year, whichever year is chosen, and it presumably increases with the number of years one is from the base-year. We have represented this with a unit root with standard error equal to 0.33 per cent p.a. cumulating away from the base-year, 1938.

5.2.6 Stockbuilding

Current prices

Stockbuilding estimates are constructed in the same way as fixed capital formation estimates, and they may be taken to be serially uncorrelated. There is one important difference. It does not make much sense to express the standard deviation as a fraction of the estimated value, because estimates close to zero do not imply accuracy. Instead the standard error may be assumed to be a fraction of some broad current price aggregate. We have assumed that it is 1.5 per cent of the trend line linking the 1920 and 1938 consumption estimates. Table 5.6 on page 87 shows the percentage standard errors which this implies in each year.

Constant prices

The constant price data are derived by deflating, and it is assumed that the standard error in the price index confers an additional unit root with standard error of 0.33 per cent p.a.

5.2.7 Public consumption

Current prices

The estimates of public consumption in current prices are derived from annual returns, and, with one or two minor exceptions, there is no suggestion of benchmarking or interpolation. Feinstein (1972) suggests B reliabilities for 1920 and A reliabilities for the period 1921 to 1938. He does, however, note problems in converting from a financial to a calendar-year basis. This might be thought to induce a moving average error process. If one year's estimate is too high, then the adjacent year's might tend to be too low, but there is no effect on any other years. We have simply assumed that this problem is too small to worry about.

These methods of data construction imply full covariance with the relevant wages and salaries data on the income side. There is a slight problem here. On the income side, public administration and defence is entirely public sector, and the covariance between this and public authorities' current expenditure is equal to the variance of the public administration and defence wages and salaries estimate. 'Other services' is only partly public consumption. One may infer from Chapman that about one quarter of the labour income in this sector is a component of public consumption. However, the low overall variance of public authorities' current expenditure estimates means that this covariance may safely be neglected.

These covariances mean that only rather small changes will be made to public authorities' current expenditure in order to reconcile the discrepancy in GDP. Since the wages and salaries components appear on both sides of the account, adjustments to them will not help to remove this discrepancy.

Constant prices

Once again, the deflation of current price data is likely to induce autocorrelation. Procurements are deflated by the most appropriate of (i) the index of building costs used for investment goods, (ii) the index of machinery costs used for investment goods, and (iii) the general consumption deflator. The first two deflators relate mainly to capital formation (although military hardware is treated as current consumption). This implies covariance between the public consumption data and the other constant price figures. We have neglected this, and our disaggregate results do not suggest that this is an important source of error because the overall changes to public consumption in our balancing exercise are small.

The labour component of constant price consumption is calculated by using 1938 rates of pay and the relevant employment level for central government employment. The local authority payroll is deflated by Chapman's index of wages and salaries for the appropriate sector. In both cases this induces autocorrelation of the type set out in section 3.5. For the central government data the autocorrelation arises through possible mismeasurement of the 1938 component of output. For local authorities it might stem both from errors in the 1938 level and from possible mismeasurement in the index. However, average local authority salaries are calculated by dividing independent estimates of the wage bill into the employment estimate. The method of calculation of constant price output is therefore equivalent to the method for central government. However, the employment figures are less accurate than for central government, with the police forces being counted directly, and with other employment being extrapolated on the basis of unemployment insurance with the 1931 census as a base. This creates a rather awkward hybrid situation. For the inaccurate employment data, it would seem that section 4.3.1 should be applied, with the base-year 1931 as amended by adjustment (4.20). However, for reasons of simplicity, bearing in mind that the data are reasonably reliable, we have decided simply to work back from the 1938 base.

The constant price measure is therefore calculated from 1938 as a base with a value of $\sigma_n = 1.25$ per cent (an A rating for the value data). It is assumed to rise asymptotically to the midpoint of the rating, with $\rho = 0.6$.[7] An additional unit root with a standard error of 0.33 per cent p.a. is added to this.

There is covariance between these data and the output data for public administration and defence and 'other services' for the same reason as that found in the current price data. However, the output series measure the volume of added value, and do not distinguish wages from profits. This does not affect public administration and defence – there are no profits. The covariance between the public administration and defence data and constant-price public authorities' current expenditure is equal to the estimated variance of the public administration and defence data, and has the implication that the discrepancy in the constant price accounts cannot be corrected by a change in public administration and defence because that would imply an equal change in public authorities' current expenditure on the other side of the account. There is a small public sector component of 'other services', but given also the small size of the adjustment to public authorities' current expenditure which we make, this covariance can again be neglected.

There is no covariance between the constant and current price data except in 1938 (the base-year) when it is obviously equal to the variance of each estimate.

5.2.8 Imports and exports

Goods at current and constant prices

Imports and exports of goods in current prices are compiled from trade data. The areas in which adjustments were made (such as second-hand

7 See section 5.3.

ships) are assumed to be too small to induce autocorrelation. The volume series are, in effect, derived using the method of section 4.3.1 working from 1938 as the base-year. We assume values of A for the current price data, and a unit root of 0.33 per cent p.a. is added on for the constant price data.

Services at current and constant prices

The financial services, travel and government components of service trade are probably measured without too much autocorrelation. The shipping figures are derived from benchmark estimates using 1936 and 1931 as reference points. The structure of section 4.3.2 thus applies between 1931 and 1936, while that of section 4.3.1 applies outside this period. There is some covariance between shipping exports and the current price data for imports on account of the way in which c.i.f. imports were broken down, but since this is a consequence of data construction and not due to any statistical link between the two series, it may be neglected.[8] We have simply given the estimates of service flows standard errors of 7.5 per cent. Once again, a unit root with standard error of 0.33 per cent p.a. has been added on for the constant price data.

5.2.9 Property income and transfer payments

These do not enter into the GDP identities and are therefore not relevant to the balancing exercise. They are derived from the accounting identities and cannot therefore be improved by balancing (see section 2.4).

5.2.10 Consumption

The construction of the consumption data leads to what is probably the most complicated type of error process. For those items which can be fitted into the framework of the censuses of production, the basic method is to derive consumption as a residual. Imports and output are added together and exports are deducted so as to produce sales to domestic final demand. The classification is done at a level of output sufficiently fine to be able to say that the sales to final demand is then a sale to consumption rather than to investment.

Outside the census years indicators of output change are used. The work predates Lomax's (1959) study of industrial output. Since it was carried out independently, it is quite likely that different indicators were

8 This can be contrasted with the treatment of consumption of domestic service where there is a clear economic link between the expenditure and income data. See section 4.3.4.

used. These indicators are used to project changes in output at constant prices, and the retail price indices are used to revalue them to current prices. Adjustments are again made to allow for foreign trade, and the outcome is an interpolated value for current consumption. This process is mostly used in the years before 1930. From 1930 onwards retail sales indices (in current prices) were used for interpolation instead. In both cases the interpolation is done on the assumption of constant distributive margins. The censuses of production, which provide evidence on this, seem to support this assumption. For these data we have assumed that the error process is a modified version of the method of section 4.3.2 which was used for wages and salaries. Once again, we have assumed that the benchmark data have standard errors at the bottom of the reliability range concerned and that if they were extrapolated rather than interpolated, they would rise to the top of the range. The value which this implies for σ_u^2 is then given from equation (4.18) and is as described in section 4.3.2. Once again, where two different values of σ_w^2 are implied the geometric mean is used. The value of ρ which we have used is 0.8 because the basic interpoland is an output series.[9] The volume measures are assumed to add on unit roots with standard errors of 0.66 per cent p.a.

The variance arising from uncertainty in the deflator is assumed to add on to the variance arising from interpolation so that the overall standard errors are slightly higher than those given by the limits of the ranges, but with a unit root having standard error of 0.33 per cent p.a. the effect is small.[10] There are, however, a number of areas to which this general approach does not apply. Consumption of alcohol and tobacco is measured in quantities from excise returns and is revalued to current prices by means of the appropriate component of the retail price index. Consumption of public transport is calculated from returns made by the firms involved. Consumption of services is calculated from rather poorly defined benchmarks and is extrapolated on the basis of employment data in the industries concerned.

The general method of data construction implies that the data follow the same sort of error process as the output data. However, a complication arises. The benchmark data derived from the censuses of production are current price data, while the interpolation is carried out on the basis of reflated constant price data. This means that, for interpolated data, the method of section 4.3.2 should be modified somewhat. Interpolation

[9] See section 5.3.

[10] Over twenty years the two unit roots taken together cumulate to a standard error of less than 2 per cent. With a standard error of 10 per cent, an additional error of 2 per cent takes the overall standard error to $(10^2 + 3.3^2)^{\frac{1}{2}} = 10.5$ per cent.

using constant price data and subsequent reflation ought to imply a rather complicated pattern of unit roots in both constant and current price data. However, the periods between censuses are relatively short, and with the values for the unit roots which we use, their cumulated effect is not that great.

We have therefore neglected the pattern of unit roots in the current price data, and assumed that that arising in the volume data is similar to that generated by the use of deflators elsewhere.[11] Nevertheless, recognising the role of the volume data in the interpolation process, we have assumed that the main serial correlation process (excluding the unit root) has a standard error of 0.8 as for the output series.

A final point arises with the adjustment made to reflect net tourists' expenditure and the like. This is rather like stockbuilding in that it is the difference of two large numbers; it makes little sense to express the standard error as a proportion of the estimated value. We have taken the current price estimate to have a standard deviation of 0.5 per cent of trend consumption, and assumed that the deflation of this adds a unit root with a standard error of 0.33 per cent p.a.

Table 5.5 shows the reliabilities which we have extracted from the figures quoted by Stone and Rowe (1966). The two columns with each year show the lower and upper limits of the percentage standard errors (σ_{u_1} and σ_{u_2}) associated with each of the benchmark years. These standard errors are taken from the reliability classification offered by Stone and Rowe (who present error margins representing twice standard errors) but they reflect gradual changes in reliability where this seems to have taken place; there is also a certain amount of reclassification involved compared with the reliabilities presented by Stone and Rowe for aggregate groupings. Where only one benchmark is shown, the extrapolative method of section 4.3.1 is used to calculate the error pattern, while if two or more benchmarks are shown, the interpolative methods of sections 4.3.2 and 4.3.3 are used. Where there is believed to be no serial correlation, the standard errors in the last column are used.

5.2.11 The Mahalanobis score

We can now use these standard errors to calculate the Mahalanobis score. The value obviously depends on the serial correlation parameters chosen. In principle each error term could have its own serial correlation parameter associated with it, but obviously it is impossible to work

[11] In other words the unit root pattern is generated by the deflation of the current price census of production data. The volume index only affects things between censuses of production.

Table 5.5 *Consumption reliabilites (% standard errors)*

Category	1921		1924		1930		1931		1933		1934		1935		1937		Constant
	σ_{u_1}	σ_{u_2}	σ_{u_1}	σ_{u_2}	σ_{u_1}	σ_{u_2}	σ_{u_1}	σ_{u_2}	σ_{u_1}	σ_{u_2}	σ_{u_1}	σ_{u_2}	σ_{u_1}	σ_{u_2}	σ_{u_1}	σ_{u_2}	
Food			1.0	2.0	0.8	2.0			0.5	2.0	0.5	2.0	0.5	2.0			
Drink																	1.3
Tobacco																	1.3
Housing															1.3	5.0	
Fuel and light															1.3	5.0	
Clothing			5.0	12.5			3.8	7.5								2.5	5.0
Motor cars					3.5	10.0							2.5	5.0			
Furniture			5.0	10.2	3.8	7.5							2.5	5.0			
Textiles			9.0	16.5	9.0	16.5							5.0	12.5			
Matches etc.			7.5	15.0	6.0	14.0							5.0	12.5	5.0	12.5	
Books			7.5	15.0	6.0	14.0							5.0	12.5			
Chemist's goods etc.	5.0	12.5					5.0	12.5									
Public transport																	3.8*
Vehicle running costs			7.5	12.5	7.5	12.5			7.5	12.5	7.5	12.5	7.5	12.5			
Domestic service	12.5	20.0					12.5	20.0									
Other services									12.5	20							
Adjustment																	0.5†

Note: *6.3% before 1924. †As a percentage of trend consumption.

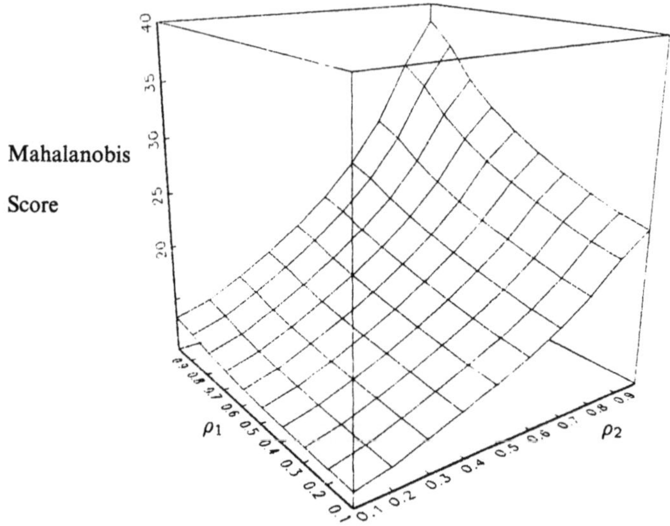

Figure 5.1 The Mahalanobis score, 1920–1938

without some degree of restriction. Since statements on measurement error suggest that there is probably greater serial correlation associated with the output variables than with the others, we have limited ourselves to examining the behaviour of the Mahalanobis score with only two serial correlation parameters, one for the output indices and one for everything else. Figures 5.1 and 5.2 show how the Mahalanobis score varies with these two parameters.

Since there are thirty-seven degrees of freedom, the median value for the score is 36.33. The 95 per cent confidence interval is given by the range 22.1–55.7. From figure 5.1 we can see that with high serial correlation parameters, it would be possible to satisfy the criterion. However, high serial correlation parameters tend to imply that the data standard errors can decline rather than increase between the benchmark years. We have therefore instead chosen values of 0.8 for the serial correlation parameter associated with output and 0.6 for the value associated with everything else. This is intended to reflect the view that there is greater serial correlation in the output measures. The Mahalanobis score is 18.3, and all the standard errors are therefore multiplied by $(18.3/36.33)^{0.5}=0.7$ so as to ensure that the score takes its median value. Thus the residuals in the accounts are consistent with standard errors only 70 per cent of those identified by those compiling the statistics.

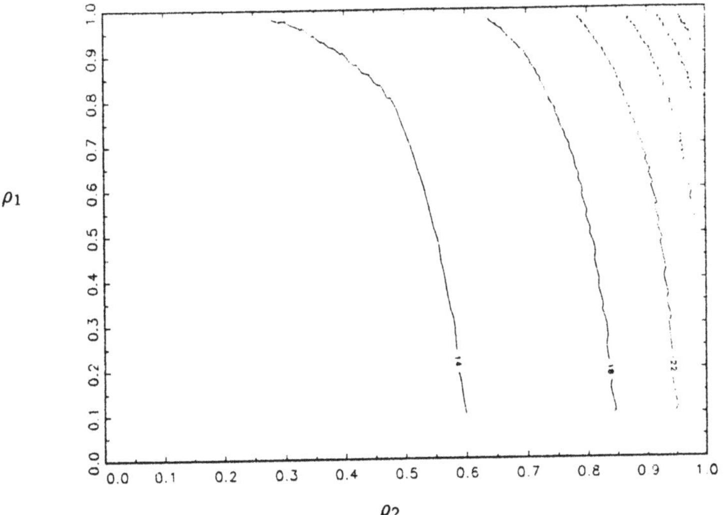

Figure 5.2 A contour map of the Mahalanobis score, 1920–1938

5.2.12 Data standard errors

Tables 5.8 and 5.9 near the end of this chapter present the standard errors associated with the levels of aggregates in the dataset for the period from 1920 to 1947, with the latter standard errors being derived as discussed subsequently. In order to save space, the corresponding data for the disaggregate components have not been presented, but they are available on request.

5.3 Data reliability, 1939–1948

The *Statistical Digest of the War* does not give any indication of the reliability with which the wartime data were believed to be measured, and we have therefore used the following parameters which are consistent with the information available on the data before and after the war. The reliabilities for the 1946–8 data are broadly consistent with those used in the years just after 1948 and discussed in chapter 6. It appears from the residual errors of the war years (figure 1.1, page 4) that the wartime data are much less reliable than the interwar and postwar data. Nevertheless, the interwar data reliabilities seem the most obvious starting point.

Tables 5.6 and 5.7 summarise the standard errors and serial correlation patterns which we have used for 1938–48. Once again σ_{u_1} refers to the lower limit of the standard error associated with the benchmark year, and σ_{u_2} to the upper limit. Where no benchmark years are shown, the standard error is assumed constant. The last column of table 5.5 shows the serial correlation parameter used in estimating the errors associated with current price output. The figures of tables 5.5 and 5.6 give error patterns which are consistent with the interwar errors after those were scaled satisfy the Mahalanobis criterion.

Table 5.7 shows similar data for the constant price series. The magnitude of the percentage unit root is shown. σ_a indicates an additional component of white noise error which is added in to the serially correlated process.

The standard errors associated with the aggregate data which are calculated from these are shown in tables 5.8 and 5.9 at the end of this chapter for the period 1939 to 1947. The relevant errors for 1948 are those presented in chapter 6.

5.3.1 The Mahalanobis criterion, 1938–1948

In balancing the interwar data we have to satisfy the current price income constraint for each year, 1939–47. We also have to satisfy the constant price constraint (in 1938 prices) for 1946–8. It is also necessary to constrain the data in 1938 and 1948 so that they are consistent with the interwar and postwar balanced data. In 1938 both constant and current price data must equal the output of the interwar exercise. The postwar data were balanced in 1985, not 1938 prices, and therefore it is only the current price data which should be equated to the results of the postwar balancing exercise. This gives a total of ninety-six constraints.

It is worth noting that, in 1946 and 1947 when both constraints are relevant, the current price data show almost no discrepancy. The reason for this is not that they are highly accurate, but simply that the CSO allocated the discrepancy in some manner which is not now known (see Feinstein, 1972, p. T13).

The score parameter which emerges is 36.9, as compared with a median value of 95.3. Nevertheless, we have not produced scaled estimates of the interwar reliabilities. In view of how little is known about measurement error in this period we do not feel that this can be justified.

On the face of it, the low score is something of a surprise, given the large errors in the current price data for 1940–44. However, the fact that, before 1946, it is not necessary to satisfy current and constant price restrictions simultaneously is likely to explain this outcome.

Table 5.6 *Income and expenditure standard errors, 1938–1948 (%)*

Item	Benchmark years	σ_{u_1}	σ_{u_2}	ρ
Components of income				
Income from employment	1938, 1948	2.3	5.0	0.6
Self-employed income	1938, 1948	7.0	10.0	0.6
Gross trading prof. cos	1938, 1948	7.0	10.0	0.6
Gross trading prof. P.C.	1938, 1948	1.8	5.0	0.6
Rent	1938, 1948	7.0	10.0	0.6
Stock appreciation	n.a.	1.1*		
Components of expenditure				
Exports of goods	n.a.	1.2		
Public authority consumption	n.a.	1.2		
Imports of goods	n.a.	1.2		
Increase in stocks	n.a.	1.1*		
Exports of services	n.a.	7.1		
Imports of services	n.a.	7.1		
Taxes on expenditure	1938, 1948	1.0	3.0	0.6
Subsidies	1938, 1948	1.0	3.0	0.6
Gross fixed capital formation				
Ships	n.a.	7.7		
Other vehicles	n.a.	3.3		
Plant	n.a.	1.3		
Buildings and works	n.a.	1.1		
Consumers' expenditure				
Food	1938, 1948	1.7	5.0	0.6
Drink	n.a.	1.0		
Tobacco	n.a.	1.0		
Housing	1938, 1948	2.1	5.0	0.6
Fuel and light	1938, 1948	2.1	5.0	0.6
Clothing	1938, 1948	3.1	7.0	0.6
Motor cars	1938, 1948	3.1	7.0	0.6
Textiles	1938, 1948	5.0	15.0	0.6
Public transport	n.a.	2.9		
Vehicle running costs	1938, 1948	7.3	12.0	0.6
Other services	1938, 1948	7.3	20.0	0.6
Adjustment	n.a.	0.7*		

Notes: *Calculated as a proportion of trend consumption.

The constant-price reliabilites are calculated by assuming that the price indices used to deflate impose additional errors with unit roots of 0.33 per cent p.a. as they move away from the base-year, 1938.

Table 5.7 *Output standard errors, 1938–1948 (%)*

Item	Benchmark years	σ_{u_1}	σ_{u_2}	ρ	Unit root	σ_a
Agriculture	1938, 1948	10.0	20.0	0.8	0.66	5.0
Components of manufacturing	1938, 1948	3.4	7.7	0.8	0.66	10.0
Utilities	n.a.	1.3			0.66	
Housing	n.a.	5.2			0.66	
Public administration and defence	n.a.	5.2			0.66	
Other industries	1938, 1948	7.7	13.0	0.8	0.66	5.0

5.4 Conclusions

Specification of the error structure associated with the data in the period 1920 to 1948 provides us with the variance matrix needed to balance the UK national accounts. There is less information available about the period 1939 to 1947 than about earlier and later years, and this obliges us to treat 1939–47 as linking datasets for 1920–38 and 1948–90.

The Mahalanobis criterion, applied to the period 1920 to 1938, allows us to verify our assumptions about data reliability. It suggests that either serial correlation was more powerful than we have assumed, or that the errors are generally smaller than we have inferred from our source material. We have chosen the second interpretation and scaled our variance matrix. The errors associated with the matrix after scaling are shown in tables 5.8 and 5.9.

There is no information on data reliability provided with the data for the war years, and we have therefore not presented scaled estimates of the standard errors associated with the data for these years. Indeed, the error pattern shown in figure 1.1 (page 4) suggests that in the early part of the war the absolute errors were much larger than later on. This may suggest heteroscedasticity, but there are simply too few observations to be able to come to any helpful conclusions on this. Our assumptions about data errors are necessary in order to complete the exercise, but they do not have the same status as those for 1920–38 or 1948–90.

Table 5.8 *Percentage standard errors in components of current price GDP:1920–1947*

	Employ ment income	Operating surplus	Factor cost adjust- ment	GDP(I)	Consumers' expend- iture	Gross fixed capital formation	Stock- building	Public authorities' current expenditure	Exports	Imports	GDP(E)
1920	3.3	5.9	1.5	3.0	2.2	1.1	n.a.	1.1	1.6	1.2	2.3
1921	3.2	5.7	1.5	2.9	2.2	1.3	n.a.	1.1	1.8	1.3	2.4
1922	3.2	5.6	1.3	2.9	2.2	1.9	n.a.	1.1	1.6	1.3	2.4
1923	3.2	5.6	1.1	2.9	2.1	1.3	n.a.	1.1	1.6	1.2	2.5
1924	3.1	5.7	1.1	2.9	2.0	1.3	n.a.	1.1	1.6	1.2	2.4
1925	3.0	5.8	1.1	2.9	2.0	1.3	n.a.	1.1	1.5	1.2	2.3
1926	2.9	5.8	1.1	2.9	2.1	1.5	n.a.	1.1	1.6	1.2	2.5
1927	2.4	3.7	1.1	2.0	2.0	1.5	n.a.	1.1	1.7	1.2	2.4
1928	2.6	4.2	1.1	2.3	2.0	1.4	n.a.	1.1	1.6	1.2	2.3
1929	2.5	4.2	1.1	2.3	2.0	1.4	n.a.	1.1	1.7	1.2	2.3
1930	2.3	3.9	1.1	2.1	1.9	1.3	n.a.	1.1	1.8	1.3	2.2
1931	1.5	3.9	1.1	1.7	1.9	1.3	n.a.	1.1	1.9	1.3	2.3
1932	1.5	3.6	1.1	1.6	1.9	1.4	n.a.	1.1	1.9	1.4	2.3
1933	1.9	3.7	1.1	1.8	1.7	1.7	n.a.	1.1	1.8	1.4	2.2
1934	2.1	3.6	1.1	1.9	1.9	1.6	n.a.	1.1	1.7	1.3	2.2
1935	2.2	3.7	1.1	1.9	1.9	1.5	n.a.	1.1	1.6	1.3	2.2
1936	2.1	3.5	1.1	1.8	2.0	1.4	n.a.	1.1	1.8	1.3	2.2
1937	2.2	4.2	1.1	2.1	2.1	1.3	n.a.	1.1	1.9	1.3	2.2
1938	2.3	4.5	1.1	2.2	2.1	1.3	n.a.	1.1	1.8	1.3	2.2
1939	3.7	6.0	2.5	3.2	2.4	1.0	n.a.	1.2	2.5	2.6	2.0

Table 5.8 (*cont.*)

	Employ ment income	Operating surplus	Factor cost adjust- ment	GDP(I)	Consumers' expend- iture	Gross fixed capital formation	Stock- building	Public authorities' current expenditure	Exports	Imports	GDP(E)
1940	3.9	5.2	2.8	3.1	2.4	1.0	n.a.	1.2	2.5	2.2	1.9
1941	4.0	5.2	3.0	3.2	2.3	1.4	n.a.	1.2	3.6	3.0	1.9
1942	4.1	5.3	3.1	3.3	2.3	1.5	n.a.	1.2	4.8	3.4	1.9
1943	4.2	5.5	3.2	3.3	2.3	1.5	n.a.	1.2	5.1	3.4	2.0
1944	4.2	5.7	3.3	3.4	2.3	1.2	n.a.	1.2	3.2	4.2	2.2
1945	4.0	5.8	3.3	3.3	2.4	0.9	n.a.	1.2	2.5	3.0	2.3
1946	3.5	6.0	2.9	3.1	2.2	0.9	n.a.	1.2	2.2	2.3	2.2
1947	2.3	5.1	1.7	2.3	1.5	0.9	n.a.	1.2	2.0	2.1	1.6

Table 5.9 *Percentage standard errors in components of GDP at 1938 prices: 1920–1947*

	Manufacturing output	GDP(O)	Factor cost adjustment	Consumers' expenditure	Gross fixed capital formation	Stock-building	Public authorities' current expenditure	Exports	Imports	GDP(E)
1920	4.1	4.4	1.5	2.3	1.3	n.a.	1.4	1.8	1.5	2.6
1921	4.2	4.4	1.4	2.3	1.3	n.a.	1.4	1.9	1.6	2.6
1922	4.2	4.4	1.4	2.2	1.4	n.a.	1.4	1.7	1.5	2.5
1923	3.9	4.4	1.4	2.1	1.2	n.a.	1.4	1.7	1.5	2.4
1924	3.7	4.3	1.4	2.0	1.3	n.a.	1.4	1.6	1.4	2.3
1925	3.7	4.3	1.4	2.0	1.4	n.a.	1.4	1.5	1.4	2.3
1926	3.8	4.3	1.3	2.1	1.5	n.a.	1.4	1.6	1.4	2.4
1927	3.7	4.2	1.3	2.0	1.5	n.a.	1.3	1.7	1.4	2.3
1928	3.7	4.3	1.3	2.0	1.4	n.a.	1.3	1.6	1.4	2.2
1929	3.6	4.2	1.3	2.0	1.4	n.a.	1.3	1.6	1.4	2.2
1930	3.6	4.2	1.3	1.9	1.3	n.a.	1.7	1.4	2.2	
1931	3.7	4.1	1.2	1.9	1.3	n.a.	1.9	1.4	2.3	
1932	3.8	4.1	1.2	1.8	1.4	n.a.	1.3	1.9	1.5	2.2
1933	3.7	4.0	1.2	1.7	1.7	n.a.	1.2	1.9	1.5	2.1
1934	3.6	3.9	1.2	1.8	1.6	n.a.	1.2	1.8	1.4	2.1
1935	3.4	3.8	1.1	1.9	1.5	n.a.	1.2	1.6	1.4	2.1
1936	3.2	3.6	1.1	2.0	1.4	n.a.	1.1	1.8	1.3	2.2
1937	3.1	3.4	1.1	2.1	1.3	n.a.	1.1	1.9	1.3	2.2
1938	3.0	2.9	1.1	2.1	1.3	n.a.	1.1	1.8	1.3	2.2
1939	n.a.	n.a.	2.0	2.5	1.0	n.a.	1.3	2.5	2.7	2.0

Table 5.9 (*cont.*)

	Manufacturing output	GDP(O)	Factor cost adjustment	Consumers' expenditure	Gross fixed capital formation	Stock-building	Public authorities' current expenditure	Exports	Imports	GDP(E)
1940	n.a.	n.a.	2.0	2.5	1.1	n.a.	1.3	2.5	2.3	1.9
1941	n.a.	n.a.	2.0	2.5	1.3	n.a.	1.4	3.6	3.0	1.9
1942	n.a.	n.a.	2.0	2.5	1.4	n.a.	1.4	4.8	3.4	1.9
1943	n.a.	n.a.	2.1	2.5	1.7	n.a.	1.4	5.2	3.5	2.1
1944	n.a.	n.a.	2.1	2.5	1.2	n.a.	1.5	3.2	4.3	2.3
1945	n.a.	n.a.	2.1	2.4	1.1	n.a.	1.5	2.6	3.1	2.4
1946	5.6	5.0	2.2	2.2	1.1	n.a.	1.6	2.3	2.5	2.4
1947	5.6	5.0	2.2	1.7	1.1	n.a.	1.6	2.2	2.2	2.0

6 The data and their reliability, 1948–1990

6.1 Introduction

While the data for this period are drawn from official sources, the problems in producing a coherent set of data from which to work are more severe than in the interwar years. There are two main reasons for this. First of all, the longer time period means that there have been changes in classification of industrial data. The most marked of these changes was between the 1968 Standard Industrial Classification (SIC) and the 1980 SIC. There were also a number of changes made to the classification of consumers' expenditure at the same time.

The reclassification of the consumption data was straightforward to correct for. We have simply added up the subcomponents provided on the CSO tape going back to 1948 in a manner compatible with the classification shown in table 5.5 on page 83. Beyond this only very minor adjustments were needed. An account of this is given in section 6.2.2.

More work was needed on the industrial data to arrive at a coherent series, covering wages and profits in the current price accounts and the output components in the constant price accounts. We have aimed to work to the 1980 industrial classifications for the whole of the period from 1948 to 1990 so as to provide continuous disaggregate time series. This means, inevitably, that there are breaks in the series at 1948 and that we have had to make changes to the disaggregate data in the period 1948 to 1970. The source of the data from 1948 to 1970 was the CSO *Blue Books*. Every attempt was made to use the final revised estimates for each series. Practically this meant that nearly every annual *Blue Book* from 1948 to 1970 was used. Beyond 1970 official estimates are available to the current classification. The changes we have made are described in section 6.2.6 below.

A second problem arises from the method of construction of the constant price data. The CSO estimates its long-run aggregate price deflators and volume indices by chainlinking the disaggregate series with the weights being rebased every five years approximately. This means that aggregate output, consumption, investment, exports and imports in constant prices are not equal to the sum of their components before 1983, the first year estimates were produced using the 1985 weights.

We could have treated these discrepancies as components of the residuals to be allocated by the balancing process. Instead, however, we took the view that the best estimates of expenditure or output in constant prices were those aggregates provided by the CSO and we scaled the components of each aggregate category to be compatible with the CSO's estimate of that aggregate. This is discussed in more detail in the next section.

6.2 The collection of the data

This section outlines the problems arising in the construction of the initial data for the period 1948 to 1990.

6.2.1 Chainlinking the constant price series

It is obviously a desirable property in constructing a set of national accounts that the subtotals should sum to the value of the total series. Unfortunately, as a consequence of chainlinking, the CSO constant price series do not satisfy this additive property. This results in the rather paradoxical observation that since 1948, the total output of the UK economy has grown faster than the vast majority of its industries. The best practical way to rectify this problem to some degree was to chainlink the subseries of output in an identical manner to the CSO but then to scale the subseries so that they summed up to the total estimate of output. In this way the total output estimate of GDP at constant prices was similar to the CSO and the paradox described earlier was avoided. It is worth noting that this scaling only becomes significant before 1963.[1]

This procedure was repeated for the expenditure series at constant prices. However, this had only a negligible effect after 1951, and was only slightly significant before. Why the chainlinking affects the expenditure series less than the output appears difficult to quantify. However, a

[1] The totals were slightly different from those of the CSO as they have the peculiar convention of updating the volume measurements but not the weights when constructing a chainlinked index after a data revision.

possible reason is that the expenditure estimate is chainlinked in stages whereas the output series, which are more disaggregate, are chainlinked in one go.[2]

6.2.2 Consumers' expenditure in constant and current prices

The primary problem in constructing consistent time series for the subtotals of consumer expenditure from 1948 to 1990 was the change in classifications in 1967 and 1980. It was an aim of this exercise to conform to the classification presented by Feinstein (1972) so as to eventually allow the construction of consistent tables of consumers' expenditure for the whole period 1900 to 1990. However, rather than use Feinstein's data for the period 1948 to 1965, every attempt was made to use the final revised estimates in the *Blue Books*. For this reason the expenditure series post 1963 under the 1980 classification of the CSO were grouped in totals that matched as closely as possible the classification of Feinstein. This was possible to a large extent. It was necessary though to make estimates of the nation's consumption of toilet soap due to its upwardly mobile reclassification from cleaning materials to pharmaceutical goods, but these adjustments are almost negligible.

The classification of the consumers' expenditure tables in Feinstein for the years 1948 to 1965 is based on the 1968 SIC. The consumption data for the years 1963 to 1990 are held on tape and are classified according to the 1980 SIC. However, the main division headings have also been subdivided for this period and it is possible to reallocate these subseries to different division headings to maintain consistent series in both current and constant prices. It shows where the subcategories have been allocated so as to produce a classification compatible with that for the years 1948–65. Table 6.1 gives a summary of the precise grouping of the present subseries of consumers' expenditure in order to match closely the 1968 classification groupings. The comments in the remarks column indicate the problem areas. They state when a particular commodity item is included or excluded in the series pre-1963 as compared to the series post-1963. As no information to our knowledge is available on the precise expenditure on these items before 1963 it was not possible to correct the series for these inconsistencies.

The only adjustment that was likely to cause large errors was the

[2] In constructing the expenditure estimate of GDP at constant prices, the individual series of consumer expenditure are chainlinked to estimate the total consumer expenditure, the individual investment series are chainlinked to give an estimate of total gross fixed capital formation and then these subtotals are all chainlinked with total government expenditure etc. to give the final estimate of GDP.

change in accounting procedure of consumer expenditure on food in catering establishments in the reclassification of 1967. Precise details of the change are recorded in Feinstein (1972), p. 42. Of concern here is that it was necessary to estimate the consumer expenditure in catering establishments pre-1952. The CSO had published data adjusted for this classification change in *Economic Trends Annual Supplement* post-1952. The inconsistency of the CSO series pre-1952 can be seen at a glance on p. 45 of the *Economic Trends Annual Supplement* 1992. After consultation with the CSO the decision was taken to extrapolate back their latest figure for 1952 using the estimates in Feinstein (1972) as an indicator. The justification for this approach was that the figure post-1952 can be considered more reliable, and therefore should be treated as a base.

In the period 1948 to 1963 we have used the estimates presented by Feinstein (1972) which are taken from the 1968 and earlier *Blue Books*. However, at constant prices, these are no longer compatible with the revisions the CSO has made to the estimate of aggregate consumption, and we have therefore scaled the components to agree with the aggregates.

From inspection of the series for the interval 1962–4 and comparison with the *Blue Book* 1968, it would seem that about £25m worth of cleaning commodities should be transferred to the category of chemist's goods before 1963. This would correspond to the toilet soap industry, if it was worth £25m in 1962. Vehicle running costs seem to be underestimated by about £50m; however we cannot account for this inconsistency. Otherwise the series appear consistent, implying the cycle, caravan, etc. markets were not worth a great deal in 1962.

Exactly the same procedure was adopted for constant price data, which is published at the same disaggregate detail as the current price data. These series appear consistent under inspection. It was necessary to scale these series, owing to the chainlinking problem discussed earlier, so that the total expenditure on consumption equalled the aggregate total published by the CSO.

The codes are those of the CSO (1991) data bank and the 1991 *Blue Book*. The constant price estimates were derived by aggregating the corresponding constant price data series.

6.2.3 Capital formation

These data were available for the period 1970 to 1990 on the CSO data tape. Before 1970 the data were found in the CSO *Blue Books*. It was necessary to link the data at constant prices that were based in different years. The constant price figures were, however, scaled to ensure

Table 6.1 *The classification of consumers' expenditure, 1948–1990*

1968 SIC	1980 SIC		
Table heading	Series heading	CSO Code	Remarks
Food	Food	CCDW	Excludes food bought in hotels, etc.
Drink	Alcoholic drink	CDCZ	No change
Tobacco	Tobacco	CCDZ	”
Housing	Housing	CDDK	”
Fuel and light	Fuel and light	CDDP	”
Clothing	Clothing	CDDE	”
Motor vehicles	Cars, motorcycles, etc.	CCDT	1968 excl. caravans, cycles, cycle acc.
Furniture, floor	Furniture, pictures	CDDQ	pre-1968 excl. pictures
	Carpets and other cov.	CDDR	
TV, radio and elec.	Radio and TV and durables	CDEI	1968 excl. photo and non-med. opt. eqpt
	Major house appl.	CDDS	1968 incl. cycles
Textiles, hardware	Textiles and furnish.	CDDT	1968 incl. cycle acc.
Matches, cleaning	Cleaning mat; matches	CDDV	1968 incl. toilet soap
Books, rec. goods	Books	CDEO	1968 incl. photo, non-med. opt. eqpt
	Newspapers and mags	CDEP	caravans
	Sports goods, toys	CDEK	
	Other rec. goods	CDEL	
Chemist, misc. goods	Pharm. and med. goods	CDES	1968 excl. toilet soap
	Toilet articles	CDEU	1968 incl. pictures
	Jewellery, silver	CDEW	
	Other goods	CDEX	

Table 6.1 (*cont.*)

1968 SIC	1980 SIC		
Table heading	Series heading	CSO Code	Remarks
Public transport	Rail travel	CDEB	
	Buses, coaches	CDEC	
	Air travel	CDED	
	Other travel	CDEE	
Vehicle run. cost	Petrol, oil	CDDY	
	Vehicle excise duty	CDDZ	
	Other run costs	CDEA	
Telecommunications	Postal services	CDEF	
	Telecommunications	CDEG	
Catering	Catering	CDEY	
Other serv. entertainment	Hhld domest serv.	CDDW	
Insurance	TV and video hire	CDEJ	
Domestic service, inc. in kind.	Betting and gaming	CDEM	
	Other rec. services	CDEN	
	Education	CDEQ	
	NHS payments	CDET	
	Life insurance, pensions	CDEZ	
	Hairdressing	CDEV	
	Other services	CDFA	
	Exp. by non-profit org.	CDFG	
Adjustment	Hhld exp. abroad	CDFE	
	Exp. by tourists	CDFD	

consistency with the CSO estimates of expenditure GDP in constant prices.

6.2.4 *Exports and imports*

These data were available for the whole of the period 1948 to 1990 on the CSO data tape. Goods were distinguished from services in both constant and current prices. The constant price figures were, however, scaled to ensure consistency with the CSO estimates of expenditure GDP in constant prices.

6.2.5 *Public authorities' current expenditure*

These estimates were taken off the data bank tape. Once again, the constant price estimates were scaled to ensure consistency of the expenditure components of GDP.

6.2.6 *Income and output data*

These series were considerably more difficult to standardise. The primary problem of constructing a consistent time-series was the change in the SIC in 1980. There existed series back to 1970 using the 1980 SIC. These series are the division totals of the SIC. Pre-1970, it was necessary to reconcile the series in the *Blue Book* with the latest classification. Unfortunately this reconciliation was not as straightforward as it was for the expenditure series and some rough estimates had to be made. The implications of these estimates are that the income series before 1970 can be regarded as less reliable.

From the information available it was only possible to make very rough estimates of the value added in various industries. The group industrial headings were kept the same as in Feinstein (1972), and industries were classified to these groups according to the 1980 SIC. Mining and quarrying was assumed to incorporate all those industries involved in the category 'coal and coke'. The utilities were assumed to be those industries involved in the category 'other energy and water supply'.

Table 6.2 shows the industries which jumped between classifications in 1968 and 1980. Adjusted data on the 1980 SIC were available on the CSO tape back to 1970. Before this it was necessary to find the data in the previous editions of the *Blue Book* and adjust the series for the change in classifications.

The following list is a precise description of how the estimates were

Table 6.2 *Industrial reclassification*

Industry	1968 SIC	1980 SIC	Remarks
Catering, hotels	Other services	Distribution	Est. from consumption data
Motor repairs, distr, filling st.	Other services	Distribution	Est. from census of prod.
Boot and shoe repair	Other services	Distribution	Est. annual stat.
Slaughtering	Distribution	Manufacturing	Est. from meat consumption
Open cast mining	Construction	Manufacturing	Neglected
Accountancy, legal services	Other services	Finance	Est. income tax returns
Other professions, scientific dev.	Other services	Finance	Neglected
Hire, rental services			
Agric., office, TV	Distribution	Finance	Neglected
Car, taxis, transport	Transport	Finance	Neglected
Construction machinery	Construction	Finance	Neglected
Nat. coal board, min. research	Other services	Mining and quarr.	Neglected
Manuf. of solid fuels	Manufacturing	Mining and quarr.	Neglected
Coke manufacture	Manufacturing	Mining and quarr.	Est. in growth project
Nuclear energy	Manufacturing	Utilities	Neglected
Extraction of multifer. ores	Mining and quarr.	Manufacturing	Neglected
Industrial training board	Finance	Other services	Neglected
Health auth., G.P. comm.	Edu. and health	PAD	Neglected
British Council	Other services	PAD	Neglected
Loc. auth. sanitary and sewerage	PAD	Other services	Est. LA expenditure
Driving, flying schools	Transport	Edu and health	Neglected
Vets	Other services	Edu. and health	Rough guess
Acas, Brit. tourist board	PAD	Other services	Neglected
Libraries	PAD	Other services	Est. LA expenditure

made of the labour income and profits in the various industries which jumped categories.

- Catering, hotels: From the amount consumed by the personal sector on food in catering establishments, and hotel rooms, etc. but not including alcoholic drink, is subtracted the amount paid by the catering industry for the food at wholesale prices (other personal expenditure on food in the *Blue Book*). This is the first estimate of the value added by this industry, and it was split between profits and income in the same ratio as the other distributive industries. It was thought necessary then to double these figures to allow for the value added due to the trade in alcoholic drink and official business functions.
- Motor repairs and distribution, filling stations: The value added by large industries for repair work on vehicles is estimated in the Censuses of production for 1948, 1954, 1963 and 1968. The intervening years were estimated by interpolation, and then this amount was assigned in the ratio 6:4 between labour income and profits. No attempt was made to estimate the value added due to small industries involved in repair work or those industries involved in distribution or filling stations.
- Boot and shoe repair: In the *Annual Abstract of Statistics* there is an estimate of the turnover of the industry. Labour income was estimated to be 30 per cent of the turnover and profits as 15 per cent of the turnover.
- Hire services (construction industry): There are estimates in the census of production of output in these industries, which could be interpolated in the intervening years. It was assumed that these industries are capital intensive and so we allocated 80 per cent of this adjustment to profits and 20 per cent to income.
- Slaughtering: Labour income in this industry was estimated to be 20 per cent and profits 10 per cent of the total amount spent on meat consumption by the personal sector in any year.
- Accountancy and legal services : Labour income was estimated to be 35 per cent of the total income from employment due to the professional services in income tax schedule E given by *Inland Revenue Statistics*. The profits were estimated as 15 per cent of the estimate of the adjustment due to financial services in the *Blue Book*. The reason for this is discussed later.
- Coke manufacture: Both the labour income and profits of this industry were provided by CSO to the Cambridge Growth Project.
- Local authority spending on sanitary and sewerage facilities: The income from this industry was estimated as 60 per cent of total expenditure on these facilities (*Blue Book* data).

- Vets: Guessed as the approximate complete shortfall in the education and health profit figure between 1969 and 1970. This was the only possible cause for this inconsistency except perhaps for the profits from private education. The amount was then reduced in proportion to the RPI.
- Libraries: Income generated by this service estimated as 60% of the local authority expenditure on libraries quoted in the *Blue Book*.
- Unassigned: 10 per cent of the income of other services was transferred to the income in education and health. A possible reason for this was the income earned by vets and their staff and also the income earned in private education.

Between the 1968 and 1980 classifications there was a change in the accounting procedure for financial services. In 1980 the margin earned by lending out at a higher rate than that paid on deposits, which is not a part of factor income, is shown as a specific adjustment item. In calculating the value added by financial services, this figure is ignored. Estimates on this basis are available back to 1970. In the data available for 1948 to 1969 profits and rent are shown gross of the adjustment for financial services and the latter is simply deducted in the calculation of aggregate GDP. In order to make the pre-1970 estimates compatible with those post-1970 it is necessary to subtract from the figures for profits and rent the proportion of this amount that was due to interest payments etc. An examination of the period for which data were available on both bases suggested that one should deduct 30 per cent of the adjustment for financial services from rent and 70 per cent from profits. However, note that of this 70 per cent, 15 per cent was removed from the profits in other services accredited to the change in classification of accountancy and the legal professions.

The final problem was accounting for stock appreciation in the various industries. On the CSO tape estimates are given for the stock appreciation in each industry back to 1970 and so it is simply necessary to subtract this figure from the profits to give the amount of value added by that industry to GDP in its profit account. However, before 1970 there is only one figure for the total amount of stock appreciation in the economy. It is therefore necessary to allocate a proportion of this total to each industry. An estimate of the stock appreciation in manufacturing (1950–70) and distribution (1958–70) is available in the *Blue Book* as the *increase in book value of stocks—physical increase in stocks*. The remaining proportion of the total unaccounted for was then assigned to each of the remaining industries according to their proportion of the total value of stocks held by these industries in 1954 for the years 1948–58 and in 1965 for the years 1959–70.

From inspection of the series there do not look to be any serious inconsistencies.

6.3 Data reliability

The data collected from the CSO blue books are graded A–D for their reliability. We adopt an identical grading system here using the reliability ranges provided by the Central Statistical Office (1985). In table 6.3, we give the 90 per cent confidence limit, the figure quoted by the CSO, and the corresponding standard error.

If the error in the data is assumed to be uncorrelated from one year to the next then the standard error of the data in each year is assumed to be at the mid point of its respective grade. If the data are constructed by extrapolation or interpolation from a benchmark year on the basis of an indicator then the standard error of the data in the benchmark year is assumed to be at the lower limit of the grade rising asymptotically to the upper limit as the data are extrapolated further away from this year.

In addition to these general codings, further comments are offered on the reliability of the output and expenditure measures in constant prices. The CSO states that 'the output measure of GDP should be regarded as good for up to 5 years and fair on a longer term', whereas the expenditure series can be regarded as more accurate over the longer term. Now the constant price output series are generally calculated as a volume index times the value of output in the base-year, whereas the expenditure series are generally calculated as the current price expenditure times a deflator. This results in the output series tending to 'go off' faster than the expenditure series. The reason is that any errors in the output volume indices are uncorrelated with the error in the current price income series and are therefore not anchored and will be free to wander. Conversely the errors in the constant price expenditure series over the current price

Table 6.3 *Reliability codes (by percentage)*

Reliability	Lower limit		Upper limit	
	90%	SE	90%	SE
A	1.0	0.6	3.0	1.8
B	3.0	1.8	10.0	6.0
C	10.0	6.0	20.0	12.0
D	20.0	12.0	35.0	21.0

series are due to errors in the deflator, but because of rebasing these series are 're-anchored' every base-year. Another reason is because of the observation discussed earlier, that the output series is more susceptible to consistent errors from chainlinking.

On the other hand, the output data are generally thought of as superior indicators of short-term growth, simply because they measure volume changes rather than deflated value changes.

This information has been incorporated into the model. Two processes are used to model the complete error-generating process of the constant price data. The first process models the short-term errors or the errors associated with the value data or volume index. The error process here is assumed to be stationary and benchmarked in census years (see section 4.3.2). The key parameter in this model is the serial correlation parameter $0 < \rho < 1$. If ρ is large then the errors are highly correlated from one year to the next and so the data indicate short-term change better than if ρ were small. Hence we have chosen a value of ρ for the volume or output data higher than for the value data. The second process is non-stationary and models the long-term errors due to the price deflator or volume index drift. The key parameter here is the size of the innovation process σ_z^2 (see section 4.3.5). The bigger the innovation the larger the drift. We have therefore made the size of the innovation process larger for the output or volume data than for the deflated value data.

6.3.1 Income from employment: current prices

Data on income from employment are compiled from three main sources,

(i) the datasets from the Department of Employment based on PAYE tax returns. This has been the preferred source since 1976. The data are accurate, A grade, and as the data are compiled annually any errors will only be correlated owing to the necessary approximations from sampling such as the estimates of income in small firms. This results in an error process described in section 4.2.

(ii) estimates calculated from either the *Censuses of production* in 1948, 1951, 1954, 1958, 1963, 1968, 1973, 1978, 1983, 1985 or the *Censuses of distribution* 1950, 1957, 1961, 1966, 1971, 1976 ,1980 and 1986 or the *Censuses of population* in 1951, 1961, 1971, 1981 and interpolated on the basis of estimated employment in the intervening years. This results in the error process described in section 4.3.2.

(iii) Estimates based on employment figures multiplied by estimates of the average wage. This leads to the error process in section 4.3.1.

Reliability estimates for pre-1976 are given on p. 141 of *Sources and*

Methods (CSO, 1968), where it is noted that the combined estimate of the total wage and salary bill tends to be more accurate than the estimate of each subtotal. After 1976 all income data are assumed to be A grade (see table 6.4).

It is worth noting the following points:

(1) There is no estimate of the income from ownership of dwellings before 1957. This was therefore estimated by linear extrapolation giving rise to a high level of uncertainty in these estimates.

(2) Owing to the change in SIC classifications there is a break in the series estimates of education and health, PAD, and distribution incomes at 1972. This break was incorporated into the model of the error processes giving a lower reliability to the estimates before 1972 compared with afterwards.

(3) The other income attributed to the 'other services' industry is calculated partly as the residue of total income from employment minus the income in the other named industries. Therefore the error in this series will be correlated with the other series. This is, however, ignored as it causes only a negligible change in the results.

6.3.2 *Profits by industry*

These are almost universally estimated from information collected by the Inland Revenue in the course of assessing liability to income and corporation tax. There is error in these figures due to the need to adjust for profits abroad, debts, depreciation and the shift between the financial and calendar year. It is also noted in the *Sources and Methods Handbook* that the differences are measured more accurately than the levels. This information suggests that the error process is modelled most accurately by the process described in section 4.2. In this model the data are collected annually but there is correlation in the errors from year to year arising from sampling or in this case estimates of income from self-employment. Though the CSO regard the estimates of company profits to be rated A, the estimates of income from self-employment and stock depreciation are rated C, implying the total to be rated B. The serial correlation parameter ρ is taken to be 0.6.

6.3.3 *Output*

The estimate of the output of agricultural data is arrived at by double deflation, that is, price indices being used for input and output. These estimates tend to more accurate A grades; however, the errors will be autocorrelated as the price indices deteriorate with time.

Table 6.4 *Reliability of income from employment*

Industry	Period	Method	Reliability	Correlation (ρ)
Agriculture	1948–89	(iii)	A	0.6
Mining and quarrying	1948–89	(ii) (Production census)	A	0.6
Manufacturing	1948–89	(ii) (Production census)	A	0.6
Oil and gas extraction	1948–89	(ii) (Production census)	A	0.6
Construction	1948–76	(ii) (Production census)	A	0.6
	1976–89	(i)	A	0.6
Utilities	1948–89	(ii) (Production census)	A	0.6
Transport and communications	1948–76	(iii)	A	0.6
	1976–89	(i)	A	0.6
Distribution	1948–76	(ii) (Distribution census)	B	0.6
	1976–89	(i)	A	0.6
Finance	1948–76	(ii) (Population census)	B	0.6
	1976–89	(i)	A	0.6
PAD	1948–72	(i)	B	0.6
	1972–89	(i)	A	0.6
Education and health	1948–72	(i)	B	0.6
	1972–89	(i)	B	0.6
Other services	1948–72	(ii)	B	0.6
	1973–89	(ii)	A	0.6

Estimates of output of the production industries usually use gross output measures as indicators combined using weights rebased every five years or so. These weights are estimated from the census of production. The error process is therefore modelled as in sections 4.3.1 and 4.3.2. On p. 45 of *Sources and Methods* (CSO, 1985), it is claimed that estimates of output of agriculture, utilities, manufacturing, mining and quarrying and gas and oil extraction are good for short periods and slowly deteriorate over long periods, whereas construction, distribution and transport are 'on the good side of fair' for short periods and deteriorate quickly. The output for the service industries is harder to measure and is generally indexed by labour inputs with the assumption of no productivity growth. These estimates are poor at best and deteriorate quickly. It is also noted that the change from the 1968 to 1980 SIC classification would reduce the reliability of the series before 1973. Employing this qualitative information, table 6.5 summarises the reliability grades for the output series. As a guide to this table, the grading for the benchmark year periods gives the short-run reliability, and the size of the innovation process σ_z describes the speed of deterioration of the index over the long run.

There is only a little information on the reliability of the components of manufacturing industry. It is expected that metal and food manufacture and the paper and printing industries were more accurately measured than the average, and the residual categories of other transport equipment and other manufacturing were slightly less accurate. This information was incorporated into the model under the restriction that the reliability of the aggregate manufactruing series was as stated in table 6.5.

6.3.4 *Gross fixed capital formation*

The data for gross fixed capital formation are collected from annual data, and it seems that benchmarking is not involved. Nevertheless, some degree of error persistence may be present. We shall therefore use the model described in section 4.2 to describe the error process with a serial correlation parameter $\rho = 0.6$. *Sources and Methods* (CSO, 1985), p. 198, gives a precise grading of the data reliabilities for the the disaggregated categories of investment. Taking the mid-range value of each grade and weighting the categories in proportion to the expenditure on the respective goods in 1980 gives reliability estimates in table 6.6.

The constant price series are produced by deflating the current series by a price index. This price index is assumed to 'go off'. This is modelled by a random walk. This source of error is assumed to introduce an

Table 6.5 *Reliability of output estimates*

Industry	Period between benchmark years								ρ	σ_z^2
	1948 1954	1954 1958	1958 1963	1963 1968	1968 1975	1975 1980	1980 1985	1985 1990		
Agriculture	B	B	B	B	B	A	A	B	0.8	0.60
Mining and quarrying	B	B	B	B	B	A	A	B	0.8	0.60
Oil and gas extraction	C	C	B	B	B	A	A	B	0.8	0.60
Manufacturing	B	B	B	B	B	A	A	B	0.8	0.60
Construction	C	C	C	C	C	B	A	B	0.8	0.66
Utilities	B	B	B	B	B	A	A	B	0.8	0.66
Trans. and communic.	B	B	B	B	B	B	A	B	0.8	0.66
Distribution	C	C	C	C	C	B	A	B	0.8	0.66
Financial services	C	C	C	C	C	B	A	B	0.8	0.80
Ownership of dwellings	C	C	C	C	C	B	A	B	0.8	0.80
PAD	B	B	B	B	B	B	A	B	0.8	0.66
Educat. and health	B	B	B	B	B	B	A	B	0.8	0.66
Other services	C	C	C	C	C	B	A	B	0.8	0.80
Adjust. to financial services	C	C	C	C	C	B	A	B	0.8	0.80

Table 6.6 *Reliability of gross fixed capital formation*

Type of asset	Standard error (%)	ρ
Vehicles, ships and aircraft	2.5	0.6
Plant and machinery	2.5	0
Dwellings	2.6	0.6
Other buildings	2.5	0.6
Transfer costs of land	3.9	0.6

additional error of 4 per cent in 1948 on the constant price series as compared to the current price series. This is equivalent to the innovation process described in section 4.3.5 having a standard error of 0.33.

6.3.5 Stockbuilding

The method adopted for estimating the error in the estimate of the increase in stocks is identical to the method adopted for the pre-war years in section 5.2.6. The error from year to year is assumed to be uncorrelated and equal to 0.15 per cent of the trend line linking the total consumption at current prices in 1948 to that in 1985, and then 1985 to 1989. The kink in this trend line at 1985 is necessary to ensure that any adjustment to the value increase in stocks series at current prices is identical to the adjustment to the constant price series in 1985.

Similarly the standard error in the constant price series is assumed to be 0.15 per cent of trend line of total consumption at constant prices, also adjusted to ensure that at 1985 its value is equal to the value of the trend line used for the current price series. In addition, the constant price series has a correlated error component due to deflating the current price series. This is assumed to add-in a separate error with a unit root of 0.33 per cent p.a.

6.3.6 Public consumption

Estimates of the four categories of public consumption, defence, education and health and other consumption, are derived from the annual returns. As most of the components of these series are estimated every year without interpolation or benchmarking techniques, it is assumed that the series are uncorrelated and of at least A-grade reliability.

It is noted that the errors in defence, other consumption and education and health will be correlated with the errors in the estimates of income generated in public administration and defence and education and health, respectively. However, in the postwar data we assume that these series are not correlated. The errors in the income series are assumed to be errors in disaggregation, partly due to the change in SIC classifications between 1968 and 1980, and not therefore due to errors in the aggregate total.

Sources and Methods (CSO, 1985, p. 183) states that over three-quarters of public expenditure at constant prices is estimated by deflating current prices by indices of pay and prices. Under a quarter is therefore evaluated as output volume index multiplied by a unit price in the base-year. It is therefore a reasonable assumption that the error process is of the form in section 4.2. In each of the constant price series the deflation process is assumed to add a unit root error of 0.33 per cent p.a. It is assumed that these price and pay indices are calculated explicitly to deflate only the public consumption figures, and therefore any errors are uncorrelated with the errors in other series. Though this is not entirely accurate, it is a reasonable assumption that will cause little or no further error.

6.3.7 Exports and imports

The export and import of goods at current prices are compiled from trade statistics. Any error in the adjustments to these figures is 'thought to be small'.[3] The constant price estimates are calculated using a different price index for each of the 900 different categories. These estimates are considered to be A grade, with the errors in the current prices series being uncorrelated. The constant price series have an additional error due to the deflation modelled by a random walk that increases the standard error by 1.5 per cent in 1948.

The export and import of services, financial, travel, etc., are more difficult to estimate as only in a few cases are there volume data as well as value data, especially in the financial and other services where the data can only be 'regarded as poor'.[4] Constant price data are again calculated by deflation of the current price series by suitable indices.

It is therefore assumed that the estimates of exports and imports are of B-grade reliability, and in addition the constant price series has an extra 1.5 per cent error in 1948 resulting from the deflation process.

6.3.8 Indirect taxes and subsidies

Estimates of the income received from indirect taxes and the income transferred in subsidies can be calculated with A-grade reliability from Customs and Excise statistics. The majority of this total is deflated by the

3 *Sources and Methods* (CSO, 1985, p. 243).
4 *Ibid.*

relevant retail price index to give an estimate at constant prices. This deflation is assumed to increase the expected standard error linearly to a maximum of an additional 1.5 per cent in 1948.

6.3.9 Consumers' expenditure

The consumption data in each category are calculated using one of the following three methods:

(i) Estimating annually from survey sample information, such as *Family Expenditure Survey*, *National Food Survey* and the *International Passenger Survey* or from VAT returns. This would result in an uncorrelated error process if it assumed that these surveys are not biased. The constant price data can then be calculated by either
   (a) multiplying any volume data in the survey by the unit price in the base-year, or
   (b) deflating the current price series by a suitable price index.

(ii) Using benchmark estimates for consumer expenditure in the years of the census of distribution and interpolating on the basis of a suitable indicator based on movements in the turnover. This results in the pattern described in section 4.3.2. The constant price series is calculated by deflating the current price series with a suitable index.[5]

Table 6.7 summarises the estimation method used for each category, the reliability grade of the data, and the correlation parameters where relevant. A comprehensive list of the reliability grades of the various series is given in *Sources and Methods* (CSO, 1985), p. 84. This also states that 'only a few of the constant price estimates are markedly less reliable than the corresponding current prices series'. Generally our estimates of the standard errors of these series are slightly lower than the CSO's, so that the standard error of the aggregate series agrees with the estimates of the CSO. We feel this highlights a degree of inconsistency in the CSO reliability grades.

The following points should be noted:

(i) The change in reliability in the vehicle running costs is due to the discontinuity in the series resulting from the changes between the 1968 and 1980 SIC.

(ii) The reliability change in the food series is caused by the effect of rationing before 1954, see *Sources and Methods*, (CSO, 1968).

(iii) The change in the accounting method for catering is comprehensively documented in *Ibid.*, and this accounts for the change in the error process in these series.

[5] In some cases the interpolation is made using volume rather than value indicators. We have not taken any account of the extra complexity that this may generate.

Table 6.7 *Reliability of consumers' expenditure*

Category	Period	Method	Reliability	ρ	σ_z
Food	1948–55	(i) (a)	B	0.6	0.33
	1955–90	(i) (a)	A	0.6	0.33
Tobacco	1948–90	(i) (a)	A	0.6	0.33
Housing	1948–90	(i) (b)	B	0.6	0.33
Fuel and light	1948–90	(i) (b)	A	0.6	0.33
Clothing	1948–90	(ii)	A	0.6	0.33
Motor vehicles	1948–90	(i) (b)	A	0.6	0.33
Furniture, floor coverings	1948–90	(ii)	A	0.6	0.33
T.V, radio and electrical goods	1948–90	(ii)	B	0.6	0.33
Textiles, hardware	1948–90	(ii)	B	0.6	0.33
Matches, cleaning materials	1948–90	(i) (b)	B	0.6	0.33
Books, recreational goods	1948–90	(ii)	B	0.6	0.33
Chemist, other goods	1948–90	(ii)	B	0.6	0.33
Public transport	1948–90	(i) (a)	A	0.6	0.33
Vehicle running costs	1948–68	(i) (a)	B	0.6	0.33
	1968–90	(i) (a)	A	0.6	0.33
Telecommunications	1948–90	(i) (b)	A	0.6	0.33
Catering	1948–64	(ii)	B	0.6	0.33
	1964–80	(ii)	A	0.6	0.33
	1980–90	(i) (b)	A	0.6	0.33
Other services	1948–90	(i) (b)	B	0.6	0.33

(iv) The error process in the adjustment for tourists' expenditure is modelled in an identical manner to the approach adopted for stock-building. It is assumed that the error in the current price series is uncorrelated and its standard error equal to 0.05 per cent of the total consumption in each year.

(v) We have assumed that the process of deflation introduces an extra unit root with a standard error of 0.33 per cent p.a. This is shown under σ_z.

6.4 The Mahalanobis criterion

As with the earlier data, we can assess the effect of the serial correlation parameters on the Mahalanobis score. Once again, in order to keep the exercise to manageable proportions, we have assumed that there are just two types of serial correlation parameters. One, ρ_1, applies to the income and expenditure data and the other, ρ_2, applies to the output data.

Figures 6.1 and 6.2 show how the value of the score depends on the serial correlation parameters. There are eighty-five degrees of freedom, so the median value of the criterion is 84.33 and the lower and upper limits of the 95 per cent confidence range are 61.4 and 112.4. Once again, rather than rely on very high serial correlation, we have chosen values of 0.8 for the parameter associated with the output variables and 0.6 for the parameter associated with all other variables. This gives a score of 53.2. We have multiplied all the standard errors by $(53.2/84.33)^{0.5}$ so as to deliver a specification of the standard errors which delivers the Mahalanobis score at its median (maximum-likelihood) value.

It is obviously not possible to explore the sensitivity of all the variables to the way in which the Mahalanobis criterion is satisfied. However, there is some evidence to suggest a degree of robustness in the resulting standard errors. This is discussed in chapter 8.

6.5 Data standard errors

Tables 6.8 and 6.9 show the data standard errors calculated using an expenditure serial correlation parameter of 0.6, an output serial correlation parameter of 0.8 and after scaling.

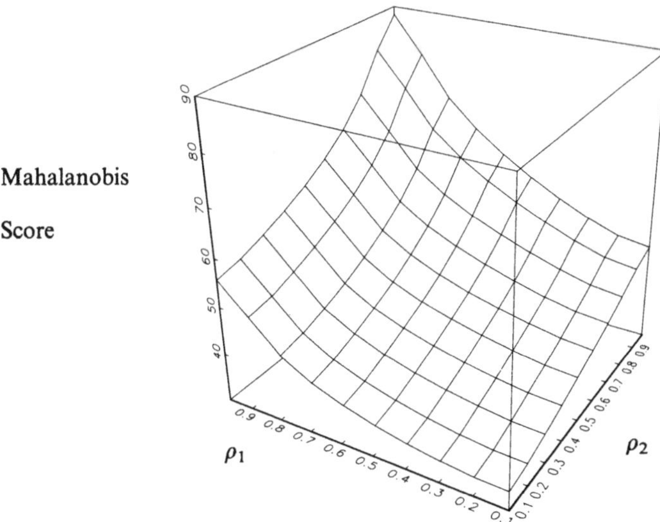

Figure 6.1 The Mahalanobis score, 1948–1990

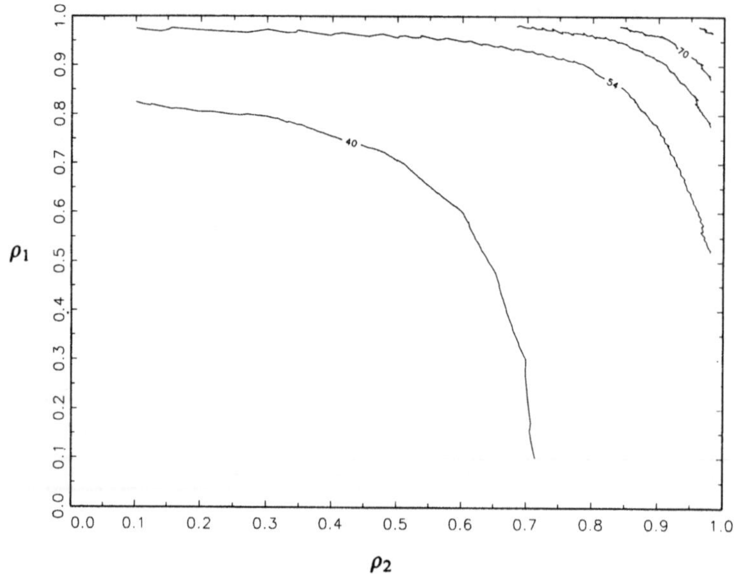

Figure 6.2 A contour map of the Mahalanobis score, 1948–1990

Table 6.8 *Percentage standard errors in components of current price GDP: 1948–1990*

	Employment income	Operating surplus	Factor cost adjustment	GDP(I)	Consumers' expenditure	Gross fixed capital formation	Stockbuilding	Public authorities' current expenditure	Exports	Imports	GDP(E)
1948	0.7	2.8	0.1	1.1	1.0	1.2	n.a.	0.9	0.7	0.6	0.9
1949	0.9	2.8	0.1	1.2	1.0	1.2	n.a.	0.9	0.7	0.6	0.9
1950	0.9	2.9	0.1	1.2	1.0	1.2	n.a.	0.9	0.7	0.6	0.9
1951	0.8	3.0	0.1	1.1	0.9	1.2	n.a.	0.9	0.7	0.5	0.9
1952	1.0	2.7	0.1	1.2	0.9	1.2	n.a.	0.9	0.7	0.5	0.8
1953	1.1	2.7	0.1	1.2	0.6	1.2	n.a.	0.9	0.7	0.6	0.7
1954	0.9	2.7	0.1	1.1	0.6	1.2	n.a.	0.9	0.7	0.6	0.7
1955	1.1	2.7	0.1	1.2	0.6	1.2	n.a.	0.9	0.7	0.6	0.7
1956	1.1	2.7	0.1	1.1	0.6	1.2	n.a.	0.9	0.7	0.6	0.7
1957	1.0	2.6	0.1	1.1	0.5	1.2	n.a.	0.9	0.7	0.6	0.7
1958	0.8	2.6	0.1	1.0	0.5	1.2	n.a.	0.9	0.7	0.6	0.8
1959	1.1	2.5	0.1	1.1	0.5	1.2	n.a.	0.8	0.7	0.6	0.8
1960	1.1	2.5	0.1	1.1	0.5	1.2	n.a.	0.8	0.7	0.6	0.8
1961	1.1	2.5	0.1	1.1	0.5	1.3	n.a.	0.8	0.7	0.6	0.8
1962	1.1	2.4	0.1	1.1	0.5	1.3	n.a.	0.8	0.7	0.6	0.8
1963	0.9	2.4	0.1	1.0	0.5	1.3	n.a.	0.8	0.7	0.6	0.8
1964	1.1	2.4	0.1	1.1	0.5	1.2	n.a.	0.8	0.7	0.6	0.8
1965	1.1	2.4	0.1	1.1	0.6	1.3	n.a.	0.8	0.7	0.6	0.8
1966	1.1	2.3	0.1	1.0	0.6	1.3	n.a.	0.8	0.7	0.6	0.8
1967	1.0	2.3	0.1	1.0	0.6	1.3	n.a.	0.8	0.7	0.6	0.8
1968	0.8	2.2	0.1	0.9	0.6	1.2	n.a.	0.8	0.7	0.6	0.8
1969	0.9	2.2	0.1	1.0	0.6	1.3	n.a.	0.8	0.7	0.6	0.8

Table 6.8 (*cont.*)

	Employment income	Operating surplus	Factor cost adjustment	GDP(I)	Consumers' expenditure	Gross fixed capital formation	Stockbuilding	Public authorities' current expenditure	Exports	Imports	GDP(E)
1970	1.0	2.1	0.1	1.0	0.6	1.3	n.a.	0.7	0.7	0.6	0.8
1971	0.9	2.1	0.1	0.9	0.6	1.3	n.a.	0.7	0.7	0.6	0.7
1972	0.9	2.1	0.1	0.9	0.6	1.2	n.a.	0.4	0.7	0.6	0.7
1973	0.6	2.1	0.1	0.8	0.6	1.2	n.a.	0.4	0.7	0.6	0.7
1974	0.8	2.0	0.1	0.8	0.6	1.2	n.a.	0.3	0.7	0.5	0.7
1975	0.9	1.9	0.1	0.8	0.6	1.2	n.a.	0.4	0.7	0.5	0.6
1976	0.9	1.8	0.1	0.8	0.6	1.2	n.a.	0.4	0.7	0.5	0.6
1977	0.7	1.7	0.1	0.8	0.6	1.2	n.a.	0.4	0.7	0.5	0.6
1978	0.5	1.8	0.1	0.7	0.6	1.2	n.a.	0.4	0.7	0.5	0.6
1979	0.7	1.7	0.1	0.7	0.6	1.2	n.a.	0.4	0.7	0.5	0.6
1980	0.7	1.7	0.1	0.7	0.6	1.2	n.a.	0.4	0.7	0.5	0.6
1981	0.7	1.8	0.1	0.7	0.6	1.3	n.a.	0.4	0.7	0.5	0.6
1982	0.7	1.8	0.1	0.7	0.7	1.2	n.a.	0.4	0.6	0.5	0.6
1983	0.4	1.8	0.1	0.7	0.7	1.2	n.a.	0.4	0.7	0.5	0.6
1984	0.6	1.8	0.1	0.7	0.7	1.2	n.a.	0.4	0.6	0.5	0.6
1985	0.4	1.8	0.1	0.7	0.7	1.3	n.a.	0.4	0.6	0.5	0.6
1986	0.7	1.7	0.1	0.8	0.7	1.2	n.a.	0.4	0.7	0.5	0.6
1987	0.8	1.7	0.1	0.8	0.7	1.2	n.a.	0.4	0.7	0.5	0.6
1988	0.8	1.8	0.1	0.8	0.7	1.2	n.a.	0.4	0.7	0.5	0.6
1989	0.8	1.8	0.1	0.8	0.7	1.2	n.a.	0.4	0.7	0.5	0.7
1990	0.8	1.8	0.1	0.8	0.7	1.3	n.a.	0.4	0.6	0.5	0.6

Table 6.9 *Percentage standard errors in components of GDP at 1985 prices: 1948–1990*

	Manufacturing output	GDP(O)	Factor cost adjustment	Consumers' expenditure	Gross fixed capital formation	Stockbuilding	Public authorities' current expenditure	Exports	Imports	GDP(E)
1948	2.7	2.1	2.0	1.4	1.5	n.a.	2.0	1.7	1.7	1.4
1949	2.8	2.0	2.0	1.4	1.5	n.a.	1.9	1.7	1.7	1.4
1950	2.8	1.9	2.0	1.4	1.6	n.a.	1.9	1.7	1.6	1.3
1951	2.6	1.9	1.9	1.4	1.6	n.a.	1.9	1.7	1.6	1.3
1952	2.8	1.9	1.9	1.3	1.5	n.a.	2.0	1.7	1.6	1.3
1953	2.8	1.9	1.9	1.2	1.5	n.a.	2.0	1.6	1.6	1.2
1954	2.6	1.9	1.8	1.1	1.5	n.a.	1.9	1.6	1.6	1.2
1955	2.8	2.0	1.8	1.1	1.5	n.a.	1.9	1.6	1.5	1.1
1956	2.9	1.9	1.8	1.1	1.5	n.a.	1.9	1.6	1.5	1.1
1957	2.8	1.9	1.8	1.0	1.5	n.a.	1.8	1.5	1.5	1.1
1958	2.5	1.9	1.7	1.0	1.5	n.a.	1.6	1.5	1.5	1.0
1959	2.7	1.9	1.7	1.0	1.4	n.a.	1.7	1.5	1.5	1.0
1960	2.9	1.9	1.7	0.9	1.4	n.a.	1.7	1.5	1.4	1.0
1961	2.9	1.9	1.6	0.9	1.4	n.a.	1.7	1.4	1.4	1.0
1962	2.7	1.9	1.6	0.9	1.4	n.a.	1.7	1.4	1.4	1.0
1963	2.4	1.9	1.6	0.9	1.4	n.a.	1.5	1.4	1.4	1.0
1964	2.7	1.9	1.5	0.9	1.4	n.a.	1.6	1.4	1.3	1.0
1965	2.8	1.9	1.5	0.9	1.4	n.a.	1.6	1.3	1.3	0.9
1966	2.8	1.9	1.4	0.9	1.4	n.a.	1.6	1.3	1.3	0.9
1967	2.7	1.9	1.4	0.9	1.4	n.a.	1.5	1.3	1.3	0.9
1968	2.4	1.9	1.4	0.9	1.4	n.a.	1.4	1.3	1.2	0.9
1969	2.7	1.9	1.3	0.9	1.4	n.a.	1.4	1.2	1.2	0.9

Table 6.9 (*cont.*)

	Manufacturing output	GDP(O)	Factor cost adjustment	Consumers' expenditure	Gross fixed capital formation	Stock-building	Public authorities' current expenditure	Exports	Imports	GDP(E)
1970	2.8	1.9	1.3	0.8	1.4	n.a.	1.5	1.2	1.2	0.9
1971	2.8	1.8	1.2	0.8	1.3	n.a.	1.5	1.2	1.1	0.9
1972	2.6	1.8	1.2	0.8	1.3	n.a.	1.4	1.2	1.1	0.9
1973	2.3	1.8	1.2	0.8	1.3	n.a.	1.2	1.1	1.1	0.8
1974	2.6	1.7	1.1	0.8	1.3	n.a.	1.3	1.1	1.0	0.8
1975	2.7	1.6	1.1	0.8	1.3	n.a.	1.3	1.1	1.0	0.8
1976	2.7	1.6	1.0	0.8	1.3	n.a.	1.3	1.0	1.0	0.8
1977	2.6	1.5	0.9	0.8	1.3	n.a.	1.2	1.0	0.9	0.8
1978	2.3	1.5	0.9	0.8	1.3	n.a.	1.0	1.0	0.9	0.8
1979	2.5	1.5	0.8	0.7	1.3	n.a.	1.1	0.9	0.8	0.8
1980	2.7	1.5	0.7	0.7	1.3	n.a.	1.2	0.9	0.8	0.8
1981	2.7	1.5	0.7	0.7	1.3	n.a.	1.1	0.9	0.8	0.7
1982	2.5	1.4	0.6	0.7	1.3	n.a.	1.0	0.8	0.7	0.7
1983	2.2	1.4	0.5	0.7	1.2	n.a.	0.8	0.8	0.6	0.7
1984	2.1	1.2	0.4	0.7	1.2	n.a.	0.8	0.7	0.6	0.7
1985	1.7	0.8	0.1	0.7	1.3	n.a.	0.4	0.6	0.5	0.6
1986	2.3	1.3	0.4	0.7	1.3	n.a.	0.8	0.7	0.6	0.7
1987	2.6	1.5	0.5	0.7	1.3	n.a.	1.0	0.8	0.6	0.7
1988	2.9	1.6	0.6	0.7	1.3	n.a.	1.2	0.8	0.7	0.8
1989	3.1	1.7	0.7	0.7	1.3	n.a.	1.3	0.8	0.7	0.8
1990	3.3	1.8	0.7	0.7	1.4	n.a.	1.4	0.9	0.8	0.8

7 Sectoral income/expenditure and capital accounts

7.1 Introduction

Using the standard errors described in chapters 5 and 6 we can now balance the UK national accounts, ensuring that the GDP identity is satisfied. But an important part of national income accounting is the estimation of the incomes accruing to the institutional sectors of the economy, the personal sector, companies, public corporations, the government sectors and the rest of the world. One may also wish to identify current and capital expenditure by the institutional sector making it.

In principle this could have been done simply by extending our classification. Operating surplus could have been split into five categories as accruing to persons, companies, public corporations and central and local government.[1] Capital formation could have been decomposed in the same way.

But there were two practical reasons for not doing this. First of all the introduction of the extra categories would have made the variance matrix unreasonably large. Second, it would have been necessary to take account of the covariances between the various sectoral estimates since they are clearly not independent of the industrial estimates.[2] These covariances could have been calculated, but since all the calculations were performed with a sparse **V** matrix, they would once again have led to a substantial increase in the effective size of the matrix. Accordingly, some way has to be found of allocating the adjustments to income and expenditure to the respective sectors if consistent sectoral accounts are to be produced.

1 With none accruing to the rest of the world by convention. Income on direct investment is treated as being paid by the company sector and not as a direct payment of factor income.

2 If they were, operating surplus calculated by industry would not equal the same aggregate calculated by institutional sector.

With the major components of income and expenditure there is no problem. All the changes to employment income affect the incomes of the personal sector, and all the changes to personal consumption affect its expenditure. But adjustments to operating surplus, public consumption and capital formation must be classified by institutional sector in order to produce sector accounts. In fact this is quite consistent with the general approach we have adopted because, as noted in chapter 2, section 2.9, there are no independent estimates of sectoral financial saving. Adjustment of factor incomes leads to offsetting changes in the estimates of financial saving and, when the GDP account is balanced, it is also true that financial saving will add to zero across the sectors (including the rest of the world).

This means that we can apply the step-by-step approach to data reconciliation described in chapter 2, section 2.2.2. Having calculated the adjustments by industry, these adjustments can then be allocated across the sectors on the basis of estimates of the reliability of sectoral components.

7.2 Initial estimates of sectoral income and expenditure

The aim of this chapter is to provide a basis for sectoral accounts consistent with the balanced estimates of GDP, by allocating the changes to factor incomes and expenditures. The receipts and payments of transfer or intermediate incomes, dividends and interest, direct taxes, social security contributions and payments, net property income from abroad and other transfers should not require any adjustments: our presumption had been that, in the source statistics, total receipts equal total payments for each type of transfer income. Indeed one would expect this to be the case if the personal sector is derived as a residual. Nevertheless, a certain amount of work was needed before the data satisfied these basic identities. The difficulties arose because some types of transfer are classified in one way by the paying sector and in a different way by the receiving sector. In the tables we have presented we have maintained the classifications of the official sources, but it was nevertheless necessary to unravel these effects so as to verify the data which were entered.

7.2.1 1920–1938

For the interwar years there were relatively few problems. The accounts were compiled on a payments basis rather than an accruals basis. This is consistent with the current treatment in the *Blue Book* and indeed the current definition of personal saving. One reason for preferring a payments basis throughout is that accruals information tends to be available for the paying sector but not for the receiving sector, and it is therefore impossible to produce a coherent set of accounts on an accruals basis. Personal sector accruals accounts show the build-up of tax liabilities but not the build-up of dividend receipts. The latter may be as important as the former in influencing personal sector behaviour, and the two types of accrual are certainly offsetting.

Using the payments basis data (Feinstein, 1972, tables 10, 12–15 and 32), the intermediate incomes can be broken down into three groups: property income, taxes and other transfers. Total net receipts of property income (including net property income received by the rest of the world) should equal rent generated by the ownership of dwellings and financial and business services sectors. As the data in table 7.1 show, there are in fact some small discrepancies in each of these identities. However, these discrepancies add to zero over the three types of payments.

In fact it is possible to identify the reasons for some of the discrepancies. UK taxes paid by foreigners, shown at £3m in 1920 and £6m in 1938, are exactly equal to the discrepancy in property income in every year, 1920–38; it is therefore reasonable to assume that they are treated as a tax on the payment side but as property income on the receipt side. They have been reclassified as a payment of property income by the rest of the world. This is consistent with the figure of net property income paid by the rest of the world shown in table 1 of Feinstein (1972). The figure shown for taxes paid by the company sector is assumed to include taxes paid on profits due to the rest of the world. This is consistent with current *Blue Book* treatment.

There then remains a residual of £2m of unaccounted direct tax payments in each year. This is offset by an excess of other transfers paid over other transfers received of the same amount. The reason for this is that personal sector transfer receipts from abroad represent a figure net of taxes paid abroad. If the net personal sector transfer from abroad is calculated from the table for international transactions (table 15 in Feinstein, 1972), which shows the sum of personal and public sector transactions and the table for central government alone (table 12 in *ibid.*), a figure for transfers alone of £2m higher is obtained. This leaves a residual of £2m in the direct tax account. The estimated tax payments of the corporate sector are simply raised by £2m to correct this gap.

The change made to the property income account has no effect on the external sector balance, because the net property income figure is already calculated on that basis. However, personal savings are raised by £2m and the company sector balance is reduced by £2m as compared with Feinstein's figures.

Table 7.1 *Transfer payments, 1920 and 1938, £m*

		1920	1938
Property income			
Receipts			
Personal sector	Rent, dividends and interest	926	1,157
Company sector	Domestic	128	190
	From abroad	184	148
Central government		26	34
Local authorities		21	74
Rest of world	Property income	49	43
	Taxes	22	18
Total		1,356	1,664
Payments			
Company sector	Dividends and interest	443	618
	Profits due abroad	26	33
Central government	Debt interest	320	232
Local autorities	Debt interest	26	68
Rest of world		314	247
Rent		224	460
Residual		3	6
Total		1,356	1,664
Direct Taxes			
Receipts			
Central government		609	383
Payments			
Personal sector		333	293
Company sector		274	88
Rest of world		3	6
Residual		−1	−4
Total		609	383
Other transfers			
Receipts			
Personal sector	From government	160	280
	From abroad	1	2
Central Government	From personal sector	28	109
	From rest of world	7	1
Local authorities		66	142
Rest of world		29	17
Total		291	551

Table 7.1 (*cont.*)

		1920	1938
Payments			
Personal sector		28	109
Central government	To personal sector	152	254
	To local authorities	66	142
	To rest of world	11	8
Local authorities	To personal sector	8	26
Rest of world		28	14
Residual		−2	−2
Total		291	551

7.2.2 1939–1945

For this period Feinstein continues to publish income and expenditure accounts of the public sector and of the rest of the world. The *Statistical Abstract of the War* presents a personal sector income and expenditure account. Feinstein published factor income, expenditure and international transaction figures for 1939 to 1945. These incorporate a number of modifications to the data from the *Statistical Abstract* to deal with omissions from the original estimates. In fact the only variables not available in Feinstein's tables needed to complete the personal sector income/expenditure account are estimates of receipts of rent, dividends and net interest and of income taxes paid. With these in place an estimate of personal saving can be produced by subtraction. We have therefore used the data from the *Statistical Abstract of the War* so as to build up a complete account on the same basis as the prewar data. The combination of income and expenditure figures from these two different sources means that our estimates of sectoral saving differ from those shown in the *Statistical Abstract of the War*.

We cannot infer figures for the company sector in the same way. However, taxes paid by companies can be calculated as the difference between the *Statistical Abstract* figure for income taxes paid by persons and the total receipts identified by Feinstein. It is not possible to produce a gross estimate of dividends and interest paid and rent, dividends and interest received. However, a net figure can be calculated as a balancing item so as to ensure that all property income is accounted for. The resulting figure for saving by companies is then consistent with the estimates for saving of the economy as a whole.

7.2.3 1946–1990

The CSO databank does not provide a coherent set of estimates for this period. However, it has been possible to exploit the accounting identities of the data in order to fill the gaps.

Property income

There are two missing items of property income. First of all, although the tape gives information on payment of dividends from 1946 onwards, it does not give any information on other payments of property income by companies. Second, the tape gives consolidated information on receipts of rent dividends and interest for all sectors except central government from 1946. For central government the series begins in 1963.

The property income payments of the company sector (inclusive of dividends) are calculated as shown in table 7.2.

Dividends and, from 1951 onwards only, profits due abroad, can be deducted from the total of property income paid to give a balance of interest income paid out. Before 1951 interest and property income paid abroad cannot be distinguished. The derived data are shown in table 7.3.

Table 7.2 *Derivation of payments of property income net of dividends by companies*

		CSO Code
	Total income	CIDB
Less	Taxes paid	CIDC
	Dividends paid	CIKB
	Retained balance	CIDA
Equals	Property income paid net of dividends	

Table 7.3 *Property income excluding dividends paid by companies, 1946–1954*

	£m		£m
1946	451	1951	255
1947	458	1952	284
1948	474	1953	300
1949	476	1954	318
1950	499		

Note: The data before 1951 include profits paid abroad. These were: 1951 £119m, 1952 £111m, 1953 £114m, 1954 £115m.

Table 7.4 *Derivation of central government receipts of property income*

		CSO Code
Payments		
Companies	Dividends	CIKB
	Other payments	Table 7.1
Public corporations		ADRP
Central government	Debt interest	ACHL
Local authority	Debt interest	ADAM
Rest of world (net)	UK taxes paid by foreigners	DKGN
	Other (net)	CGOA
Rent component of GDP		DIDS
Total payments		
Receipts		
Personal sector (net)		CFAM
Company sector	Domestic	CICN
	From abroad	CIBU
Public corporations		ADRF
Local authorities		CTMZ
Central government	Balance	
Total receipts = Total payments.		

Table 7.5 *Estimates of central government receipts of property income 1946–1962*

	£m		£m
1946	−8	1955	225
1947	−15	1956	254
1948	74	1957	260
1949	97	1958	301
1950	98	1959	338
1951	136	1960	361
1952	165	1961	433
1953	186	1962	524
1954	204		

In order to complete the picture we also have to calculate the rent, dividend and interest receipts of central government. This is done as the residual needed to equate receipts of property income to payments. The calculations are performed taking account of the fact that taxes on income due abroad must, as in the inter-war years, be reclassified. They have to be debited from property income payments by the corporate sector and credited to taxes paid. This puts corporate tax payments on the same basis as in the interwar years and avoids any discrepancies from this source. Beyond 1973 no taxes are shown on income due abroad, so no adjustment is necessary.

The calculations of central government property income are shown in table 7.4 with the data in table 7.5.

Transfers from central government to the personal sector

The tape does not provide estimates of payments of transfers to the personal sector by central government before 1955. Nor is information given on receipts by the personal sector (which is the only recipient of such payments). However, personal sector receipts of such transfer payments can be calculated as a residual from the data on total personal income and its components. The calculations are shown in table 7.6 and the result is in table 7.7.

Saving

When these changes are made, sectoral savings figures are consistent with those shown on the CSO tape, with the exception of central government savings figures for the period 1946 to 1953 and local authorities for 1946 and 1947. Table 7.8 shows the two estimates for central government for 1946–53.

Table 7.6 *Derivation of transfer payments by central government to personal sector*

		CSO Code
	Total personal incomes	AIIA
Less	Income from employment	DJAO
	Self-employment income	CFAN
	Property income	CFAM
	Other transfers	CFBR
	Capital consumption	CFBM
Equals	Transfers from government	
Less	Payments by local authorities	ADAL
Equals	Payments by central government	

Table 7.7 *Transfer payments by central government to persons, 1946–1954*

	£m		£m
1946	608	1951	705
1947	606	1952	819
1948	632	1953	907
1949	673	1954	924
1950	683		

Table 7.8 *Estimates of central government saving, 1946–1953*

	CSO tape £m	Derived £m
1946	−433	−269
1947	155	284
1948	507	603
1949	590	625
1950	663	690
1951	577	612
1952	341	376
1953	201	218

The explanation of this discrepancy is to be found in the 1968 *Blue Book*. For the period 1948 to 1953 this shows capital transfers equal to the discrepancy. A comparison with the most recent estimates for current transfers from abroad shows that these capital transfers have now been reclassified as central government receipts of current transfers. With this redefinition current income, and therefore saving, is raised. One can thus infer that the discrepancy arises because the published figures for central government saving have not been revised to reflect the reclassification of these transfers to the current account. In 1954 and 1955 the amounts reclassified are £1m. There is no discrepancy, either because savings have been redefined or because the change has simply been lost in rounding.[3]

In 1946 and 1947 the figures for saving by local authorities were £32m and £34m higher than the data provided on the CSO tape. There was a

[3] Although it has a counterpart in the implicit estimate of payments by companies to charities. See page 129.

corresponding discrepancy between aggregate saving and aggregate investment. Since these amounts were exactly equal to the estimate shown on the CSO tape for capital consumption by local authorities, we concluded that imputed capital consumption was double-counted. Not only was it shown explicitly, but also, in the local government data, it was included in the rent receipts. We therefore replaced the CSO estimates of rent received by local authorities of £77m and £80m in 1946 and 1947 respectively with figures of £45m and £46m.

The user of these data should thus bear in mind that, before 1946, imputed capital consumption is included in rent receipts for both central and local government and for the non-profit-making bodies included in the personal sector. After 1946 it is shown explicitly.

There remains a discrepancy between overall saving and overall investment plus capital transfers paid in 1955, 1957 and 1960. The discrepancies are £5m, £1m and −£4m respectively. There are corresponding errors in the balance of property income received as against property income paid. We have not been able to find any explanation of this. In view of the fact that personal sector transfers are calculated as residuals in the preparation of the data, we have deducted the errors from rent, dividends and interest receipts of the personal sector, with knock-on effects on personal saving.

Advance corporation tax

The advance corporation tax system, introduced as from 1973, means that companies pay tax on behalf of the personal sector. Personal sector receipts are shown gross of this tax, which is then shown in the published personal sector account as tax paid. At the same time most of the advance corporation tax is shown as being paid by the company sector. In consequence total taxes paid exceed total taxes received, and property income received exceeds property income paid. Table 3.7 of the *Blue Book* shows the amount of tax which is double-counted and the CSO data bank takes the series for the amount double-counted back to 1973. Our sectoral accounts are constructed to the *Blue Book* definition and therefore also include double-counting. The amounts involved are shown in table 7.9. These should be deducted from advance corporation tax payments in table A.28, and added to corporate payments of dividends and interest in order to produce a corporate sector account on the same basis as the personal sector account. However, the tables of part three retain the *Blue Book* classification for the sake of consistency. In order to make the data balance, royalties paid by companies and public corporations after 1980 have to be included as a component of property income paid out.

Table 7.9 *Personal income tax paid by companies, 1973–1990*

	£m		£m
1973	345	1983	1864
1974	585	1984	2202
1975	683	1985	2687
1976	767	1986	3109
1977	932	1987	3506
1978	935	1988	4452
1979	1411	1989	5362
1980	1346	1990	6329
1981	1379		
1982	1573		

Note: These data are drawn from the 1991 CSO tape.

Company transfers to charities

There is an excess of transfers to charities received over transfers paid. The amount is equal to current transfers to charities from companies, except that, in the first two years for which these data are published, the most recent amount shown in a *Blue Book* is £9m, while the discrepancy is £8m. The calculation of other interest payments as a residual led to the inclusion of this amount with these payments until 1980, when tape data became available. Interest paid by companies is reduced by the discrepancy and transfers paid are increased by the same amount.

This change means that receipts of property income, taxes and other transfer incomes are equated to payments. The residual error in the production account has a counterpart in the discrepancy between saving and investment. The data, reconstructed in this way, provide a starting point to which the adjustments on the production account can be allocated.

7.3 Sectoral capital accounts

The official sources publish sectoral capital accounts, showing the allocation of saving among gross fixed capital formation, the value of increases in stocks, and financial saving for the period 1962 to 1990. We were, however, able to construct estimates of sectoral capital accounts for the period 1948 to 1961, so that the tables of part three are able to present sectoral accounts for 1948–90. Before 1948 there is not enough information to do more than to construct an aggregate capital account similar in structure to that presented by Feinstein (1972, table 16). Such a table is presented for the whole period from 1920 to 1990.

It proved possible to construct sectoral capital accounts for the period 1948 to 1961 because the *Blue Books* for the period give estimates of fixed capital formation and value of increase in stocks by sector, even though these figures have not found their way to the CSO tape. The CSO tape does, however, give estimates of financial balances for the personal, company and local authority sectors; the financial balance of the rest of the world is simply the UK balance of payments deficit.

This means that we can, once again, apply the method of least squares with the aim of producing sectoral capital accounts consistent with the published macroeconomic aggregates. For each of the five domestic sectors we have known estimates of saving and for three of the five we have estimates of financial balances. We have to adjust the figures for gross capital formation and increase in the value of stocks to be consistent with saving less financial balances where they are known. The financial balances of the public corporations and central government have to be treated as derived data in the manner described in chapter 2, section 2.9, subject to the overall constraint that financial balances including the financial balance of the rest of the world should sum to the residual error of the production account.

The data position can be summarised as in table 7.10. The available sectoral data are represented in italics; the row totals are also published. The gross fixed capital formation data are shown in heavy type to indicate that they represent vectors of the four types of asset.

The data have to be adjusted to satisfy the following accounting constraints

$$\mathbf{i}'\mathbf{X_1} + V_1 = S_1 - F_1 - T_1 \quad (7.1)$$

$$\mathbf{i}'\mathbf{X_2} + V_2 = S_2 F_2 - T_2 \quad (7.2)$$

$$\mathbf{i}'\mathbf{X_3} + V_3 + F_3 = S_3 - T_3 \quad (7.3)$$

$$\mathbf{i}'\mathbf{X_4} + V_4 + F_4 = S_4 - T_4 \quad (7.4)$$

$$\mathbf{i}'\mathbf{X_5} + V_5 = S_5 - F_5 - T_5 \quad (7.5)$$

$$'\mathbf{X_1} + \mathbf{X_2} + \mathbf{X_3} + \mathbf{X_4} + \mathbf{X_5} = \mathbf{R_3} \quad (7.6)$$

$$V_1 + V_2 + V_3 + V_4 + V_5 = R_4, \quad (7.7)$$

where $\mathbf{i}'$ is the vector (1 1 1 1).

In each of these constraints, the adjustments have to be made to the

Table 7.10 *Data availability for sectoral capital accounts*

	Institutional sector						
	Personal	Company	Public corp.	Cent. govt	Local auth.	Rest of world	Total
Saving	S_1^*	S_2^*	S_3^*	S_4^*	S_5^*	S_6^*	R_1^*
Net capital transfers received	T_1^*	T_2^*	T_3^*	T_4^*	T_5^*	T_6^*	R_2^*
Gross fixed capital formation	X_1	X_2	X_3	X_4	X_5	0	R_3^*
Value of increase in stocks	V_1	V_2	V_3	V_4	V_5	0	R_4^*
Financial Balances	F_1^*	F_2^*	F_3	F_4	F_5^*	F_6^*	R_5^*

Notes: *Indicates data available consistent with 1991 CSO tape for period 1948 to 1961.

initial estimates of the variables shown on the left-hand side of the constraints. The restriction $F_3 + F_4 = R_4 - F_1 - F_2 - F_5 - F_6$ does not need to be included explicitly, since it is a linear transformation of the other restrictions.

In this exercise the least-squares adjustment is simply allocating revisions made to the aggregate row totals across the components shown in the 1958 and 1968 *Blue Books*. There is no reason to believe that the revisions are related to the overall reliability of the data, and we have therefore simply assumed that the notional standard errors are proportional to the data. However, the two unknown financial balances are given very large standard errors. This ensures that they are estimated as unobserved components.

The domestic capital accounts derived in this way are shown in tables 7.11–7.15. These are used as the basis for allocating the adjustments to capital formation calculated from the reconciliation of the production account as described in section 7.4.

Table 7.11 *Personal sector capital account (£m):1948–1961*

	Savings	Gross fixed capital formation	Increase in value of stocks etc.	Net capital transfers paid	Net acquisition of financial assets
1948	78	226	94	99	−341
1949	155	253	70	160	−327
1950	196	264	105	106	−279
1951	217	356	218	124	−481
1952	443	341	−5	97	10
1953	515	421	40	116	*−2*
1954	436	520	67	144	*−295*
1955	526	598	81	117	−270
1956	808	588	67	106	48
1957	779	589	62	125	3
1958	680	656	30	128	−134
1959	845	703	68	155	−81
1960	1,365	802	93	172	298
1961	1,805	876	86	185	659

Table 7.12 *Company sector capital account (£m): 1948–1961*

	Savings	Gross fixed capital formation	Increase in value of stocks etc.	Net capital transfers paid	Net acquisition of financial assets
1948	1,146	540	412	−64	258
1949	1,047	575	218	−55	309
1950	1,458	636	415	−51	458
1951	1,822	577	852	−32	425
1952	1,246	643	−84	−32	719
1953	1,361	688	22	−42	693
1954	1,755	798	259	−23	721
1955	1,915	980	476	−26	485
1956	2,108	1,226	400	−18	500
1957	2,156	1,415	332	−11	420
1958	2,049	1,464	51	−10	544
1959	2,241	1,559	208	−7	481
1960	2,663	1,788	617	−15	273
1961	2,373	2,054	350	−9	−22

Table 7.13 *Public corporations' capital account (£m): 1948–1961*

	Savings	Gross fixed capital formation	Increase in value of stocks etc.	Net capital transfers paid	Net acquisition of financial assets
1948	77	179	32	−4	−130
1949	86	261	33	−42	−166
1950	127	284	14	−3	−168
1951	171	353	85	−5	−262
1952	183	410	45	−5	−267
1953	194	485	−31	−7	−253
1954	204	537	−65	−7	−261
1955	166	569	39	−12	−430
1956	205	584	27	−16	−390
1957	166	658	68	−9	−550
1958	149	690	33	−7	−567
1959	185	753	10	−7	−571
1960	309	775	−10	−7	−449
1961	364	894	8	−8	−530

Table 7.14 *Central government capital account (£m):1948–1961*

	Savings	Gross fixed capital formation	Increase in value of stocks etc.	Net capital transfers paid	Net acquisition of financial assets
1948	603	116	−38	−145	670
1949	625	117	−56	−172	736
1950	690	128	−94	−176	832
1951	612	173	170	−117	386
1952	376	219	44	−45	158
1953	218	222	19	−37	14
1954	233	194	−131	−87	256
1955	504	201	−100	−64	467
1956	416	228	−26	−58	272
1957	527	250	−36	−85	398
1958	622	250	−8	−85	465
1959	492	259	−10	−114	357
1960	202	262	−16	−119	75
1961	369	225	6	−137	275

Table 7.15 *Local authorities' capital account (£m):1948–1961*

	Savings	Gross fixed capital formation	Increase in value of stocks etc.	Net capital transfers paid	Net acquisition of financial assets
1948	78	372	0	−24	−270
1949	81	383	0	−45	−257
1950	79	406	0	−16	−311
1951	82	460	0	−13	−365
1952	82	540	0	−15	−443
1953	114	607	0	−30	−463
1954	117	575	0	−27	−431
1955	111	563	0	−15	−437
1956	126	567	0	−14	−427
1957	167	569	0	−20	−382
1958	171	544	0	−26	−347
1959	207	582	0	−27	−348
1960	245	604	0	−31	−328
1961	187	702	0	−31	−484

7.4 Allocation of the adjustments from the production accounts

The next step in the calculation of sectoral accounts consistent with the balanced production accounts is the allocation of the adjustments needed in the production accounts to the relevant institutional sectors. For some of the entries in the production account, such as employment income or consumers' expenditure, the whole of the adjustment is applied to one sector. For other entries, such as profit classified by industry, the adjustment has to be split between a number of sectors. This section describes the way in which such adjustments are allocated by sector.

7.4.1 Classification of industrial profits by institutional sector

The basis of the allocation of the industrial profits' adjustment, and indeed all the other similar adjustments, is that each sector should be allocated a component of the adjustment in proportion to the variance of the measurement error associated with the profits earned by each sector in the industry concerned. Each industry is treated separately and independently of the other industries. So an obvious assumption is that the percentage standard errors associated with the estimated value of profits earned by each sector in the industry concerned are proportional to the overall reliability attributed to self-employment income or trading profits.

In order to do this, it is necessary to have a classification of profits by sector and industry. There is no published classification; the classification by sector and industry has been derived in different ways for different periods. These are discussed in turn, starting with 1970–90 because estimates for the period before 1970 are calculated recursively from the information available in 1970.

1970–1990

For 1970–90 the CSO has kindly provided estimates of each type of sectoral income classified by industry (see table 7.16).[4]

1948–1969

In this period there are no available estimates of operating surplus classified by sector and industry. These have to be produced before the reliabilities set out in table 7.16 can be applied. The method used is that described by Weale (1986). It works recursively back from the CSO 1970 estimates and is inspired by the problem of updating an input–output table to be consistent with known marginal totals (see Stone *et al.*, 1963; Bacharach, 1971). Stone devised the RAS method to solve this problem, but, in an account of the application of least-squares adjustment, it is more natural to use the method of chapter 1 to produce estimates of the cross-classification of operating surplus by sector and industry.

The 1970 data can be considered in the form shown in table 7.16. In each of the years from 1948 to 1969 there are estimates of the row and column totals; the sectoral classification should be consistent with these. This is achieved as follows.

With the 1970 data the elements of the table are divided by the 1970 row totals to give the proportions of industrial profit accruing to each sector. These proportions are then multiplied by industrial profits in 1969 so as to give an estimate of the table for 1969. In this estimate the column totals will normally be wrong because the proportion of profits accruing to each sector will not be constant in each industry. The data are therefore adjusted to rectify this.

[4] These estimates are inclusive of stock appreciation whereas we are concerned with allocating adjustments net of stock appreciation. However, there is no basis for allocating this by sector as well as by industry. It is unlikely that the use of data including stock appreciation is a significant source of error.

Table 7.16 *Sectoral classification of industrial profits*

Industry	Personal	Company	Public corp.	Cent. govt	Local auth.	Total
	Institutional sector					
Agriculture	$B_{1,1}$	$B_{1,2}$	$B_{1,3}$	$B_{1,4}$	$B_{1,5}$	R_1
Mining and quarrying	$B_{2,1}$	$B_{2,2}$	$B_{2,3}$	$B_{2,4}$	$B_{2,5}$	R_2
Oil and gas	$B_{3,1}$	$B_{3,2}$	$B_{3,3}$	$B_{3,4}$	$B_{3,5}$	R_3
Manufacturing	$B_{4,1}$	$B_{4,2}$	$B_{4,3}$	$B_{4,4}$	$B_{4,5}$	R_4
Construction	$B_{5,1}$	$B_{5,2}$	$B_{5,3}$	$B_{5,4}$	$B_{5,5}$	R_5
Utilities	$B_{6,1}$	$B_{6,2}$	$B_{6,3}$	$B_{6,4}$	$B_{6,5}$	R_6
Transport and communication	$B_{7,1}$	$B_{7,2}$	$B_{7,3}$	$B_{7,4}$	$B_{7,5}$	R_7
Distribution	$B_{8,1}$	$B_{8,2}$	$B_{8,3}$	$B_{8,4}$	$B_{8,5}$	R_8
Finance and business	$B_{9,1}$	$B_{9,2}$	$B_{9,3}$	$B_{9,4}$	$B_{9,5}$	R_9
Financial services adjustment	$B_{10,1}$	$B_{10,2}$	$B_{10,3}$	$B_{10,4}$	$B_{10,5}$	R_{10}
Education and health	$B_{11,1}$	$B_{11,2}$	$B_{11,3}$	$B_{11,4}$	$B_{11,5}$	R_{11}
Other services	$B_{12,1}$	$B_{12,2}$	$B_{12,3}$	$B_{12,4}$	$B_{12,5}$	R_{12}
Total	C_1	C_2	C_3	C_4	C_5	

If $\hat{\mathbf{B}}_{70}$ represents proportions set out as the 60 ×12 matrix

$$\hat{\mathbf{B}}_{70} = \begin{pmatrix} B_{1,1} & 0 & \cdots & 0 \\ B_{1,2} & 0 & \cdots & 0 \\ B_{1,3} & 0 & \cdots & 0 \\ B_{1,4} & 0 & \cdots & 0 \\ B_{1,5} & 0 & \cdots & 0 \\ 0 & B_{2,1} & \cdots & 0 \\ \cdots & \cdots & \cdots & \cdots \\ 0 & 0 & \cdots & B_{12,1} \\ 0 & 0 & \cdots & B_{12,2} \\ 0 & 0 & \cdots & B_{12,4} \\ 0 & 0 & \cdots & B_{12,5} \end{pmatrix} \tag{7.8}$$

then, if $\mathbf{r}_{69}$ is the vector of industry totals

$$\mathbf{x}_{69} = \hat{\mathbf{B}}_{70}\mathbf{r}_{69} \tag{7.9}$$

gives the first estimate of the table cells as a column vector.

We now adjust $\mathbf{x}_{69}$ to ensure that both row and column totals are satisfied. Denote by $\mathbf{A}$ the matrix of linear constraints which are met by the true data $\mathbf{x}^*_{69}$, so that, where $\mathbf{c}_{69}$ is the vector of the first four column totals, then

$$\mathbf{A}\mathbf{x}^*_{69} = \begin{bmatrix} \mathbf{r}_{69} \\ \mathbf{c}_{69} \end{bmatrix}. \tag{7.10}$$

The fifth column total is omitted because it is redundant: if all the industrial totals are satisfied and the first four sectoral totals are met, then the fifth sectoral total will also be met.

Given a variance matrix $\mathbf{V}$ for the vector $\mathbf{x}_{69}$ it is a simple matter to calculate the least-squares estimate $\mathbf{x}^{**}_{69}$ (see chapter 2, section 2.2) as

$$\mathbf{x}^{**}_{69} = \mathbf{x}_{69} - \mathbf{V}\mathbf{A}'(\mathbf{A}\mathbf{V}\mathbf{A}')^{-1}\left(\mathbf{A}\mathbf{x}_{69} - \begin{bmatrix} \mathbf{r}_{69} \\ \mathbf{c}_{69} \end{bmatrix}\right) \tag{7.11}$$

The variance matrix is assumed to be diagonal, with each element given by the square of the relevant element of $\mathbf{x}_{69}$. No allowance has been made for differing sectoral reliabilities associated with the preliminary vector $\mathbf{x}_{69}$ because no information is provided on the reliability of its components.

The new estimate $\mathbf{x}^{**}_{69}$ of the sectoral classification of industrial profits is then used as the starting point to which the CSO sectoral reliabilities are applied; with these data the adjustments to industrial profits can be allocated across the sectors in the manner described in chapter 2, section 2.2.

The exercise then proceeds recursively. A new matrix of proportions, $\hat{\mathbf{B}}_{69}$ is calculated from $\mathbf{x}^{**}_{69}$ and from the row totals $\mathbf{r}_{69}$. This is applied to the 1968 row totals, to give an initial estimate, $\mathbf{x}_{68}$. From the reconciled estimate for 1968, $\mathbf{x}^{**}_{68}$, one can calculate $\hat{\mathbf{B}}_{68}$ and so the exercise proceeds back to 1948.

These data are not presented in the *Blue Book* and neither are their balanced estimates presented in part three. They are used simply as a basis for allocating adjustments calculated by industry to the various institutional sectors. Accordingly we do not present the cross-classification of profits by sector, derived as described here, in the text.

1939–1947

In this period there are no estimates of industrial profits in the production account. Profits are instead disaggregated by receiving sector. The question of allocating industrial profits therefore does not arise.

1920–1938

The period 1920 to 1938 is treated in much the same way as 1948–69. However, no 1938 estimate exists, so it is not possible to work back recursively. Instead of a recursive exercise, we have taken the average of the proportions implied by Feinstein's sectoral allocations for 1927 and 1937 as our starting point, and used these to provide estimates $\mathbf{x}_{20} \ldots \mathbf{x}_{38}$ for each of the years 1920–38.

There is, however, one important difference between the treatment of the 1920–38 data and those for 1948–69. In the postwar years estimates of both row and column totals were available net of stock appreciation, even though the proportions matrix for 1970 was based on industrial profits gross of stock appreciation. For 1920–38 the estimates of sectoral income include stock appreciation. This means that the reconciliation exercise can be done only with stock appreciation treated as an extra 'industry' with known row total, but with no basis for allocation by sector.

This has the implication that, since total profits by industry plus stock appreciation equals total profit by sector inclusive of stock appreciation, the value of stock appreciation for each sector is calculated as a residual. Both row and column totals are reconciled without any adjustments to the individual cells being needed. Although this leads to estimates of sectoral stock appreciation, we do not consider they are sufficiently reliable to merit inclusion in the data tables.

7.4.2 *Adjustments to sectoral profits*

We are now able to use the cross-classification of industrial profits by industry and by sector to allocate the adjustments to industrial profits, calculated in chapters 5 and 6, to the institutional sectors. In each industry we assume that the estimate of sectoral profit has a standard error proportional to that given by the CSO (post-1948) or Feinstein (pre-1938) for the relevant category of sectoral income. The relevant reliabilities are shown in tables 7.17 and 7.18.

These reliabilities are not consistent with those calculated after application of the Mahalanobis criterion, but this does not matter, since it is only relative reliabilities which affect the allocation of the discrepancy. Making the assumption that the pattern of serial correlation is common across the sectors, no attention needs to be paid to this in calculating the changes which need to be made to sectoral income.

Accordingly, the standard deviations of the sectoral components of industry profits are simply assumed to be given by applying the percentages of tables 7.17 and 7.18 to our estimates of industrial profits earned

Table 7.17 *Reliability codes for sectoral operating surplus, 1948–1990*

Sector	Type of income	Reliability code	% standard error
Personal	Self-employment income	C	9.1
Company	Gross trading profit	B	4.0
Public corp.	Gross trading surplus	A	0.9
Central govt	Gross trading surplus	A	0.9
Local govt	Gross trading surplus	A	0.9

Table 7.18 *Reliability codes for sectoral operating surplus, 1920–1938*

Sector	Type of income	Reliability code	% standard error
Personal	Self-employment income	B	6.1
Companies	Gross trading profit	B	6.1
Central govt	Gross trading surplus	B	6.1
Local govt	Gross trading surplus	B	6.1

by each sector. The least-squares approach then simply implies that the adjustments are allocated in proportion to the resulting variances. The aggregate sectoral adjustments are calculated by adding up the adjustments allocated on an industry-by-industry basis.

7.4.3 Sectoral classification of rent

Unfortunately, the same information is not available for the allocation of the sectoral classification of rent. This appears as factor income in two industries, ownership of dwellings and business and financial services.[5] A large part of the rent on ownership of dwellings is imputed rent. None of the adjustment should be attributed to this because it implies equal adjustments to expenditure and income. The two adjustments to rent have been added together and allocated across the sectors using standard deviations calculated from the reliabilities of sectoral profits and from estimates of sectoral receipts of rent excluding imputed rent. These data

[5] Feinstein's prewar data identify a third source of rent earned in agriculture. This appears to be paid to the personal sector and we have credited it with the self-employment income of the personal sector in agriculture.

can be derived from the CSO tape back to 1963. For the period 1948 to 1962 the 1963 standard deviations are used.

Feinstein (1972, table 8.1) gives a classification of rent by category for the years 1920, 1925, 1930, 1935 and 1938. His classification does not fit the institutional sectors exactly. Rents received by central and local government are identified without difficulty. There are four categories shown as accruing to the private sector. The largest component, on property occupied by persons as consumers, is assumed not to bear any adjustment. The reason for this is that the data presented by Feinstein as incomes were the basis for Stone and Rowe's (1966) estimation of expenditure. Of the remaining rentals, farm income is already included in the income of the agricultural sector. Of the balance 80 per cent of rent on buildings and 20 per cent of ground rent and property is assumed to accrue to the personal sector, with the remainder accruing to companies. These proportions are, unfortunately arbitrary. Linear interpolation was used to estimate sectoral income for the years for which Feinstein does not provide data and the resulting 'estimates' were used as a basis for allocating the total adjustment to rent identified in the two industries.

Table 7.19 compares the proportions of rent received by each sector excluding imputed rent in the post-war years and all rent on property occupied by consumers as persons in the prewar years. There seems to be a reasonable degree of stability, validating the use of fixed ratios for the period when no data are available.

For the period 1939 to 1947, the reconciliation of income and expenditure is based on factor income classified by type instead of industrial value added. This means that the estimate of rent includes rent on farms (which is classified as profits of agriculture in the periods 1920–1938 and 1948–1990). Accordingly, since this is assumed to be received by the personal sector, a larger share of the adjustment to rent must be allocated to personal sector incomes in 1939–47. The proportions used are also shown in table 7.19.

7.4.4 Allocation of public consumption

While all the adjustments to personal consumption find their way to the personal sector, the changes to public consumption need to be split between central government and local authorities. The *Blue Book* provides the information which is needed for the period 1948 to 1990, showing each of the four categories of public expenditure split between central and local government. The total adjustment to each category of expenditure is allocated between central and local government, making the assumption that the measurement errors in the published data have

Table 7.19 *Sectoral allocation of rent (receipts as % of total)*

	1938		1963
	Excluding farms	Including farms	
Personal sector	39	46	33
Companies	20	17	21
Public corporations			5
Central government	4	3	2
Local authorities	37	33	38

Note: In 1938 public corporations are included with companies.

standard errors proportional to the data themselves (i.e. that they have equal proportional reliability).

Between 1920 and 1938 the adjustments to public expenditure are minimal, being never more than £1m. They are split between central and local government on the assumption that standard errors are proportional to the expenditures identified by Feinstein (1972).

7.4.5 Sectoral allocation of adjustments to capital formation

The sectoral allocation of the adjustments to capital formation is needed to complete the sectoral capital accounts. This is done in the same way as the sectoral adjustments to profits and to public consumption. Section 7.3 described how we obtained estimates of capital formation by sector for the period 1948 to 1970. We have assumed that these have reliabilities as shown in table 7.20, and used these reliabilities to allocate the adjustments to capital formation by asset derived in the reconciliation of the GDP accounts.

In the period before 1938 the adjustments to capital formation in current prices are never more than £1m. We have simply split the adjustment equally between company and personal sectors.

7.5 Conclusions

These techniques allow us to allocate the adjustments across the sectoral current and capital accounts. The results are shown in tables A.25–A.39 of part three. That the residual has been allocated in a consistent manner can be seen from the financial reconciliation account. When the financial

Table 7.20 *Reliability codes for sectoral capital formation, 1948–1960*

Sector	Reliability code	% SE
Personal sector	C	9.1
Companies	B	4.0
Public corporations	A	0.9
Central government	A	0.9
Local government	A	0.9

balances are calculated as residuals, as in the *Blue Book* or in tables 7.11–7.15, the residual error is equal to the sum of the financial balances (including the financial balance of the rest of the world). Table A.43 in part three shows that this now sums to zero.

Transfer payments from one sector to another do not enter into the GDP identity. Nevertheless, the revisions to factor incomes and to final demand mean that sectoral accounts may be changed substantially as a consequence of the balancing exercise. Section 8.3 of chapter 8 provides a good illustration of this. In this chapter we have described some of the problems faced in constructing sectoral accounts for the full period. The outcome has been a fuller set of sectoral income/expenditure and capital accounts than has hitherto been available.

8 The results of the balancing exercise

8.1 Introduction

The standard errors which we described in chapters 5 and 6 allowed us to construct the variance matrices needed to balance the UK national accounts in three stages. We treated the periods 1920 to 1938 and 1948 to 1990 quite independently of each other. We then took the period 1938 to 1948, constraining the data to satisfy the accounting identities and also restricting the 1938 and 1948 estimates to equal those calculated using the two earlier exercises. This gave a balanced set of national accounts for the period 1920 to 1990. We were able to allocate the adjustments across the sectoral accounts as described in chapter 7, so as to produce full sectoral accounts. Less detail is, however, available during the war years, and we are not able to produce sectoral capital accounts before 1948.

In this chapter we draw attention to some of the properties of the balanced dataset, indicating how the new estimates of national income differ from those provided by the standard sources and providing estimates of their reliability. The new data themselves are presented in part three of the book.

We do not present the adjustments to each of the components of national income and expenditure shown in the tables of part three; this would require an appendix of similar magnitude showing the adjustments. Instead we limit ourselves to presenting the adjustments to the main aggregate components of the national accounts. We also avoid presenting a standard error for each observation of each variable. An adequate guide can be given by period averages. We do, however, provide indicators of the reliability with which year-on-year percentage changes in variables are measured.

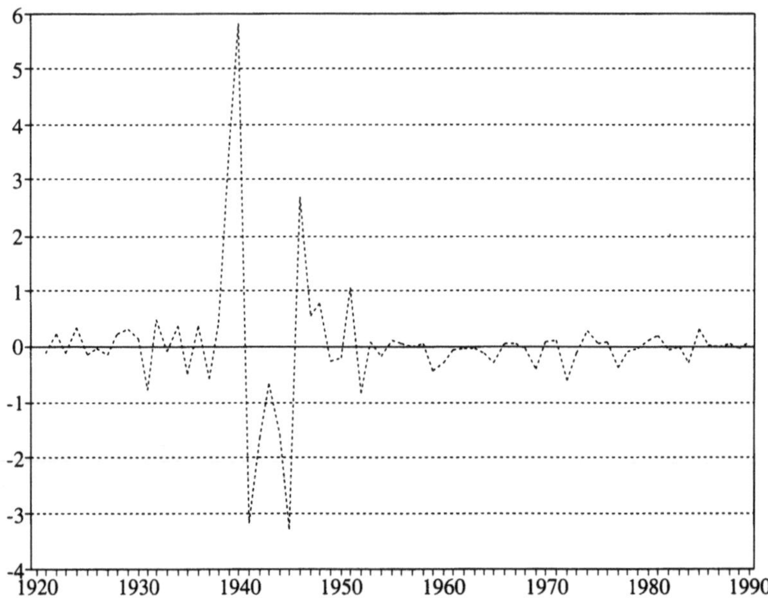

Figure 8.1 Change in GDP(B) minus change in GDP(A) (%)

8.2 Analysis of the adjustments to the main aggregates

The adjustments to the main components of GDP are presented in current and then constant prices in tables 8.4 and 8.5. This section describes some of the differences between the original data and the balanced data.

8.2.1 Growth in GDP

As figure 8.1 shows, the estimated growth in the balanced estimate of GDP, GDP(B), at constant prices is in most years not very different from that of the average estimate, GDP(A), presented by Feinstein (1972) and on the CSO tape. This suggests that, although arbitrary, the averaging process used in calculating the average estimate is reasonably close to what would emerge from a least-squares approach. Certainly tables 5.9 and 6.9 suggest that the reliabilities of the expenditure and output measures are not very different. The current price income and expenditure estimates (tables 5.8 and 6.8) also have broadly similar reliabilities and the residuals to be allocated are, at least in the postwar period, much smaller.

Table 8.1 *Growth rates in average and balanced estimates of GDP (% p.a.)*

	GDP(A)	GDP(B)
1920–1930	1.59	1.42
1930–1938	2.20	2.13
1938–1948	1.26	1.67
1948–1960	2.76	2.71
1960–1970	2.97	2.82
1970–1980	1.80	1.74
1980–1990	2.48	2.50
1920–1990	2.17	2.16

Thus the use of an average gives, approximately speaking, two weights to the similar income/expenditure estimates and only one to the output estimate. Since the least-squares estimate places much less weight on the income estimate, because it has to be deflated using a deflator derived from the expenditure constant and current price measures, it is likely to lie closer to the output measure than does GDP(A). Between 1950 and 1975 the output measure grew more slowly than the expenditure measure, and this explains why figure 8.1 shows GDP(B) growing more slowly than GDP(A) at this time.

Between 1939 and 1945 there is no output measure. The current price measures of income and expenditure are reconciled and the constant price measure of expenditure also moves as a consequence of the covariance between the constant price and current price expenditure data. But since a part of the discrepancy in the current price accounts is implicitly attributed to price effects rather than to volume effects, the adjustment to the expenditure estimate is lower than one would find if the standard deflator were simply applied to the current price figures. This leads to large movements in estimated year-on-year growth.

As table 8.1 shows, the growth rates over long periods are not changed very much by the balancing. The estimated growth rate is raised by 0.4 per cent p.a. during the period 1938 to 1948, but this is offset by slightly lower growth estimates in most other periods so that from 1920 to 1990 there is no change in the annual average growth rate.

8.2.2 Growth in manufacturing and other output

The use of GDP(A) does not allow the error to be allocated across the data. Thus, although GDP(A) and GDP(B) show broadly similar growth

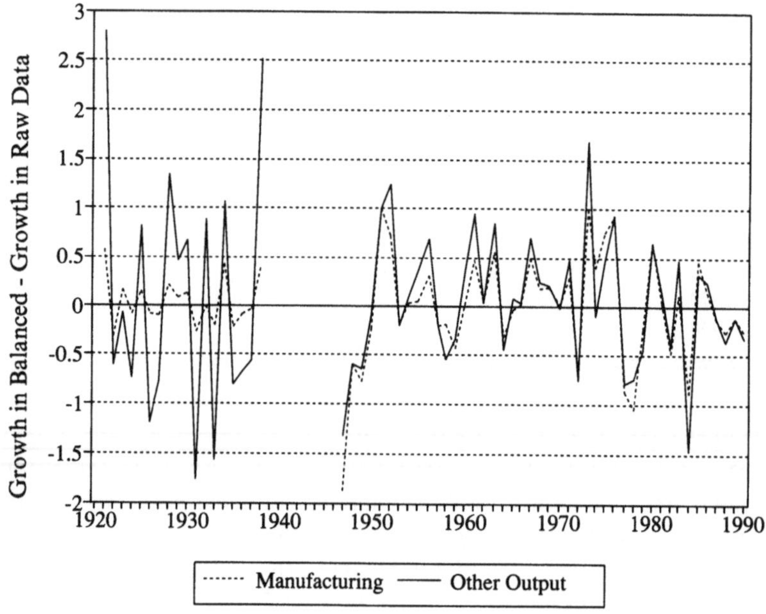

Figure 8.2 Balanced minus original actual change in manufacturing and other output (% p.a.)

rates, the same cannot be said of the output series which make up the components of the output measure of GDP(B). Figure 8.2 shows the difference in the growth rate of the balanced estimates of manufacturing and other output and the growth rates of the original estimates. No data are available for the Second World War.

In the postwar period in particular, the output series was considerably higher than the expenditure estimate for most of the period, but the gap had more or less closed by 1980. In order to reconcile the estimates it is necessary to depress the levels of the output estimates in the earlier part of the period, and this has the effect of raising the growth rates of the output estimates. As figure 8.2 shows, the percentage adjustments to manufacturing and to other output are broadly similar.

In the interwar period the adjustments do not show the same bias. The proportionate adjustments to manufacturing are much smaller than postwar, with the adjustments to other output being slightly larger in absolute magnitude. This reflects the fact that, while manufacturing

Table 8.2 *Growth rates in manufacturing and other output (% p.a.)*

	Manufacturing		Other output	
	Original	Balanced	Original	Balanced
1920–1930	1.58	1.66	1.07	1.34
1930–1938	3.73	3.73	1.52	1.50
1938–1948	1.88	2.62	0.55	1.23
1948–1960	4.17	4.18	2.02	2.17
1960–1970	3.08	3.25	2.38	2.65
1970–1980	−0.17	−0.05	2.30	2.44
1980–1990	2.25	2.11	2.79	2.63
1920–1990	2.41	2.51	1.86	2.01

output was measured more accurately postwar than between 1920 and 1938, the accuracy with which other output was measured increased much more substantially. Relative to other output manufacturing was measured more reliably interwar than postwar. This leads to a smaller proportionate adjustment. From table 8.2 we can see that growth rates of both manufacturing and other output are altered, markedly in some cases. This reflects the fact that the components of the output estimate have to be changed to reconcile them with the expenditure estimates.

8.2.3 *Change in stocks and work in progress*

Figure 8.3 shows the difference between the balanced estimate of change in stocks and the original estimate measured as a fraction of balanced GDP at current market prices. Before 1940 there were substantial adjustments to stockbuilding. These were smaller after the war and became almost insignificant after 1980.

8.2.4 *Consumers' expenditure and the consumption deflator*

The differences between the balanced and initial estimates of growth in consumers' expenditure in constant prices are shown in figure 8.4. The graph also shows the differences between increases in the balanced and initial estimates of the private consumption deflator. In the interwar

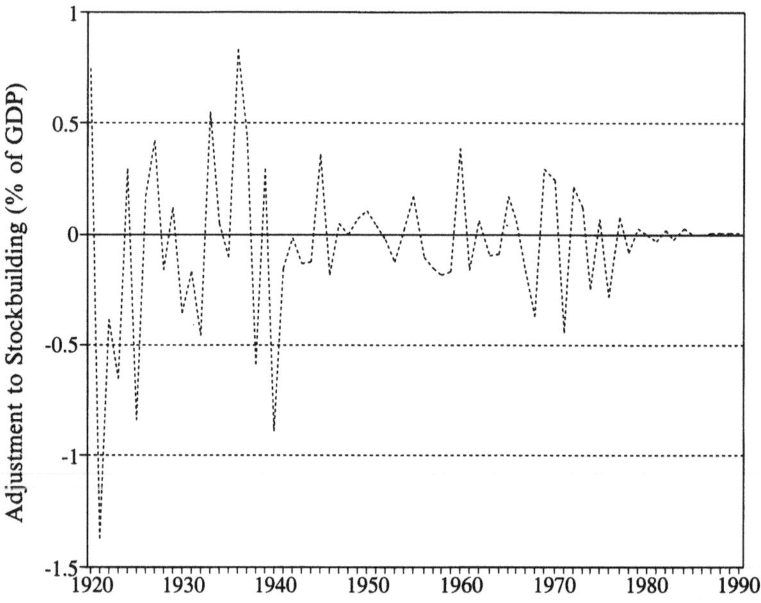

Figure 8.3 Balanced minus original change in stocks (% of GDP at current market prices)

years the differences are larger than postwar. This reflects the fact that for much of the period the adjustments to both constant and current price data had to be in the same direction. The covariance between constant and current price expenditure data made it more attractive for expenditure items to bear the brunt in this case. It can be seen that the adjustments in the deflator are generally in the same direction as those to the growth of constant price consumers' expenditure.

By contrast, in the postwar years the adjustments to current price data are much smaller than those to constant price data and are often in the opposite direction. In such circumstances it becomes more sensible to adjust output estimates relatively more and expenditure estimates relatively less (as is implicit in figure 8.2). The adjustments to the deflator tend to offset those to the consumption estimate.

These points are borne out in table 8.3. Except during the Second World War, the changes to the estimated growth rate of consumption are small and, over each of the 'decades' balancing never changes the deflator growth rate by more than 0.15 per cent p.a.

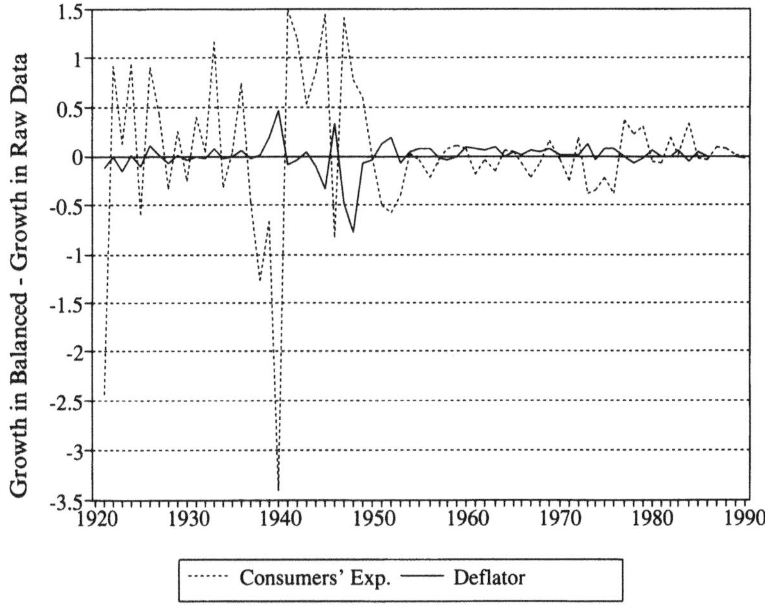

Figure 8.4 Balanced minus original change in consumers' expenditure and in the private consumption deflator (% p.a.)

Table 8.3 *Growth in consumers' expenditure and in the consumption deflator (% p.a.)*

	Consumers' expenditure		Consumption deflator	
	Original	Balanced	Original	Balanced
1920–1930	1.34	1.33	−3.78	−3.82
1930–1938	1.74	1.78	0.40	0.40
1938–1948	0.72	0.89	6.02	6.12
1948–1960	2.39	2.49	3.33	3.18
1960–1970	2.39	2.33	3.90	3.95
1970–1980	2.22	2.16	12.46	12.50
1980–1990	3.34	3.40	5.84	5.83
1920–1990	2.04	2.09	4.02	4.01

8.2.5 Implications of balancing for savings data

The data for sectoral saving and the financial balances of each sector emerge downstream from the balancing and allocation process. Since there are no comprehensive estimates of financial saving, these data are pure residuals. Figure 8.5 shows the estimates of the personal savings ratio which emerge from the balanced data, and compares them with the initial estimates. It can be seen that, particularly in the period 1920 to 1938, the balanced data suggest a reasonably stable picture of savings behaviour; some might regard this as more plausible. In particular, in the period 1920 to 1924, the negative savings ratios identified by Feinstein (1972) disappear. The reason for this is quite straightforward. In this period the expenditure estimate of GDP was considerably above the income estimate. Any reconciliation will reduce expenditure relative to income; it is almost certain that personal consumption, the largest component of expenditure, will be reduced while incomes, and therefore personal income, will be raised. In consequence the savings ratio is raised to the values shown in figure 8.5.

8.3 Adjustments to the main aggregates

Tables 8.4 and 8.5 show the adjustments to the main aggregates which result from the balancing exercise. In general the adjustments to expenditure and to income/output are in opposite directions. This is what would be expected. The balanced data lie between the two. However, the constant price data for the period 1920 to 1938 do not fit this pattern. For much of this period there are negative adjustments to both variables, giving balanced estimates which lie outside the interval between the initial output and expenditure estimates.

Solomou and Weale (1993) discuss the point at some length. The finding appears to be reasonably robust to the specification used. A balanced estimate between output and expenditure is only found if the covariance between constant and current price expenditure is reduced much below the values generated by the pattern which we have assumed.

The reason for the result can be inferred from figure 1.1 (page 4). For 1920–38 the discrepancy in the current price series is larger than in the constant price series. The expenditure components have to adjust considerably in order to correct this. We are implicitly assuming that the underlying price indices are reasonably reliable so that these adjustments are transmitted to the constant price expenditure measure. It is dragged down so far that the output measure must also be reduced in order to reconcile constant price GDP.

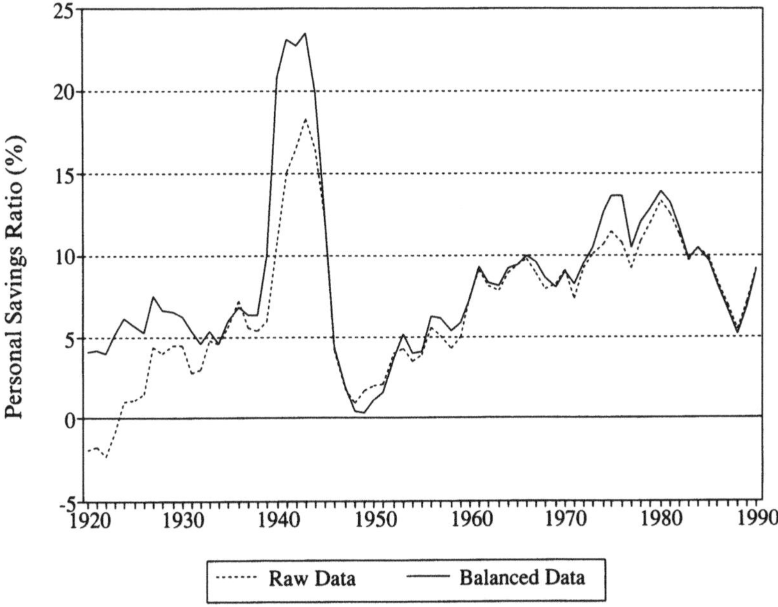

Figure 8.5 Original and balanced estimates of the savings ratio (%)

In the postwar years it might be expected that the large adustments required to constant price expenditure would cast a similar shadow over current price expenditure. But the biggest problems arise when the series are further from the 1985 base-year. By this time the cumulated errors in the price indices are much greater so that the effect is less marked. The phenomenon can, however, be observed in the current price data between 1950 and 1952 as well as in some other years.

Table 8.4 *Adjustments to published data, current price GDP (£m): 1920–1990*

	Employment income	Operating surplus	Factor cost adjustment	GDP(I)	Consumers' expenditure	Gross fixed capital formation	Stock-building	Public authorities' current expenditure	Exports	Imports	GDP(E)
1920	154	134	0	288	−91	0	44	1	−10	3	−58
1921	96	−58	1	39	−186	−1	−67	−1	−10	5	−270
1922	91	38	0	130	−132	0	−17	0	−7	3	−160
1923	86	22	0	108	−129	0	−28	0	−8	4	−169
1924	85	50	0	135	−96	0	12	0	−5	2	−90
1925	67	−37	0	30	−126	−1	−38	0	−7	4	−175
1926	61	9	0	69	−87	0	7	0	−4	2	−85
1927	51	16	0	67	−70	1	19	0	−3	1	−54
1928	30	−4	0	26	−87	0	−7	0	−4	2	−100
1929	17	−18	0	−2	−78	0	6	0	−3	1	−76
1930	1	−24	0	−23	−88	0	−16	0	−3	2	−110
1931	27	8	0	35	−71	0	−7	0	−1	1	−80
1932	−1	−9	0	−11	−68	0	−19	0	−1	1	−91
1933	8	−12	0	−4	−23	1	23	0	0	−1	2
1934	−16	−38	0	−54	−37	0	2	0	0	0	−35
1935	−5	−33	0	−38	−37	0	−5	0	0	0	−42
1936	−8	−34	−1	−42	−6	1	41	1	1	−2	40
1937	15	−16	0	−2	−27	1	23	1	1	−1	−1
1938	−13	−52	1	−65	−82	−1	−32	−1	−1	1	−119
1939	79	13	2	93	−113	0	14	2	2	−5	−93

Table 8.4 (*cont.*)

	Employment income	Operating surplus	Factor cost adjustment	GDP(I)	Consumers' expenditure	Gross fixed capital formation	Stockbuilding	Public authorities' current expenditure	Exports	Imports	GDP(E)
1940	324	181	8	505	−284	−1	−44	−29	−5	38	−408
1941	313	126	9	439	−232	0	−8	−8	−1	4	−262
1942	261	101	8	362	−189	0	−1	−1	0	0	−199
1943	232	100	7	332	−170	0	−10	−12	−4	8	−210
1944	124	68	4	192	−142	0	−10	−11	−7	10	−184
1945	−91	−29	−2	−120	−82	0	23	15	4	−31	−7
1946	−133	−41	−3	−174	−142	0	−26	−3	−2	4	−174
1947	−77	−7	−2	−84	−90	0	1	0	1	−2	−84
1948	5	33	0	38	63	2	0	−5	0	−1	61
1949	−10	−3	0	−13	113	6	9	−5	4	−3	129
1950	10	42	0	52	115	6	14	−5	3	−3	136
1951	14	49	0	63	85	4	5	−6	2	−2	92
1952	7	16	0	23	46	1	−4	−7	1	−1	37
1953	58	114	0	172	−7	−2	−22	−9	−3	1	−44
1954	37	83	0	121	0	0	2	−9	0	0	−6
1955	22	36	0	58	4	1	33	−8	2	−1	33
1956	55	92	0	146	−16	−6	−21	−9	−4	3	−59
1957	84	172	0	256	−25	−9	−34	−10	−5	4	−87
1958	92	207	0	299	−22	−8	−43	−11	−4	3	−90
1959	96	168	0	264	−6	−2	−41	−11	−2	1	−62

Table 8.4 (*cont.*)

	Employment income	Operating surplus	Factor cost adjustment	GDP(I)	Consumers' expenditure	Gross fixed capital formation	Stock-building	Public authorities' current expenditure	Exports	Imports	GDP(E)
1960	4	19	0	23	22	8	99	−9	5	−3	128
1961	25	51	0	76	−1	−3	−44	−11	−2	0	−61
1962	31	45	0	76	−1	0	17	−11	1	0	7
1963	25	39	0	63	−17	−8	−30	−11	−4	2	−72
1964	51	59	0	110	−8	−2	−30	−12	−1	1	−53
1965	7	1	0	8	10	5	60	−13	2	−1	66
1966	49	58	0	108	−3	0	24	−14	2	0	9
1967	93	130	0	224	−46	−24	−66	−17	−7	5	−165
1968	82	157	0	239	−63	−33	−163	−18	−13	8	−297
1969	−58	−52	0	−110	−2	0	137	−14	4	0	125
1970	−38	−38	0	−75	−9	0	127	−14	6	0	110
1971	150	177	0	327	−98	−60	−256	−17	−37	18	−486
1972	82	49	0	132	−35	−3	138	−12	13	2	100
1973	57	−2	0	55	−163	−76	88	0	−33	27	−211
1974	676	464	0	1,140	−394	−186	−210	−10	−96	76	−972
1975	867	469	0	1,337	−583	−229	69	−20	−79	84	−925
1976	1,319	885	0	2,204	−915	−461	−359	−31	−312	173	−2,251
1977	481	329	0	810	−735	−266	104	−31	−88	102	−1,119
1978	469	920	0	1,388	−703	−306	−143	−41	−193	109	−1,496
1979	454	561	0	1,015	−506	−164	53	−45	−32	62	−755

Table 8.4 (*cont.*)

	Employment income	Operating surplus	Factor cost adjustment	GDP(I)	Consumers' expenditure	Gross fixed capital formation	Stock-building	Public authorities' current expenditure	Exports	Imports	GDP(E)
1980	304	247	0	551	−579	−195	−4	−52	−94	74	−999
1981	420	397	0	817	−770	−241	−89	−60	−185	98	−1,442
1982	221	202	0	423	−562	−122	41	−64	−21	52	−780
1983	−51	−173	0	−224	−511	−170	−89	−64	−177	75	−1,085
1984	64	224	0	287	30	55	77	−71	101	−21	212
1985	−139	−165	0	−304	61	6	−2	−69	−12	−1	−16
1986	−241	−491	0	−731	−34	−33	−25	−74	−60	15	−241
1987	−395	−763	0	−1,158	190	48	8	−78	14	−15	197
1988	−357	−641	0	−998	382	121	13	−84	47	−40	518
1989	−354	−547	0	−902	416	135	5	−92	35	−44	543
1990	−114	67	0	−47	349	127	7	−109	52	−46	471

Table 8.5 *Adjustments to published data, GDP at constant prices (£m): 1920–1990*

	Manufacturing output	GDP(O)	Factor cost adjustment	Consumers' expenditure	Gross fixed capital formation	Stock-building	Public authorities' current expenditure	Exports	Imports	GDP(E)
					1920–1948 in 1938 prices					
1920	−23	−82	−1	−72	0	25	1	−3	1	−49
1921	−13	−6	1	−141	−1	−53	−1	−5	3	−204
1922	−18	−22	0	−118	0	−19	0	−5	2	−144
1923	−18	−25	0	−117	0	−26	0	−5	2	−152
1924	−21	−45	0	−89	0	4	0	−3	1	−89
1925	−20	−24	1	−111	−1	−34	−1	−5	3	−154
1926	−20	−56	0	−80	0	1	0	−3	1	−82
1927	−23	−83	0	−67	1	12	0	−2	0	−57
1928	−20	−44	0	−81	0	−11	0	−3	1	−96
1929	−20	−31	0	−73	0	0	0	−2	1	−76
1930	−18	−10	0	−84	0	−19	0	−3	2	−108
1931	−20	−62	0	−70	0	−9	0	−2	1	−80
1932	−20	−36	0	−68	0	−20	0	−2	1	−92
1933	−23	−84	0	−24	1	20	0	0	−1	−2
1934	−20	−54	0	−38	0	1	0	0	0	−38
1935	−25	−80	0	−37	0	−4	0	0	0	−42
1936	−28	−105	−1	−7	1	41	1	1	−2	40
1937	−30	−127	0	−27	1	25	1	1	−1	2
1938	−24	−42	1	−82	−1	−32	−1	−1	1	−119
1939	0	0	1	−117	0	13	1	2	−4	−97

Table 8.5 (*cont.*)

	Manufacturing output	GDP(O)	Factor cost adjustment	Consumers' expenditure	Gross fixed capital formation	Stockbuilding	Public authorities' current expenditure	Exports	Imports	GDP(E)
1940	0	0	1	−251	0	−56	−27	−4	28	−368
1941	0	0	1	−188	0	−19	−9	−1	3	−222
1942	0	0	1	−147	0	−16	−4	0	1	−169
1943	0	0	2	−131	0	−29	−12	−2	5	−181
1944	0	0	2	−108	0	−33	−12	−4	6	−165
1945	0	0	2	−58	0	−9	6	2	−15	−46
1946	95	291	2	−100	0	−55	−5	−1	2	−167
1947	63	229	2	−53	0	−34	−2	0	0	−91
1948	60	218	2	−10	0	−35	−2	0	1	−50
				1948–1990 in 1985 prices						
1948	−839	−4,956	−291	1,553	71	156	751	225	−248	3,296
1949	−1,163	−5,722	−295	2,118	113	370	808	277	−288	4,269
1950	−1,342	−5,900	−300	2,173	118	382	802	308	−285	4,368
1951	−1,011	−4,971	−306	1,693	93	233	799	283	−291	3,699
1952	−704	−3,688	−284	1,116	60	125	796	249	−243	2,874
1953	−822	−4,007	−290	773	42	−4	837	224	−243	2,404
1954	−859	−4,018	−298	836	61	169	806	247	−250	2,668
1955	−896	−3,693	−303	830	72	329	739	272	−273	2,819
1956	−757	−2,940	−290	609	19	36	656	235	−240	2,086
1957	−863	−3,205	−290	589	1	−12	633	223	−234	1,957
1958	−931	−3,839	−294	675	10	−38	599	212	−230	1,983
1959	−1,185	−4,338	−308	835	49	−21	616	223	−250	2,259

Table 8.5 (*cont.*)

	Manufacturing output	GDP(O)	Factor cost adjustment	Consumers' expenditure	Gross fixed capital formation	Stockbuilding	Public authorities' current expenditure	Exports	Imports	GDP(E)
1960	−1,279	−4,071	−310	963	120	445	602	268	−291	2,999
1961	−1,037	−2,952	−294	733	51	−28	556	203	−243	2,053
1962	−1,012	−2,943	−278	685	67	149	552	213	−235	2,178
1963	−743	−1,867	−267	495	9	10	476	169	−208	1,635
1964	−1,000	−2,580	−264	589	50	9	481	181	−224	1,798
1965	−1,049	−2,514	−246	654	92	215	460	188	−214	2,070
1966	−1,062	−2,512	−231	560	59	121	436	172	−190	1,770
1967	−752	−1,486	−214	243	−86	−78	387	95	−145	919
1968	−693	−1,125	−198	134	−138	−270	335	60	−122	442
1969	−590	−807	−176	364	35	300	275	138	−138	1,426
1970	−579	−845	−162	315	29	264	246	123	−115	1,255
1971	−367	−76	−144	−93	−250	−406	200	−104	−14	−496
1972	−857	−1,361	−139	211	9	251	249	109	−70	1,038
1973	−152	1,631	−111	−467	−270	154	102	−120	66	−556
1974	158	1,446	−87	−1,074	−554	−302	42	−327	199	−2,327
1975	703	2,276	−63	−1,464	−562	103	−49	−269	227	−2,404
1976	1,398	4,076	−39	−2,149	−994	−494	−163	−795	402	−4,957
1977	763	2,714	−34	−1,507	−517	136	−96	−274	242	−2,466
1978	−39	1,404	−34	−1,183	−532	−183	−25	−440	243	−2,572
1979	−217	546	−30	−665	−253	64	−21	−130	151	−1,125

Table 8.5 (*cont.*)

	Manufacturing output	GDP(O)	Factor cost adjustment	Consumers' expenditure	Gross fixed capital formation	Stock-building	Public authorities' current expenditure	Exports	Imports	GDP(E)
1980	265	1,863	−12	−770	−258	−9	−110	−229	173	−1,539
1981	287	2,189	−3	−920	−288	−106	−138	−334	194	−1,977
1982	−28	1,379	−3	−574	−145	42	−88	−94	115	−971
1983	55	2,472	7	−589	−193	−99	−121	−265	141	−1,416
1984	−567	−786	−8	124	57	79	−1	97	−17	380
1985	−254	−50	0	60	6	−2	−69	−12	−1	−17
1986	−142	538	2	−19	−33	−25	−95	−69	19	−261
1987	−249	256	−2	203	46	7	−81	19	−24	219
1988	−490	−668	−9	396	112	12	−45	69	−73	626
1989	−613	−987	−13	421	120	5	−31	64	−91	683
1990	−838	−1,882	−19	416	112	7	3	97	−116	770

8.4 Data reliability

One of the aspects of the balancing exercise is that it is possible to calculate *ex-post* estimates of reliability for the balanced data. The error structure of the data means that the reliability of both the levels and the year-on-year changes varies from one year to the next. On the other hand, it is not practical to publish, for each variable, estimates of both the standard errors of the levels of the aggregates and of the changes from any one year to any other year of our sample.

8.4.1 Confidence limits for growth in GDP

Our first results concern the reliability of the estimated growth in GDP. With our parameter estimates we find an average standard error of the growth rate in GDP of 0.97 per cent p.a. with the interwar data and 0.56 per cent p.a. with the postwar data. Figure 8.6 shows year-on-year growth in balanced GDP together with confidence limits of twice the standard errors.

8.4.2 Robustness

In figures 8.7–8.10 we show the average standard error associated with the estimates of year-on-year growth calculated from our balanced data. These estimates are shown as a function of ρ_1 and ρ_2, the two serial correlation parameters. The first relates to the serial correlation associated with the income/expenditure variables, and was set to 0.6 in both periods. The second relates to the serial correlation associated with the output variables. This was set to 0.8 in both periods. The surface and contour plots illustrate the sensitivity of our results about the reliability of GDP growth rates to these estimates. It appears that the results are not very sensitive to the choice of parameter, suggesting a satisfactory degree of robustness in our results.

The reason for this is as follows. In figures 5.1 and 5.2 and figures 6.1 and 6.2 we show the sensitivity of the Mahalanobis score to the choice of serial correlation parameter. But we have then, for the reasons given, scaled the standard errors to bring the Mahalanobis score to its maximum-likelihood value. Low serial correlation leads to a low score and thus considerable downward scaling of the errors generally. High serial correlation leads to less scaling, but reduces the standard errors associated wtih year-on-year growth rates anyway. Our results show that, as far as the standard error of growth in GDP is concerned, it does not matter very much whether one relies mainly on scaling or mainly on serial correlation to satisfy the Mahalanobis criterion. The implications for data reliability are similar.

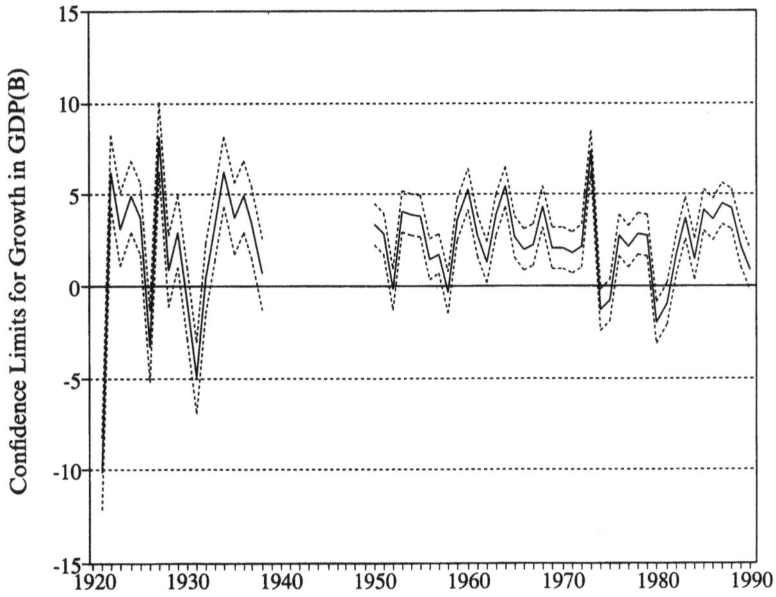

Figure 8.6 Confidence limits for growth in real GDP (%)

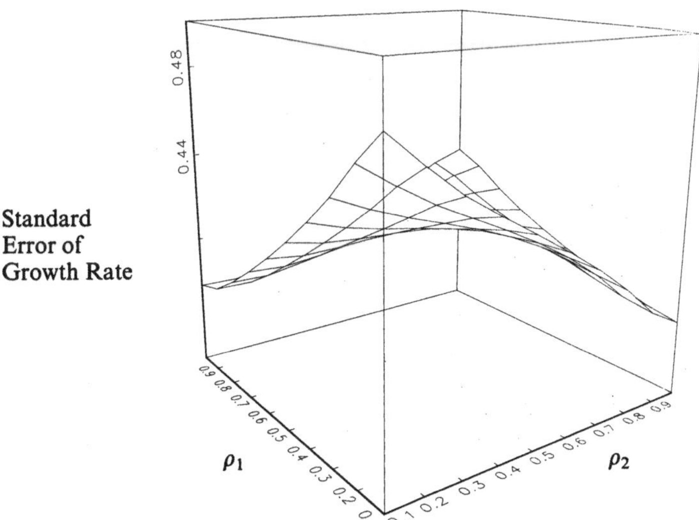

Figure 8.7 The standard error of growth in balanced GDP, 1920–1938

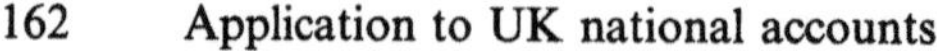

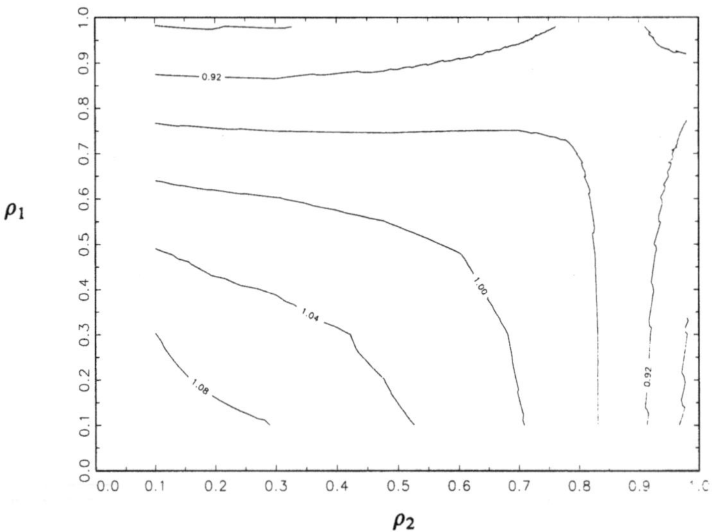

Figure 8.8 A contour map of the standard error of growth in balanced GDP, 1920–1938

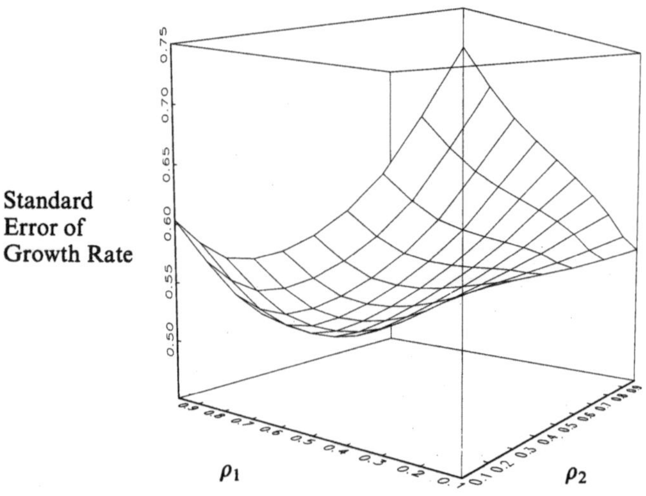

Figure 8.9 The standard error of growth in balanced GDP, 1948–1990

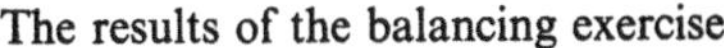

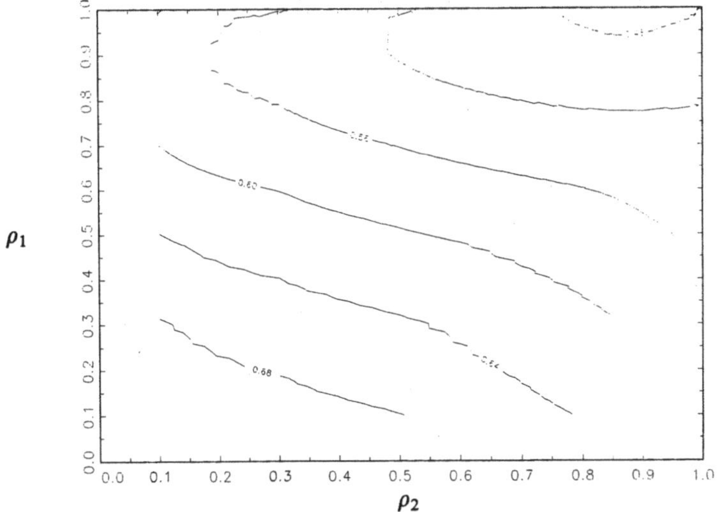

Figure 8.10 A contour map of the standard error of growth in balanced GDP, 1948–1990

8.4.3 Estimates of standard errors of components of GDP

In order to give general usable estimates of the reliability of the components of GDP in part three, we present, in tables 8.6–8.13, averages for the three data periods 1920–38, 1948–70 and 1971–90. These make it possible to assess the statistical significance of the growth in an aggregate between one year and another.

For many purposes the measurement errors associated with year-on-year changes will be the most relevant. In particular, they provide a useful check on any regression equation estimated in log differences. If the standard error of the regression is lower than, or not much higher than, the estimated measurement error, there is a real risk that the regression equation is overfitted and thus contains spurious elements.

For periods of longer than five years it is probably adequate to take the standard error for 5 years and multiply by the square root of 5/the length of the interval. Nevertheless, the presence of the unit roots in the measurement errors associated with constant price data means that this will tend to understate the measurement errors associated with long intervals.

The tables do suggest that, at a disaggregate level, balancing has no real impact on the standard errors of most variables. But the framework used for assessing the data standard errors allows us to check the consistency of statisticians' statements about data reliability against the discrepancies in the data. This gives greater coherence to the estimates than is usually found in estimates of measurement error.

Table 8.6 *Standard errors of balanced current price expenditure data, 1920–1938*

	A	B	C	D	E	F
Food	1.4	1.3	−1.5	1.6	0.8	0.4
Drink	1.5	1.5	−2.3	2.0	1.0	0.4
Tobacco	1.2	1.2	2.2	1.4	0.7	0.3
Housing	3.0	3.0	3.0	1.9	1.2	0.6
Fuel and light	3.0	3.0	0.6	1.9	1.2	0.6
Clothing	3.2	3.2	−2.6	1.9	1.3	0.7
Motor cars	4.3	4.3	3.1	2.7	1.8	1.0
Furniture	3.5	3.5	1.3	2.4	1.5	0.9
Textiles	6.7	6.7	−2.3	4.2	2.8	1.6
Matches etc.	5.8	5.8	−1.4	4.0	2.7	1.4
Books	5.9	5.9	0.2	4.0	2.7	1.4
Medical care	5.9	5.7	0.7	3.8	2.5	1.3
Public transport	3.1	3.1	0.2	4.3	2.1	0.8
Vehicle running costs	4.9	4.9	4.6	4.1	2.6	1.4
Domestic service	10.5	10.3	0.1	5.1	3.4	2.0
Other services	12.3	11.5	0.9	5.7	3.8	2.0
Travel adjustment	n.a.					
Ships	7.1	7.1	n.a.	233.2	n.a.	2.3
Other vehicles	3.0	3.0	1.0	4.4	2.2	0.9
Plant and machinery	1.2	1.2	3.3	1.8	0.9	0.4
Dwellings	3.9	3.9	8.0	6.0	2.9	1.2
Other buildings and works	1.0	1.0	0.7	1.4	0.7	0.3
Defence	1.8	1.8	5.1	2.6	1.3	0.5
Education	1.8	1.8	2.0	2.6	1.3	0.5
Other public expenditure	1.8	1.8	1.4	2.5	1.3	0.5
Exports of goods	1.1	1.1	−4.3	1.4	0.7	0.3
Exports of services	6.5	6.5	−3.4	2.9	2.0	1.1
Imports of goods	1.1	1.1	−2.9	1.5	0.7	0.3
Imports of services	6.5	6.4	−1.8	2.9	2.0	1.1
Increase in stocks	n.a.					

A Average percentage standard error, original data (%)
B Average percentage standard error, balanced data (%)
C Arithmetic average of year-on-year growth rates (% p.a.)
D Average standard error of year-on-year growth rate, as percentage of level data
E Average standard error of annual average growth rate over two years, as percentage of level data
F Average standard error of annual average growth rate over five years, as percentage of level data

Note: Gross capital formation in ships was negative in some years.

Table 8.7 *Standard errors of balanced constant price expenditure data, 1920–1938*

	A	B	C	D	E	F
Food	1.5	1.5	1.9	1.6	0.9	0.4
Drink	1.7	1.7	−1.8	2.0	1.0	0.4
Tobacco	1.2	1.2	2.3	1.4	0.7	0.3
Housing	3.1	3.2	1.7	1.9	1.2	0.6
Fuel and light	3.1	3.2	2.1	1.9	1.2	0.6
Clothing	3.8	3.8	1.1	2.7	1.7	0.9
Motor cars	4.4	4.4	9.5	2.9	1.9	1.1
Furniture	3.5	3.5	4.0	2.5	1.6	0.9
Textiles	6.7	6.7	0.6	4.3	2.9	1.7
Matches etc.	5.8	5.8	1.7	4.2	2.8	1.5
Books	5.9	5.9	1.5	4.1	2.7	1.5
Medical care	5.9	5.8	3.0	3.9	2.5	1.4
Public transport	3.1	3.1	1.6	4.4	2.2	0.9
Vehicle running costs	5.0	4.9	9.0	4.2	2.7	1.4
Domestic service	10.5	10.3	1.6	5.2	3.5	2.0
Other services	12.3	11.5	2.7	5.8	3.9	2.1
Travel adjustment	n.a.					
Ships	7.1	7.1	n.a.	14.5	5.7	2.0
Other vehicles	3.1	3.1	5.2	4.5	2.3	0.9
Plant and machinery	1.4	1.4	6.1	1.8	0.9	0.4
Dwellings	4.0	4.0	11.6	6.2	3.0	1.2
Other buildings and works	1.2	1.2	3.1	1.5	0.7	0.3
Defence	2.1	2.1	5.6	2.7	1.3	0.5
Education	2.1	2.1	1.8	2.6	1.3	0.5
Other public expenditure	2.1	2.1	1.2	2.6	1.3	0.5
Exports of goods	1.3	1.3	0.2	1.5	0.8	0.3
Exports of services	6.5	6.5	1.3	3.0	2.1	1.2
Imports of goods	1.3	1.3	1.8	1.6	0.8	0.3
Imports of services	6.5	6.4	3.8	3.0	2.1	1.2
Change in stocks	n.a.					

A Average percentage standard error, original data (%)
B Average percentage standard error, balanced data (%)
C Arithmetic average of year-on-year growth rates (% p.a.)
D Average standard error of year-on-year growth rate, as percentage of level data
E Average standard error of annual average growth rate over two years, as percentage of level data
F Average standard error of annual average growth rate over five years, as percentage of level data

Note: Gross capital formation in ships was negative in some years.

Table 8.8 *Standard errors of balanced current price income data, 1920–1938*

	A	B	C	D	E	F
Agriculture: Wages	7.9	7.8	−2.5	5.0	3.1	1.5
Profits	13.1	12.8	0.3	12.4	7.0	3.4
Mining: Wages	1.6	1.6	−2.1	2.1	1.1	0.4
Profits	8.2	n.a.	n.a.	24.3	5.4	2.1
Manufacturing: Wages	4.8	4.2	−1.5	3.1	2.0	1.0
Profits	7.6	7.0	0.9	7.8	4.3	1.9
Construction: Wages	4.5	4.5	0.4	3.6	2.3	1.1
Profits	9.1	9.1	1.7	10.1	5.5	2.5
Utilities: Wages	4.4	4.4	1.5	2.7	1.7	0.9
Profits	6.1	6.1	3.7	6.8	3.7	1.7
Transport: Wages	6.1	6.0	−1.0	8.3	4.2	1.7
Profits	6.1	6.1	0.7	6.3	3.5	1.6
Communication: Wages	0.9	0.9	1.0	1.3	0.6	0.3
Profits	6.1	6.1	6.6	7.0	3.8	1.8
Distribution: Wages	9.4	9.0	1.0	5.6	3.6	1.7
Profits	13.1	12.0	−1.0	11.8	6.8	3.3
Finance: Wages	9.4	9.2	0.3	5.6	3.6	1.8
Profits	13.1	12.7	0.2	12.9	7.4	3.6
Rent	13.6	12.9	6.3	13.9	7.9	3.8
Adjustment	13.1	12.7	0.9	12.8	7.4	3.5
Ownership of dewllings	4.3	4.3	3.7	6.3	3.2	1.3
Public administration and defence	1.6	1.6	0.8	2.2	1.1	0.5
Other services: Wages	9.4	8.6	0.6	5.4	3.4	1.7
Profits	13.1	12.5	0.5	12.7	7.3	3.5
Expenditure taxes	1.1	1.1	1.4	1.5	0.8	0.3
Subsidies	1.1	1.1	0.1	1.5	0.7	0.3

A Average percentage standard error, original data (%)
B Average percentage standard error, balanced data (%)
C Arithmetic average of year-on-year growth rates (% p.a.)
D Average standard error of year-on-year growth rate, as percentage of level data
E Average standard error of annual average growth rate over two years, as percentage of level data
F Average standard error of annual average growth rate over five years, as percentage of level data

Table 8.9 *Standard errors of balance constant price output data, 1920–1938*

	A	B	C	D	E	F
Agriculture	14.5	14.5	1.4	10.1	5.1	2.1
Mining	2.7	2.7	3.4	1.5	0.9	0.4
Chemicals	12.0	12.0	2.5	3.0	2.0	1.0
Food, drink and tobacco	11.6	11.6	2.2	3.0	1.9	1.0
Ferrous metals	13.9	13.9	5.9	3.2	2.0	1.0
Non-ferrous metals	10.1	10.1	6.6	3.1	2.0	1.0
Mechanical engineering	12.7	12.7	3.0	3.1	2.0	1.0
Electrical engineering	8.9	8.9	5.5	3.1	2.0	1.0
Shipbuilding	16.7	16.7	13.0	3.6	2.1	1.0
Other vehicles	8.7	8.7	7.2	3.2	2.0	1.0
Precision instruments	10.8	10.8	2.9	3.0	1.9	1.0
Other metal goods	9.9	9.9	3.5	3.1	2.0	1.0
Textiles	14.5	14.5	1.5	3.1	2.0	1.0
Leather	14.4	14.4	2.7	3.0	1.9	1.0
Clothing	12.8	12.8	2.8	3.0	1.9	1.0
Timber products	10.0	10.0	5.6	3.1	2.0	1.0
Paper and publishing	11.9	11.9	4.1	3.1	2.0	1.0
Building materials	10.7	10.7	4.2	3.1	2.0	1.0
Construction	3.8	3.8	7.1	1.5	0.9	0.4
Utilities	4.1	4.1	5.0	1.7	0.9	0.4
Transport and communication	10.2	10.2	2.4	5.1	3.3	1.8
Distribution	11.7	11.0	1.6	4.0	2.7	1.4
Financial services	18.5	18.3	1.1	4.2	2.8	1.5
Ownership of dwellings	4.4	4.4	1.7	6.2	3.1	1.2
Other services	10.8	9.9	1.0	3.7	2.5	1.4
Pub. administration and defence	1.7	1.7	0.6	1.6	0.8	0.4
Factor cost adjustment	1.3	1.3	1.1	1.5	0.8	0.3

A Average percentage standard error, original data (%)
B Average percentage standard error, balanced data (%)
C Arithmetic average of year-on-year growth rates (% p.a.)
D Average standard error of year-on-year growth rate, as percentage of level data
E Average standard error of annual average growth rate over two years, as percentage of level data
F Average standard error of annual average growth rate over five years, as percentage of level data

Table 8.10 *Standard errors of balanced current price expenditure data, 1948–1990*

	A	B	C	D	E	F	G	H
Food	1.5	1.4	1.0	1.0	7.6	1.2	0.7	0.3
Drink	1.0	1.0	1.0	1.0	8.3	1.0	0.6	0.3
Tobacco	0.5	0.5	0.5	0.5	6.1	0.5	0.3	0.2
Housing	4.2	4.1	3.9	3.7	10.5	3.9	2.4	1.2
Fuel and light	0.5	0.5	0.5	0.5	9.2	0.5	0.3	0.2
Clothing	0.8	0.8	0.8	0.8	7.8	0.8	0.5	0.2
Motor vehicles	1.2	1.2	1.0	1.0	16.6	1.2	0.7	0.3
Furniture and floor coverings	0.8	0.8	0.8	0.8	9.2	0.8	0.5	0.2
TV etc.	1.7	1.7	1.8	1.8	10.9	1.6	1.0	0.5
Textiles and hardware	2.3	2.3	2.3	2.3	8.6	1.8	1.2	0.6
Matches etc.	1.8	1.8	1.8	1.8	7.9	1.8	1.1	0.5
Books and recreational goods	1.7	1.8	1.8	1.8	10.0	1.6	1.0	0.5
Chemists' and other goods	1.3	1.3	0.8	0.8	9.6	1.0	0.6	0.3
Public transport	1.0	1.0	1.0	1.0	8.9	1.0	0.6	0.3
Vehicle running costs	1.4	1.4	1.0	1.0	15.8	1.3	0.8	0.4
Telecommunications	0.3	0.3	0.3	0.3	12.1	0.3	0.2	0.1
Catering	1.5	1.5	0.9	0.9	10.4	1.2	0.7	0.3
Other services	1.8	1.8	1.8	1.8	10.4	1.9	1.2	0.6
Travel adjustment	n.a.							
Vehicles, ships and aircraft	2.5	2.5	2.5	2.5	9.8	2.8	1.7	0.8
Plant and machinery	2.5	2.5	2.5	2.4	10.9	2.8	1.7	0.8
Dwellings	1.9	1.9	1.9	1.9	10.4	2.2	1.3	0.6
Other buildings	2.5	2.5	2.5	2.5	12.3	2.8	1.7	0.8
Land transfer costs	3.9	3.9	3.9	3.9	11.9	4.5	2.7	1.2
Education	1.7	1.7	0.9	0.9	11.5	1.0	0.6	0.3
National health service	1.5	1.5	0.8	0.8	13.3	0.9	0.5	0.3
Defence	1.6	1.6	0.8	0.8	8.7	0.9	0.5	0.3
Other	1.6	1.6	0.8	0.9	10.6	0.9	0.6	0.3
Exports of goods	0.6	0.6	0.6	0.6	10.7	0.9	0.5	0.2
Exports of services	2.0	2.0	2.0	2.0	10.4	2.0	1.3	0.6
Imports of goods	0.4	0.4	0.4	0.4	11.2	0.4	0.3	0.1
Imports of services	2.0	2.0	2.0	2.0	9.5	2.0	1.3	0.6
Increase in stocks	n.a.							

A Average percentage standard error, original data, 1948–1970 (%)
B Average percentage standard error, balanced data, 1948–1970 (%)
C Average percentage standard error, original data, 1971–1990 (%)
D Average percentage standard error, balanced data, 1971–1990 (%)
E Arithmetic average of year-on-year growth rates (% p.a.)
F Average standard error of year-on-year growth rate, as percentage of level data
G Average standard error of annual average growth rate over two years, as percentage of level data
H Average standard error of annual average growth rate over five years, as percentage of level data

Table 8.11 *Standard errors of balanced constant price expenditure data, 1948–1990*

	A	B	C	D	E	F	G	H
Food	2.7	2.6	1.8	1.8	1.2	1.1	0.7	0.4
Drink	2.4	2.4	1.8	1.8	2.5	1.0	0.6	0.3
Tobacco	1.9	1.9	1.1	1.1	0.2	0.6	0.4	0.2
Housing	4.7	4.7	4.0	3.8	2.2	3.7	2.3	1.1
Fuel and light	1.8	1.8	0.9	0.9	1.8	0.6	0.4	0.2
Clothing	1.9	1.9	1.1	1.1	3.3	0.9	0.5	0.3
Motor vehicles	2.8	2.9	1.8	1.8	11.1	1.2	0.8	0.4
Furniture and floor coverings	1.9	1.9	1.1	1.1	3.6	0.9	0.6	0.3
TV etc.	2.4	2.4	2.0	2.0	8.1	1.6	1.0	0.5
Textiles and hardware	2.8	2.8	2.5	2.5	3.7	1.8	1.2	0.6
Matches etc.	2.5	2.5	2.0	2.0	2.3	1.8	1.1	0.5
Books and recreational goods	2.4	2.4	2.0	2.0	3.5	1.5	1.0	0.5
Chemists' and other goods	2.1	2.1	1.1	1.1	4.7	1.1	0.7	0.3
Public transport	2.4	2.4	1.8	1.8	1.4	1.0	0.6	0.3
Vehicle running costs	3.0	3.0	1.8	1.8	8.4	1.3	0.8	0.4
Telecommunications	1.7	1.7	0.8	0.8	4.5	0.5	0.3	0.2
Catering	2.2	2.2	1.2	1.2	2.6	1.1	0.7	0.4
Other services	2.5	2.5	2.0	2.0	3.0	1.8	1.1	0.5
Adjustment	n.a.							
Vehicles, ships and aircraft	3.0	3.0	2.6	2.6	3.2	2.6	1.6	0.7
Plant and machinery	3.0	3.0	2.6	2.6	4.7	2.6	1.6	0.7
Dwellings	2.6	2.6	2.1	2.1	2.9	2.1	1.3	0.6
Other buildings	3.0	3.0	2.6	2.6	5.3	2.7	1.6	0.7
Land transfer costs	4.2	4.2	4.0	4.0	4.0	4.2	2.5	1.2
Education	3.5	3.5	2.4	2.4	2.9	1.6	1.0	0.5
National health service	3.0	3.0	2.1	2.1	4.0	1.4	0.9	0.4
Defence	3.1	3.0	2.1	2.1	0.2	1.3	0.9	0.4
Other	3.2	3.2	2.2	2.2	2.1	1.4	0.9	0.5
Exports of goods	1.8	1.8	1.0	1.0	4.4	0.9	0.5	0.2
Exports of services	2.6	2.6	2.1	2.2	4.3	2.0	1.2	0.6
Imports of goods	1.7	1.7	0.9	0.9	5.0	0.5	0.3	0.2
Imports of services	2.6	2.6	2.1	2.1	3.2	1.9	1.2	0.6
Increase in stocks	n.a.							

A Average percentage standard error, original data, 1948–1970 (%)
B Average percentage standard error, balanced data, 1948–1970 (%)
C Average percentage standard error, original data, 1971–1990 (%)
D Average percentage standard error, balanced data, 1971–1990 (%)
E Arithmetic average of year-on-year growth rates (% p.a.)
F Average standard error of year-on-year growth rate, as percentage of level data
G Average standard error of annual average growth rate over two years, as percentage of level data
H Average standard error of annual average growth rate over five years, as percentage of level data

Table 8.12 *Standard errors of balanced current price income data, 1948–1990*

	A	B	C	D	E	F	G	H
Agriculture: Wages	2.0	2.0	2.3	2.2	5.7	2.1	1.3	0.6
Profits	5.8	5.8	5.8	5.8	6.9	5.6	3.5	1.7
Mining: Wages	2.0	2.0	2.3	2.2	6.9	2.1	1.3	0.6
Profits	5.8	5.9	5.8	5.9	14.8	6.7	3.7	1.7
Oil and gas: Wages	2.1	n.a.	2.3	2.3	17.1	2.3	1.5	0.7
Profits	5.8	n.a.	5.8	5.7	45.7	8.2	4.8	2.2
Manufacturing: Wages	1.8	1.7	2.1	1.8	8.8	1.8	1.1	0.5
Profits	5.3	4.6	5.3	4.9	8.4	4.7	3.0	1.4
Construction: Wages	2.0	2.0	1.3	1.3	9.0	1.9	1.1	0.5
Profits	5.8	5.8	5.8	5.8	20.4	6.5	4.0	1.8
Utilities: Wages	2.0	2.0	2.3	2.2	9.7	2.1	1.3	0.6
Profits	5.8	5.8	5.8	5.8	12.2	5.9	3.7	1.8
Transport and Comm.:								
Wages	2.1	2.1	1.5	1.5	9.0	2.0	1.2	0.6
Profits	5.8	5.8	5.8	5.8	10.1	5.8	3.6	1.7
Distribution: Wages	4.7	4.5	1.5	1.5	10.2	3.0	1.9	0.9
Profits	7.8	7.2	6.4	6.2	8.5	6.7	4.2	2.0
Finance: Wages	2.7	2.7	1.8	1.8	12.6	2.2	1.4	0.7
Profits	7.8	7.8	6.4	6.4	97.0	16.8	5.4	2.3
Rent	7.4	7.4	6.5	6.5	16.4	6.2	3.9	2.0
Adjustment	6.3	n.a.	5.5	n.a.				
Ownership of dwellings	4.2	4.2	2.7	2.7	11.8	4.7	2.5	1.0
Public administration								
and defence: Wages	1.2	1.2	0.7	0.7	9.7	0.8	0.5	0.2
Imputed income	0.1	0.0	0.1	0.0	10.3	0.0	0.0	0.0
Education and health:								
Wages	1.4	1.4	0.7	0.7	12.1	0.8	0.5	0.2
Profit	5.5	5.5	3.0	3.0	14.0	4.7	2.9	1.4
Other services: Wages	4.7	4.7	2.5	2.5	10.2	3.6	2.3	1.1
Profit	7.7	7.7	7.7	7.7	8.6	7.5	4.8	2.3
Taxes on expenditure	0.2	0.1	0.2	0.1	9.3	0.1	0.1	0.0
Subsidies	0.2	0.1	0.2	0.1	7.4	0.1	0.1	0.0

A Average percentage standard error, original data, 1948–1970 (%)
B Average percentage standard error, balanced data, 1948–1970 (%)
C Average percentage standard error, original data, 1971–1990 (%)
D Average percentage standard error, balanced data, 1971–1990 (%)
E Arithmetic average of year-on-year growth rates (% p.a.)
F Average standard error of year-on-year growth rate, as percentage of level data
G Average standard error of annual average growth rate over two years, as percentage of level data
H Average standard error of annual average growth rate over five years, as percentage of level data

Note: In the postwar years the data are balanced with output of financial services net of the financial services adjustment.

Table 8.13 *Standard errors of balanced constant price output data, 1948–1990*

	A	B	C	D	E	F	G	H
Agriculture	5.5	5.5	4.6	4.6	2.8	1.8	1.2	0.6
Mining	4.2	4.2	2.8	2.8	−1.2	1.1	0.8	0.4
Oil and gas	6.7	0.0	6.0	5.3	n.a.	2.0	1.1	0.6
Metal manufacture	8.3	8.3	7.9	7.9	1.3	4.2	2.7	1.3
Other mineral products	8.3	8.3	7.9	7.9	2.4	4.2	2.7	1.3
Chemicals and fibres	9.0	8.9	8.6	8.4	5.2	5.0	3.2	1.6
Mechanical engineering	8.9	8.9	8.6	8.4	2.3	5.0	3.2	1.5
Electrical and instrument engineering	9.0	8.9	8.6	8.4	5.4	5.0	3.2	1.6
Motor vehicles	8.9	8.9	8.6	8.6	3.9	5.1	3.2	1.6
Other transport equipment	9.8	9.8	9.5	9.5	0.5	5.9	3.8	1.8
Food manufacture	8.3	8.3	7.9	7.9	2.1	4.2	2.7	1.3
Drink and tobacco	8.7	8.7	8.3	8.3	2.6	5.0	3.2	1.6
Textiles	8.8	8.8	8.4	8.4	0.4	5.0	3.2	1.5
Clothing and leather goods	9.1	9.1	8.7	8.7	1.1	5.0	3.2	1.5
Paper and printing	8.2	8.2	7.8	7.8	3.3	4.3	2.7	1.3
Other manufacture	9.7	9.7	9.4	9.3	3.8	5.8	3.7	1.8
Construction	4.8	4.8	3.9	3.9	2.5	1.8	1.2	0.6
Utilities	5.0	5.0	4.1	4.1	4.4	1.8	1.2	0.6
Transport and communication	4.4	4.4	3.4	3.4	3.2	1.8	1.2	0.6
Distribution	7.2	6.1	5.8	4.7	2.9	3.8	2.5	1.2
Finance	6.6	6.6	3.6	3.5	5.1	2.5	1.7	0.9
Ownership of dwellings	5.4	5.4	3.1	3.1	1.9	4.4	2.3	1.0
Public administration and defence	2.4	2.4	1.7	1.7	0.4	1.1	0.7	0.4
Education and health	2.5	2.5	1.7	1.7	2.8	1.1	0.7	0.4
Other services	6.5	6.5	4.2	4.2	2.3	3.4	2.1	1.1
Adjustment for financial services	7.6	n.a.	6.6	n.a.				
Factor cost adjustment	1.7	1.7	0.8	0.8	2.9	0.4	0.3	0.2

A Average percentage standard error, original data, 1948–1970 (%)
B Average percentage standard error, balanced data, 1948–1970 (%)
C Average percentage standard error, original data, 1971–1990 (%)
D Average percentage standard error, balanced data, 1971–1990 (%)
E Arithmetic average of year-on-year growth rates (% p.a.)
F Average standard error of year-on-year growth rate, as percentage of level data

G Average standard error of annual average growth rate over two years, as percentage of level data
H Average standard error of annual average growth rate over five years, as percentage of level data
Note: In the postwar years the data are balanced with output of financial services net of the financial services adjustment.

Table 8.14 *Standard errors of balanced aggregate data, 1920–1938*

	A	B	C	D	E	F
Employment income	2.9	2.3	0.8	2.2	1.3	0.6
Operating surplus	5.3	3.7	0.2	4.3	2.5	1.2
Factor cost adjustment	1.4	1.4	2.7	2.4	1.2	0.5
Consumption	2.4	1.7	0.6	1.8	1.0	0.4
Gross fixed capital formation	1.6	1.6	1.6	2.9	1.5	0.6
Stockbuilding	0.0	0.0	0.0	0.0	0.0	0.0
Public consumption	1.3	1.3	2.7	2.3	1.1	0.5
Exports	2.0	2.0	−4.2	1.8	1.0	0.5
Imports	1.5	1.4	−2.8	1.9	1.0	0.4
Manufacturing (1938 prices)	4.4	4.1	3.0	1.4	0.9	0.5
Other output (1938 prices)	4.8	2.6	1.5	1.8	1.1	0.5
Factor cost adj. (1938 prices)	1.5	1.5	1.1	2.2	1.1	0.5
Consumption (1938 prices)	2.4	1.7	1.6	1.7	1.0	0.4
GFCF (1938 prices)	1.6	1.6	4.5	2.8	1.4	0.6
Stockbuilding (1938 prices)	0.0	0.0	0.0	0.0	0.0	0.0
Public consumption (1938 prices)	1.5	1.5	3.1	2.3	1.2	0.5
Exports (1938 prices)	2.0	2.0	0.3	1.9	1.1	0.5
Imports (1938 prices)	1.6	1.6	2.0	2.0	1.0	0.5
GDP(Income)	2.7	1.5	0.5	1.5	0.9	0.4
GDP(Expenditure)	2.7	1.5	0.5	1.5	0.9	0.4
GDP(Output) (1938 prices)	3.7	1.6	1.9	1.3	0.8	0.4
GDP(Expenditure) (1938 prices)	2.7	1.6	1.9	1.3	0.8	0.4

A Average percentage standard error, original data (%)
B Average percentage standard error, balanced data (%)
C Arithmetic average of year-on-year growth rates (% p.a.)
D Average standard error of year-on-year growth rate, as percentage of level data
E Average standard error of annual average growth rate over two years, as percentage of level data
F Average standard error of annual average growth rate over five years, as percentage of level data

Table 8.15 *Standard errors of balanced aggregate data, 1948–1990*

	A	B	C	D	E	F	G	H
Employment income	1.0	0.9	0.7	0.6	9.7	0.7	0.5	0.2
Operating surplus	2.6	2.0	1.9	1.5	9.6	1.8	1.1	0.5
Factor cost adjustment	0.1	0.1	0.1	0.1	10.1	0.1	0.1	0.0
Consumption	0.6	0.6	0.6	0.6	9.3	0.6	0.4	0.2
Gross fixed capital formation	1.3	1.2	1.3	1.2	10.9	1.4	0.8	0.4
Stockbuilding	0.0	0.0	0.0	0.0	0.0	0.0	0.0	0.0
Public consumption	0.9	0.9	0.4	0.4	10.4	0.5	0.3	0.1
Exports	0.7	0.7	0.7	0.7	10.6	0.8	0.5	0.2
Imports	0.6	0.6	0.5	0.5	10.8	0.6	0.4	0.2
Manufacturing (1985 prices)	2.8	2.4	2.6	2.2	2.5	1.4	0.9	0.4
Output (1985 prices)	2.0	1.4	1.5	1.0	2.5	0.8	0.5	0.2
Factor cost adj. (1985 prices)	1.8	1.7	0.8	0.8	2.9	0.4	0.3	0.2
Consumption (1985 prices)	1.1	1.0	0.8	0.7	2.6	0.6	0.4	0.2
GFCF (1985 prices)	1.5	1.5	1.3	1.3	4.1	1.2	0.8	0.3
Stockbuilding (1985 prices)	0.0	0.0	0.0	0.0	0.0	0.0	0.0	0.0
Public consumption (1985 prices)	1.7	1.7	1.1	1.1	1.8	0.7	0.5	0.2
Exports (1985 prices)	1.5	1.5	0.9	0.9	4.4	0.8	0.5	0.2
Imports (1985 prices)	1.5	1.5	0.9	0.8	4.6	0.6	0.4	0.2
GDP(Income)	1.1	0.6	0.8	0.5	9.6	0.6	0.4	0.2
GDP(Expenditure)	0.8	0.6	0.7	0.5	9.6	0.6	0.4	0.2
GDP(Output) (1985 prices)	1.6	0.9	1.3	0.6	2.5	0.5	0.3	0.2
GDP(Expenditure) (1985 prices)	1.1	0.9	0.8	0.6	2.5	0.5	0.3	0.2

A Average percentage standard error, original data, 1948–1970 (%)
B Average percentage standard error, balanced data, 1948–1970 (%)
C Average percentage standard error, original data, 1971–1990 (%)
D Average percentage standard error, balanced data, 1971–1990 (%)
E Arithmetic average of year-on-year growth rates (% p.a.)
F Average standard error of year-on-year growth rate, as percentage of level data
G Average standard error of annual average growth rate over 2 years, as percentage of level data
H Average standard error of annual average growth rate over 5 years, as percentage of level data

Note: In the postwar years the data are balanced with output of financial services net of the financial services adjustment.

8.5 Conclusions

The most important result of this exercise is the set of new national accounts presented in part three. These data cannot fully replace earlier estimates. Both Feinstein (1972) and the CSO sources provide a wealth of detail which is absent from our data. Nevertheless, we have attempted to unravel some of the changes in classification in the postwar years, so that our dataset provides, at the disaggregate level, a longer coherent run of data than is available from other sources. We have also extended the sectoral capital account data on a coherent basis back to 1948 and provided sectoral current accounts for the full period.

The application of least-squares/maximum likelihood balancing methods to a long series of UK national accounts suggests that there may be important changes to a number of important variables. It seems that growth in industrial output has been understated in the past. There are substantial movements to the savings ratio in the period before 1945 and also marked movements in the mid 1970s. The implications of these for standard consumption functions remain to be assessed.

Very importantly, the balancing method and associated calculations allows for the first time the full set of national accounts presented in part three to be complemented with quantified estimates of their reliability. These will fulfil a useful role even if all they do is make data users more aware of the margins of error associated with national accounting data. We hope they will bring nearer the day when, as a matter of course, standard errors are presented with data estimates as is usual with parameter estimates.

Part three

Balanced national accounts for the United Kingdom: 1920–1990

Table A.1 *GNP and national income (£m): 1920–1990*

	GDP at factor cost	Plus net property income from abroad	Plus net transfers from abroad	Equals GNP at factor cost	Less deprec-iation	Equals national income
1920	5,554	246	−1	5,799	435	5,364
1921	4,462	178	43	4,683	352	4,331
1922	3,980	177	12	4,169	314	3,855
1923	3,762	176	3	3,941	288	3,653
1924	3,899	196	6	4,101	283	3,818
1925	4,040	232	19	4,291	283	4,008
1926	3,862	237	20	4,119	283	3,836
1927	4,080	239	26	4,345	279	4,066
1928	4,066	240	27	4,333	284	4,049
1929	4,175	243	26	4,444	293	4,151
1930	4,118	215	37	4,370	291	4,079
1931	3,820	163	28	4,011	290	3,721
1932	3,695	127	8	3,830	283	3,547
1933	3,775	154	4	3,933	283	3,650
1934	3,971	167	2	4,140	282	3,858
1935	4,157	181	0	4,338	298	4,040
1936	4,388	195	0	4,583	317	4,266
1937	4,706	205	−1	4,910	357	4,553
1938	4,867	192	−3	5,056	370	4,686
1939	5,225	165	−15	5,375	390	4,985
1940	6,310	165	−13	6,462	440	6,022
1941	7,519	140	−12	7,647	500	7,147
1942	8,241	100	−18	8,323	530	7,793
1943	8,780	90	−16	8,854	620	8,234
1944	8,876	80	−11	8,945	650	8,295
1945	8,667	80	−60	8,687	640	8,047
1946	8,700	85	80	8,865	690	8,175
1947	9,338	150	45	9,533	770	8,763
1948	10,447	235	29	10,711	900	9,811
1949	11,158	219	−18	11,359	950	10,409
1950	11,608	396	−8	11,996	1,029	10,967
1951	12,869	342	−28	13,183	1,198	11,985
1952	13,986	252	84	14,322	1,360	12,962
1953	15,010	229	64	15,303	1,411	13,892

Table A.1 (*cont.*)

	GDP at factor cost	Plus net property income from abroad	Plus net transfers from abroad	Equals GNP at factor cost	Less deprec-iation	Equals national income
1954	15,903	250	−9	16,144	1,469	14,675
1955	17,099	174	−25	17,248	1,615	15,633
1956	18,403	229	−65	18,567	1,772	16,795
1957	19,487	249	−74	19,662	1,901	17,761
1958	20,328	293	−60	20,561	2,006	18,555
1959	21,428	262	−61	21,629	2,063	19,566
1960	22,995	233	−68	23,160	2,167	20,993
1961	24,393	254	−88	24,559	2,326	22,233
1962	25,544	334	−97	25,781	2,462	23,319
1963	27,138	398	−123	27,413	2,615	24,798
1964	29,467	404	−158	29,713	2,793	26,920
1965	31,613	450	−169	31,894	3,000	28,894
1966	33,490	402	−181	33,711	3,239	30,472
1967	35,204	401	−216	35,389	3,431	31,958
1968	37,833	359	−223	37,969	3,727	34,242
1969	40,256	531	−206	40,581	4,077	36,504
1970	44,319	596	−182	44,733	4,618	40,115
1971	49,880	553	−196	50,237	5,330	44,907
1972	56,416	594	−272	56,738	6,131	50,607
1973	65,595	1,329	−443	66,481	7,329	59,152
1974	75,441	1,508	−422	76,527	9,088	67,439
1975	95,793	891	−475	96,209	11,621	84,588
1976	112,819	1,560	−786	113,593	13,976	99,617
1977	129,553	265	−1,128	128,690	16,501	112,189
1978	149,146	806	−1,791	148,161	19,378	128,783
1979	172,676	1,205	−2,210	171,671	22,827	148,844
1980	200,793	−183	−1,984	198,626	27,952	170,674
1981	218,828	1,251	−1,547	218,532	31,641	186,891
1982	238,145	1,458	−1,741	237,862	33,653	204,209
1983	261,106	2,831	−1,593	262,344	36,150	226,194
1984	279,804	4,358	−1,730	282,432	38,759	243,673
1985	306,556	2,647	−3,111	306,092	41,883	264,209
1986	326,134	5,095	−2,157	329,072	45,083	283,989
1987	358,153	4,078	−3,400	358,831	48,150	310,681

Table A.1 (*cont.*)

	GDP at factor cost	Plus net property income from abroad	Plus net transfers from abroad	Equals GNP at factor cost	Less deprec- iation	Equals national income
1988	397,180	5,048	−3,518	398,710	52,596	346,114
1989	435,912	4,087	−4,578	435,421	56,633	378,788
1990	477,540	4,029	−4,935	476,634	61,126	415,508

Table A.2 *Expenditure on the Gross Domestic Product (£m): 1920–1990*

	Consumers' expenditure	Plus gross fixed capital formation	Plus stock-building	Plus public consumption	Plus exports	Less imports	Equals GDP at market prices
1920	4,929	482	−56	489	2,118	2,039	5,923
1921	4,129	457	−167	488	1,156	1,199	4,864
1922	3,710	381	−108	435	1,106	1,104	4,419
1923	3,588	334	−93	395	1,153	1,161	4,217
1924	3,681	374	6	398	1,195	1,326	4,328
1925	3,752	419	95	412	1,151	1,361	4,469
1926	3,746	401	24	420	1,013	1,294	4,311
1927	3,817	427	63	423	1,087	1,258	4,559
1928	3,852	420	11	425	1,088	1,237	4,559
1929	3,905	442	46	435	1,093	1,270	4,651
1930	3,844	435	75	443	881	1,102	4,575
1931	3,734	408	−10	443	631	927	4,279
1932	3,615	347	−18	431	577	765	4,186
1933	3,673	358	−35	430	573	738	4,261
1934	3,765	427	31	446	608	799	4,478
1935	3,898	456	0	483	690	848	4,679
1936	4,074	518	35	537	698	917	4,944
1937	4,262	575	83	618	844	1,093	5,288
1938	4,310	591	51	748	756	1,002	5,454
1939	4,426	540	114	1,181	702	1,095	5,867

Table A.2 (*cont.*)

	Consumers' expenditure	Plus gross fixed capital formation	Plus stock-building	Plus public consumption	Plus exports	Less imports	Equals GDP at market prices
1940	4,515	519	156	2,923	595	1,588	7,121
1941	4,872	480	92	4,089	599	1,554	8,579
1942	5,221	450	−101	4,580	600	1,350	9,400
1943	5,355	360	90	4,971	736	1,508	10,005
1944	5,704	300	−210	5,045	963	1,710	10,092
1945	6,309	350	−177	4,205	804	1,669	9,822
1946	7,138	929	−128	2,345	1,428	1,829	9,882
1947	7,946	1,203	293	1,810	1,653	2,226	10,679
1948	8,680	1,435	175	1,831	2,196	2,433	11,884
1949	9,093	1,594	74	2,056	2,499	2,694	12,621
1950	9,594	1,725	−196	2,144	2,998	3,073	13,192
1951	10,323	1,923	580	2,516	3,650	4,329	14,663
1952	10,831	2,154	46	2,992	3,761	3,932	15,851
1953	11,503	2,421	103	3,127	3,684	3,836	17,002
1954	12,210	2,624	58	3,204	3,837	3,961	17,973
1955	13,176	2,912	333	3,265	4,179	4,480	19,385
1956	13,866	3,187	238	3,522	4,594	4,557	20,850
1957	14,627	3,472	204	3,671	4,831	4,782	22,023
1958	15,442	3,596	68	3,740	4,697	4,587	22,957
1959	16,290	3,854	137	3,989	4,847	4,887	24,231

Table A.2 (*cont.*)

	Consumers' expenditure	Plus gross fixed capital formation	Plus stock-building	Plus public consumption	Plus exports	Less imports	Equals GDP at market prices
1960	17,136	4,240	661	4,227	5,152	5,546	25,870
1961	18,007	4,747	235	4,559	5,378	5,511	27,415
1962	19,096	4,904	9	4,885	5,515	5,608	28,802
1963	20,337	5,136	131	5,144	5,862	6,029	30,581
1964	21,725	6,121	670	5,469	6,201	6,821	33,366
1965	23,164	6,635	521	5,998	6,616	6,971	35,964
1966	24,502	7,063	312	6,525	7,169	7,260	38,311
1967	25,715	7,684	220	7,213	7,381	7,859	40,354
1968	27,688	8,473	289	7,663	8,967	9,388	43,693
1969	29,464	8,832	674	8,004	10,091	9,930	47,135
1970	32,105	9,736	509	9,024	11,516	11,103	51,787
1971	35,912	10,834	−142	10,288	12,881	12,179	57,594
1972	40,715	11,937	163	11,739	13,634	13,742	64,447
1973	46,426	14,650	1,617	13,398	17,035	18,977	74,149
1974	53,298	17,311	835	16,706	22,783	27,225	83,708
1975	65,542	20,806	−1,285	23,097	26,784	28,887	106,058
1976	75,966	24,043	542	27,011	34,778	36,809	125,532
1977	87,140	26,770	1,928	29,438	43,210	42,484	146,001
1978	100,541	30,754	1,661	33,366	47,283	45,477	168,128
1979	119,483	36,761	2,215	38,785	54,866	54,408	197,703

Table A.2 (*cont.*)

	Consumers' expendi-ture	Plus gross fixed capital formation	Plus stock-building	Plus public consump-tion	Plus exports	Less imports	Equals GDP at market prices
1980	139,029	41,366	−2,576	48,888	62,522	57,680	231,548
1981	154,642	41,063	−2,857	55,314	67,247	60,486	254,924
1982	170,088	44,702	−1,147	60,299	72,673	67,814	278,801
1983	186,517	48,445	1,376	65,723	79,879	77,604	304,337
1984	199,455	55,022	1,373	69,689	91,953	92,648	324,844
1985	217,679	60,359	819	73,736	102,196	98,865	355,923
1986	241,241	64,481	691	79,307	98,259	101,085	382,894
1987	265,070	74,125	1,396	85,271	107,045	111,853	421,054
1988	299,178	89,079	4,813	91,645	107,881	124,844	467,751
1989	326,906	101,977	3,160	98,937	122,826	142,660	511,145
1990	349,770	105,322	−711	109,386	134,160	147,536	550,391

Note: Exports and imports do not include property income flows.

Table A.3 *Expenditure on the Gross Domestic Product (£m constant prices):1920–1990*

	Consumers' expenditure	Plus gross fixed capital formation	Plus stock-building	Plus public consumption	Plus exports	Less imports	Equals GDP market prices	Less factor cost adjustment	Equals GDP factor cost
1920–1948 in 1938 prices									
1920	3,271	284	−35	447	810	731	4,047	488	3,559
1921	3,002	325	−123	451	643	645	3,654	456	3,198
1922	3,136	300	−82	424	811	741	3,848	450	3,398
1923	3,232	308	−71	399	890	794	3,962	458	3,504
1924	3,339	359	−0	403	920	872	4,149	473	3,676
1925	3,397	409	54	416	914	896	4,295	484	3,811
1926	3,416	397	13	425	840	930	4,161	474	3,687
1927	3,564	443	45	430	946	945	4,481	494	3,988
1928	3,609	438	3	435	952	916	4,521	500	4,021
1929	3,692	461	31	444	984	962	4,650	510	4,140
1930	3,738	463	60	455	846	950	4,613	510	4,103
1931	3,793	454	−12	465	682	985	4,399	500	3,899
1932	3,771	396	−19	465	667	879	4,402	485	3,916
1933	3,913	410	−52	472	678	878	4,542	498	4,045
1934	4,013	498	35	482	704	918	4,813	517	4,296
1935	4,126	518	2	515	794	963	4,991	537	4,454
1936	4,278	566	35	563	772	985	5,229	556	4,673
1937	4,330	585	81	627	811	1,022	5,412	577	4,835
1938	4,310	592	51	748	756	1,002	5,454	588	4,867
1939	4,299	530	113	1,135	702	1,086	5,694	601	5,093

Table A.3 (*cont.*)

	Consumers' expenditure	Plus gross fixed capital formation	Plus stock-building	Plus public consumption	Plus exports	Less imports	Equals GDP market prices	Less factor cost adjustment	Equals GDP factor cost
1940	3,748	460	94	2,619	476	1,138	6,259	590	5,668
1941	3,649	370	41	3,308	409	973	6,804	611	6,192
1942	3,649	320	−66	3,474	370	821	6,926	608	6,318
1943	3,620	220	31	3,582	408	815	7,045	615	6,431
1944	3,756	170	−153	3,352	516	906	6,735	616	6,119
1945	4,050	190	−129	2,739	422	845	6,427	633	5,794
1946	4,433	480	15	1,495	709	862	6,269	645	5,624
1947	4,622	560	106	1,056	710	865	6,189	639	5,550
1948	4,709	600	45	1,015	865	846	6,388	635	5,753
				1948–1990 in 1985 prices					
1948	92,268	15,566	1,333	37,344	21,127	22,303	145,336	18,329	127,007
1949	93,638	16,911	789	39,188	23,300	23,855	149,971	18,598	131,373
1950	96,211	17,879	−907	39,111	26,622	24,071	154,846	19,047	135,799
1951	95,462	18,183	3,148	42,367	26,601	26,041	159,721	19,991	139,730
1952	92,922	17,968	430	45,533	25,510	23,629	158,735	19,241	139,494
1953	96,800	20,026	622	46,848	26,601	25,574	165,323	20,091	145,231
1954	101,324	21,883	467	46,856	28,250	26,642	172,139	21,245	150,894

Table A.3 (*cont.*)

	Consumers' expenditure	Plus gross fixed capital formation	Plus stock-building	Plus public consumption	Plus exports	Less imports	Equals GDP market prices	Less factor cost adjustment	Equals GDP factor cost
1955	106,777	23,427	2,072	46,098	30,355	29,680	179,049	22,377	156,673
1956	107,790	24,527	1,396	45,664	31,709	29,880	181,207	22,304	158,903
1957	110,412	25,939	1,389	45,068	32,624	30,757	184,675	22,965	161,709
1958	113,399	26,242	584	43,933	32,177	31,142	185,194	24,066	161,128
1959	118,891	28,410	1,151	44,875	33,207	33,314	193,219	26,226	166,993
1960	124,371	31,233	4,129	46,021	35,373	37,496	203,631	27,806	175,825
1961	126,459	34,081	1,739	47,413	36,312	37,145	208,859	28,182	180,677
1962	129,043	34,272	206	48,760	36,840	37,870	211,250	28,174	183,076
1963	134,946	34,756	1,085	49,595	38,635	39,564	219,454	29,315	190,139
1964	139,453	40,631	4,438	50,477	40,018	43,801	231,216	30,795	200,421
1965	141,540	42,738	3,093	51,729	41,681	44,150	236,631	30,908	205,724
1966	143,932	43,777	1,944	53,045	43,821	45,241	241,278	31,464	209,814
1967	146,777	47,338	1,362	55,836	43,885	48,301	246,896	32,313	214,583
1968	151,121	50,378	2,029	56,133	49,447	52,134	256,975	33,161	223,813
1969	152,619	50,362	2,851	55,168	54,499	53,949	261,550	33,134	228,416
1970	157,055	51,641	2,163	56,062	57,363	56,612	267,673	34,460	233,214
1971	161,694	52,319	197	57,675	61,111	59,715	273,280	35,796	237,484
1972	172,030	52,436	244	60,123	61,970	65,512	281,291	38,544	242,747
1973	180,547	55,680	6,765	62,683	69,234	73,288	301,621	41,097	260,524
1974	176,734	53,842	2,675	63,561	73,838	73,909	296,740	39,471	257,269

Table A.3 (*cont.*)

	Consumers' expenditure	Plus gross fixed capital formation	Plus stock-building	Plus public consumption	Plus exports	Less imports	Equals GDP market prices	Less factor cost adjustment	Equals GDP factor cost
1975	175,362	52,708	−3,291	66,959	71,726	68,986	294,479	39,274	255,205
1976	175,663	53,234	1,126	67,756	77,850	72,565	303,064	40,875	262,190
1977	175,631	52,749	3,549	66,710	83,792	73,532	308,899	41,012	267,887
1978	186,560	54,489	2,689	68,512	85,433	76,854	320,829	45,259	275,570
1979	195,340	56,321	3,399	69,911	88,994	84,153	329,813	46,684	283,129
1980	194,887	53,130	−3,378	70,727	88,454	80,915	322,904	45,271	277,632
1981	194,634	47,901	−3,299	70,793	87,538	78,544	319,023	44,146	274,877
1982	197,187	50,716	−1,237	71,513	88,616	82,381	324,414	44,847	279,567
1983	206,343	53,283	1,258	72,968	90,324	87,850	336,326	46,362	289,963
1984	210,378	58,091	1,163	73,791	95,622	96,377	342,668	48,339	294,328
1985	217,678	60,359	819	73,736	102,196	98,865	355,922	49,367	306,556
1986	231,153	61,780	712	75,011	106,983	105,681	369,959	52,314	317,645
1987	243,482	67,799	1,165	75,953	113,113	113,892	387,619	55,537	332,082
1988	261,726	76,760	4,043	76,441	113,219	127,891	404,299	58,303	345,995
1989	270,996	81,965	2,673	77,151	117,993	137,298	413,480	59,961	353,519
1990	273,720	80,005	−698	79,374	123,739	139,007	417,132	60,537	356,596

Table A.4 *Gross Domestic Product by type of income (£m): 1920–1990*

	Income from employment	Plus operating surplus	Equals GDP factor cost	Plus factor cost adjustment	Equals GDP market prices
1920	3,603	1,951	5,554	370	5,923
1921	2,931	1,530	4,462	403	4,864
1922	2,502	1,477	3,980	439	4,419
1923	2,404	1,358	3,762	454	4,217
1924	2,461	1,438	3,899	430	4,328
1925	2,486	1,554	4,040	429	4,469
1926	2,397	1,466	3,862	449	4,311
1927	2,556	1,524	4,080	479	4,559
1928	2,527	1,539	4,066	493	4,559
1929	2,562	1,614	4,175	476	4,651
1930	2,486	1,632	4,118	457	4,575
1931	2,409	1,411	3,820	459	4,279
1932	2,356	1,340	3,695	490	4,186
1933	2,410	1,365	3,775	486	4,261
1934	2,491	1,480	3,971	507	4,478
1935	2,592	1,565	4,157	522	4,679
1936	2,736	1,652	4,388	556	4,944
1937	2,923	1,784	4,706	582	5,288
1938	2,976	1,891	4,867	588	5,454
1939	3,294	1,930	5,225	642	5,867
1940	4,167	2,143	6,310	811	7,121
1941	4,848	2,671	7,519	1,059	8,579
1942	5,303	2,938	8,241	1,159	9,400
1943	5,704	3,076	8,780	1,225	10,005
1944	5,875	3,001	8,876	1,216	10,092
1945	5,798	2,869	8,667	1,155	9,822
1946	5,625	3,075	8,700	1,183	9,882
1947	6,150	3,188	9,338	1,341	10,679
1948	6,790	3,657	10,447	1,437	11,884
1949	7,236	3,922	11,158	1,463	12,621
1950	7,637	3,971	11,608	1,584	13,192
1951	8,515	4,354	12,869	1,794	14,663
1952	9,114	4,872	13,986	1,865	15,851
1953	9,692	5,318	15,010	1,992	17,002
1954	10,321	5,582	15,903	2,070	17,973

Table A.4 (*cont.*)

	Income from employment	Plus operating surplus	Equals GDP factor cost	Plus factor cost adjustment	Equals GDP market prices
1955	11,266	5,833	17,099	2,286	19,385
1956	12,322	6,082	18,403	2,447	20,850
1957	13,047	6,440	19,487	2,536	22,023
1958	13,562	6,766	20,328	2,629	22,957
1959	14,203	7,225	21,428	2,803	24,231
1960	15,164	7,831	22,995	2,875	25,870
1961	16,422	7,972	24,393	3,022	27,415
1962	17,329	8,215	25,544	3,258	28,802
1963	18,215	8,924	27,138	3,443	30,581
1964	19,781	9,685	29,467	3,899	33,366
1965	21,317	10,296	31,613	4,351	35,964
1966	22,891	10,598	33,490	4,821	38,311
1967	23,893	11,311	35,204	5,150	40,354
1968	25,538	12,295	37,833	5,860	43,693
1969	27,170	13,086	40,256	6,879	47,135
1970	30,516	13,803	44,319	7,468	51,787
1971	33,640	16,240	49,880	7,714	57,594
1972	37,953	18,463	56,416	8,031	64,447
1973	43,934	21,661	65,595	8,555	74,149
1974	53,055	22,386	75,441	8,267	83,708
1975	69,362	26,431	95,793	10,265	106,058
1976	79,324	33,495	112,819	12,712	125,532
1977	87,053	42,500	129,553	16,448	146,001
1978	99,312	49,835	149,146	18,981	168,128
1979	116,320	56,356	172,676	25,027	197,703
1980	138,087	62,706	200,793	30,755	231,548
1981	150,157	68,671	218,828	36,096	254,924
1982	159,059	79,086	238,145	40,656	278,801
1983	169,796	91,310	261,106	43,231	304,337
1984	180,947	98,858	279,804	45,039	324,844
1985	195,569	110,987	306,556	49,367	355,923
1986	211,488	114,645	326,134	56,760	382,894
1987	229,138	129,016	358,153	62,901	421,054
1988	255,000	142,180	397,180	70,571	467,751
1989	283,231	152,682	435,912	75,233	511,145

Table A.4 (*cont.*)

	Income from employment	Plus operating surplus	Equals GDP factor cost	Plus factor cost adjustment	Equals GDP market prices
1990	316,294	161,246	477,540	72,850	550,391

Note: Operating surplus is the sum of gross trading profits, gross trading surplus of public enterprises, self-employment income, rent and capital consumption of non-profit-making operations of the personal and public sectors.

Table A.5 *Summary capital account (£m): 1920–1990*

	Domestic saving	Plus transfers received	Less: Depreciation	Less: Stock appreciation	Equals total net saving	Net fixed capital formation	Plus increase in physical stocks	Plus net foreign investment	Equals total net investment
1920	551	0	435	−200	316	47	−56	324	361
1921	118	0	352	−350	116	105	−167	178	116
1922	401	0	314	−62	149	67	−108	191	149
1923	458	0	288	45	125	46	−93	171	125
1924	491	0	283	40	168	91	6	71	168
1925	417	0	283	−139	273	136	95	41	273
1926	346	0	283	−56	119	118	24	−24	119
1927	566	0	279	−18	305	148	63	94	305
1928	531	0	284	−18	265	136	11	119	265
1929	500	0	293	−80	287	149	46	92	287
1930	327	0	291	−213	249	144	75	31	249
1931	230	0	290	−63	3	118	−10	−105	3
1932	241	0	283	−34	−8	64	−18	−54	−8
1933	360	0	283	45	32	75	−35	−8	32
1934	440	0	282	5	153	145	31	−23	153
1935	505	0	298	26	181	158	0	23	181
1936	627	0	317	98	212	201	35	−24	212
1937	679	0	357	67	255	218	83	−45	255
1938	476	0	370	−109	215	221	51	−57	215
1939	628	0	390	217	20	150	114	−243	20

Table A.5 (*cont.*)

	Domestic saving	Plus transfers received	Less: Deprec-iation	Less: Stock apprec-iation	Equals total net saving	Net fixed capital formation	Plus increase in physical stocks	Plus net foreign investment	Equals total net investment
1940	278	0	440	444	−606	79	156	−841	−606
1941	−114	0	500	140	−755	−20	92	−827	−755
1942	−220	0	530	99	−849	−80	−101	−669	−849
1943	−211	0	620	38	−868	−260	90	−698	−868
1944	−551	0	650	37	−1,238	−350	−210	−678	−1,238
1945	−592	0	640	80	−1,312	−290	−177	−845	−1,312
1946	700	0	690	135	−125	239	−128	−236	−125
1947	1,560	0	770	442	349	433	293	−378	349
1948	1,962	138	900	325	875	535	175	165	875
1949	1,873	154	950	200	877	644	74	160	877
1950	2,493	140	1,029	650	954	696	−196	454	954
1951	2,888	43	1,198	750	983	725	580	−322	983
1952	2,314	0	1,360	−50	1,004	794	46	164	1,004
1953	2,590	0	1,411	−75	1,254	1,010	103	141	1,254
1954	2,874	0	1,469	75	1,330	1,155	58	117	1,330
1955	3,289	0	1,615	196	1,478	1,297	333	−152	1,478
1956	3,835	0	1,772	208	1,855	1,415	238	202	1,855
1957	4,088	0	1,901	187	2,000	1,571	204	225	2,000
1958	4,003	0	2,006	−5	2,002	1,590	68	343	2,002
1959	4,250	0	2,063	98	2,089	1,791	137	162	2,089

Table A.5 (*cont.*)

			Less						
	Domestic saving	Plus transfers received	Deprec-iation	Stock apprec-iation	Equals total net saving	Net fixed capital formation	Plus increase in physical stocks	Plus net foreign investment	Equals total net investment
1960	4,794	0	2,167	122	2,505	2,073	661	−229	2,505
1961	5,185	0	2,326	171	2,688	2,421	235	32	2,688
1962	5,210	0	2,462	152	2,596	2,442	9	145	2,596
1963	5,527	0	2,615	152	2,760	2,521	131	108	2,760
1964	6,660	0	2,793	243	3,624	3,328	670	−373	3,624
1965	7,373	0	3,000	291	4,082	3,635	521	−74	4,082
1966	7,810	0	3,239	305	4,266	3,824	312	130	4,266
1967	7,748	0	3,431	137	4,180	4,253	220	−293	4,180
1968	9,061	0	3,727	583	4,751	4,746	289	−285	4,751
1969	10,724	0	4,077	733	5,914[a]	4,755	674	486	5,915[a]
1970	12,132	0	4,618	1,061	6,453	5,118	509	827	6,453
1971	12,806	0	5,330	1,055	6,421	5,504	−142	1,060	6,421
1972	13,605	0	6,131	1,290	6,184	5,806	163	214	6,184
1973	18,018	−59	7,329	2,806	7,824	7,321	1,617	−1,115	7,824
1974	20,900	−75	9,088	6,109	5,628	8,223	835	−3,431	5,628
1975	23,355	0	11,621	5,521	6,213	9,185	−1,285	−1,687	6,213
1976	30,009	0	13,976	6,681	9,352	10,067	542	−1,257	9,352
1977	33,656	0	16,501	5,095	12,060	10,269	1,928	−137	12,060
1978	37,464	0	19,378	4,228	13,858	11,376	1,661	821	13,858
1979	47,267	0	22,827	8,837	15,603	13,934	2,215	−547	15,603

Table A.5 (*cont.*)

			Less						
	Domestic saving	Plus transfers received	Deprec-iation	Stock apprec-iation	Equals total net saving	Net fixed capital formation	Plus increase in physical stocks	Plus net foreign investment	Equals total net investment
1980	47,855	0	27,952	6,391	13,512	13,414	−2,576	2,674	13,512
1981	50,646	0	31,641	5,974	13,031	9,422	−2,857	6,466	13,031
1982	52,407	0	33,653	4,276	14,478	11,049	−1,147	4,577	14,478
1983	57,539	0	36,150	4,204	17,185	12,295	1,376	3,514	17,185
1984	62,841	0	38,759	4,513	19,569	16,263	1,373	1,933	19,569
1985	66,783	0	41,883	2,738	22,162	18,476	819	2,866	22,162
1986	67,073	0	45,083	1,790	20,200	19,398	691	112	20,200
1987	76,116	0	48,150	4,725	23,241	25,975	1,396	−4,130	23,241
1988	84,671	0	52,596	6,212	25,863	36,483	4,813	−15,433	25,863
1989	92,104	0	56,633	7,292	28,179	45,344	3,160	−20,325	28,179
1990	96,720	0	61,126	6,391	29,203	44,196	−711	−14,283	29,203

Note: [a] Totals do not agree owing to rounding errors.

Table A.6 *International transactions (£m): 1920–1990*

	Exports			Imports			Property income (net)	Net transfers received	Surplus on current account
	Goods	Services	Total	Goods	Services	Total			
1920	1,665	452	2,118	1,811	228	2,039	246	−1	324
1921	872	284	1,156	1,024	175	1,199	178	43	178
1922	887	219	1,106	952	153	1,104	177	12	191
1923	913	240	1,153	1,012	149	1,161	176	3	171
1924	959	236	1,195	1,171	154	1,326	196	6	71
1925	941	210	1,151	1,210	151	1,361	232	19	41
1926	794	219	1,013	1,140	154	1,294	237	20	−24
1927	846	241	1,087	1,114	144	1,258	239	26	94
1928	858	231	1,088	1,095	141	1,237	240	27	119
1929	854	239	1,093	1,117	153	1,270	243	26	92
1930	669	212	881	954	148	1,102	215	37	31
1931	464	166	631	786	141	927	163	28	−105
1932	425	152	577	642	124	765	127	8	−54
1933	427	146	573	618	120	738	154	4	−8
1934	463	145	608	683	116	799	167	2	−23
1935	541	149	690	724	124	848	181	0	23
1936	524	174	698	783	135	917	195	0	−24
1937	614	229	844	949	144	1,093	205	−1	−45
1938	563	193	756	850	152	1,002	192	−3	−57
1939	500	202	702	799	296	1,095	165	−15	−243

Table A.6 (*cont.*)

	Exports			Imports			Property income (net)	Net transfers received	Surplus on current account
	Goods	Services	Total	Goods	Services	Total			
1940	399	195	595	1,003	585	1,588	165	−13	−841
1941	400	199	599	1,101	453	1,554	140	−12	−827
1942	300	300	600	800	550	1,350	100	−18	−669
1943	240	496	736	800	708	1,508	90	−16	−698
1944	270	693	963	900	810	1,710	80	−11	−678
1945	450	354	804	700	969	1,669	80	−60	−845
1946	960	468	1,428	1,063	766	1,829	85	80	−236
1947	1,180	473	1,653	1,541	685	2,226	150	45	−378
1948	1,639	558	2,196	1,790	643	2,433	235	29	27
1949	1,864	634	2,499	1,999	694	2,694	219	−18	6
1950	2,262	736	2,998	2,311	761	3,073	396	−8	314
1951	2,735	914	3,650	3,423	905	4,329	342	−28	−365
1952	2,769	991	3,761	3,048	885	3,932	252	84	164
1953	2,682	1,003	3,684	2,927	909	3,836	229	64	141
1954	2,785	1,052	3,837	2,989	972	3,961	250	−9	117
1955	3,075	1,104	4,179	3,386	1,095	4,480	174	−25	−152
1956	3,376	1,219	4,594	3,325	1,232	4,557	229	−65	202
1957	3,508	1,324	4,831	3,539	1,243	4,782	249	−74	225
1958	3,405	1,292	4,697	3,378	1,209	4,587	293	−60	343
1959	3,526	1,321	4,847	3,642	1,245	4,887	262	−61	162

Table A.6 (*cont.*)

	Exports			Imports			Property income (net)	Net transfers received	Surplus on current account
	Goods	Services	Total	Goods	Services	Total			
1960	3,740	1,412	5,152	4,137	1,409	5,546	233	−68	−229
1961	3,901	1,476	5,378	4,043	1,468	5,511	254	−88	32
1962	4,004	1,511	5,515	4,103	1,505	5,608	334	−97	145
1963	4,329	1,533	5,862	4,451	1,579	6,029	398	−123	108
1964	4,568	1,633	6,201	5,111	1,710	6,821	404	−158	−373
1965	4,914	1,702	6,616	5,173	1,798	6,971	450	−169	−74
1966	5,278	1,891	7,169	5,384	1,876	7,260	402	−181	130
1967	5,239	2,142	7,381	5,841	2,018	7,859	401	−216	−293
1968	6,428	2,540	8,967	7,147	2,240	9,388	359	−223	−285
1969	7,273	2,818	10,091	7,478	2,452	9,930	531	−206	486
1970	8,135	3,381	11,516	8,142	2,961	11,103	596	−182	827
1971	9,013	3,868	12,881	8,824	3,354	12,179	553	−196	1,060
1972	9,427	4,207	13,634	10,155	3,587	13,742	594	−272	214
1973	11,877	5,158	17,035	14,459	4,518	18,977	1,329	−443	−1,056
1974	16,259	6,524	22,783	21,542	5,683	27,225	1,508	−422	−3,356
1975	19,197	7,587	26,784	22,471	6,416	28,887	891	−475	−1,687
1976	24,970	9,807	34,778	29,106	7,703	36,809	1,560	−786	−1,257
1977	31,720	11,490	43,210	34,045	8,439	42,484	265	−1,128	−137
1978	34,921	12,362	47,283	36,616	8,861	45,477	806	−1,791	821
1979	40,510	14,356	54,866	43,838	10,570	54,408	1,205	−2,210	−547

Table A.6 (*cont.*)

	Exports			Imports			Property income (net)	Net transfers received	Surplus on current account
	Goods	Services	Total	Goods	Services	Total			
1980	47,141	15,381	62,522	45,819	11,861	57,680	−183	−1,984	2,674
1981	50,597	16,650	67,247	47,450	13,035	60,486	1,251	−1,547	6,466
1982	55,369	17,304	72,673	53,440	14,374	67,814	1,458	−1,741	4,577
1983	60,608	19,271	79,879	62,266	15,338	77,604	2,831	−1,593	3,514
1984	70,361	21,592	91,953	75,590	17,058	92,648	4,358	−1,730	1,933
1985	77,989	24,207	102,196	81,335	17,530	98,865	2,647	−3,111	2,866
1986	72,592	25,667	98,259	82,193	18,893	101,085	5,095	−2,157	112
1987	79,160	27,885	107,045	90,729	21,124	111,853	4,078	−3,400	−4,130
1988	80,367	27,515	107,881	101,952	22,892	124,844	5,048	−3,518	−15,433
1989	92,395	30,431	122,826	116,967	25,693	142,660	4,087	−4,578	−20,325
1990	102,060	32,100	134,160	120,691	26,845	147,536	4,029	−4,935	−14,283

Table A.7 *Consumers' expenditure (i) (£m): 1920–1990*

	Food	Drink	Tobacco	Housing	Fuel and light	Clothing	Motor vehicles	Public transport	Running costs of motor vehicles	Travel adjustment
1920	1,545	457	120	269	173	790	40	202	42	41
1921	1,395	402	116	314	168	473	19	199	32	−38
1922	1,191	355	112	325	157	424	28	198	33	−18
1923	1,199	330	109	320	147	400	31	191	34	−28
1924	1,212	337	112	318	159	412	39	194	39	−11
1925	1,236	338	116	322	157	425	51	197	42	−31
1926	1,215	323	117	333	143	413	47	195	47	−13
1927	1,193	320	124	346	165	423	44	199	49	−14
1928	1,207	310	131	353	151	433	41	203	54	−24
1929	1,204	311	136	362	161	438	38	200	57	−16
1930	1,161	301	140	372	161	417	34	196	59	−21
1931	1,093	282	140	379	162	394	27	183	57	−9
1932	1,040	264	139	384	157	364	26	178	60	−14
1933	1,008	258	142	392	158	367	30	179	62	11
1934	1,027	262	146	401	161	372	38	183	66	−2
1935	1,054	273	153	415	164	389	44	185	73	−5
1936	1,086	283	161	430	176	403	47	192	76	14
1937	1,139	297	169	442	185	427	49	198	83	3
1938	1,155	294	176	454	188	439	43	208	88	−10
1939	1,201	311	204	510	198	458	37	190	82	43

Table A.7 (*cont.*)

	Food	Drink	Tobacco	Housing	Fuel and light	Clothing	Motor vehicles	Public transport	Running costs of motor vehicles	Travel adjustment
1940	1,200	378	260	520	221	490	5	183	46	78
1941	1,248	468	317	524	236	451	1	220	44	160
1942	1,300	550	414	530	237	490	1	255	24	192
1943	1,238	634	491	547	232	435	0	279	12	240
1944	1,323	678	507	570	240	506	0	290	13	254
1945	1,382	705	562	613	259	532	2	324	41	336
1946	1,560	697	603	688	280	635	36	360	88	213
1947	1,815	727	690	755	301	734	49	378	101	168
1948	2,025	804	766	802	328	904	48	356	57	67
1949	2,233	757	755	828	336	1,015	61	364	81	57
1950	2,459	736	768	872	357	1,066	64	362	111	46
1951	2,672	777	803	908	393	1,120	74	387	132	63
1952	2,906	781	824	943	425	1,100	117	426	152	42
1953	3,163	798	841	1,007	453	1,120	187	442	172	29
1954	3,340	798	859	1,066	493	1,212	235	446	192	45
1955	3,635	836	886	1,132	531	1,304	312	469	246	43
1956	3,836	871	940	1,184	600	1,386	270	501	275	41
1957	3,976	911	987	1,276	622	1,448	322	535	291	36
1958	4,074	914	1,040	1,458	694	1,469	428	533	347	35
1959	4,189	929	1,072	1,593	693	1,540	511	550	397	34

Table A.7 (*cont.*)

	Food	Drink	Tobacco	Housing	Fuel and light	Clothing	Motor vehicles	Public transport	Running costs of motor vehicles	Travel adjustment
1960	4,264	971	1,151	1,691	758	1,680	573	577	455	37
1961	4,394	1,083	1,226	1,797	802	1,741	519	608	528	44
1962	4,582	1,168	1,249	1,958	916	1,781	572	637	615	55
1963	4,687	1,232	1,286	2,103	1,000	1,873	700	666	707	83
1964	4,886	1,390	1,343	2,295	992	1,971	796	708	819	113
1965	5,059	1,499	1,428	2,558	1,076	2,099	770	753	975	143
1966	5,294	1,626	1,504	2,780	1,149	2,154	765	805	1,124	143
1967	5,479	1,738	1,512	2,954	1,196	2,218	843	833	1,271	83
1968	5,688	1,869	1,578	3,198	1,328	2,374	951	877	1,485	11
1969	6,038	2,029	1,694	3,495	1,416	2,506	880	953	1,641	−35
1970	6,431	2,300	1,720	3,871	1,480	2,754	1,081	1,021	1,758	−94
1971	7,095	2,592	1,691	4,338	1,605	2,990	1,544	1,164	1,948	−121
1972	7,610	2,909	1,808	5,019	1,781	3,371	1,924	1,296	2,199	−98
1973	8,748	3,423	1,938	5,744	1,880	3,859	1,938	1,471	2,669	−102
1974	10,000	3,911	2,229	6,838	2,248	4,495	1,720	1,660	3,342	−302
1975	12,283	4,843	2,735	8,311	2,886	5,204	2,325	2,104	4,290	−431
1976	14,402	5,705	3,091	9,526	3,555	5,795	2,868	2,513	4,975	−932
1977	16,565	6,540	3,628	11,056	4,218	6,629	3,197	2,897	5,736	−1,490
1978	18,319	7,274	3,884	12,718	4,612	7,827	4,807	3,399	6,242	−1,304
1979	20,953	8,659	4,234	15,254	5,291	9,167	6,490	4,074	7,733	−1,126

Table A.7 (*cont.*)

	Food	Drink	Tobacco	Housing	Fuel and light	Clothing	Motor vehicles	Public transport	Running costs of motor vehicles	Travel adjustment
1980	23,642	9,952	4,821	18,446	6,354	9,872	6,509	5,100	9,639	−788
1981	24,929	11,147	5,515	22,074	7,726	10,151	6,555	5,569	11,284	−385
1982	26,490	12,000	5,881	25,566	8,695	10,923	7,405	5,911	12,403	−308
1983	28,086	13,270	6,209	27,611	9,347	12,117	9,111	6,515	13,476	−809
1984	29,303	14,312	6,623	29,515	9,478	13,160	8,982	6,935	14,344	−1,067
1985	30,726	15,648	7,007	32,416	10,512	14,913	9,916	7,487	15,558	−1,842
1986	32,609	16,404	7,472	36,171	10,882	16,661	11,495	8,298	15,862	−805
1987	34,514	17,454	7,654	39,949	10,754	17,687	13,461	9,394	17,426	−515
1988	36,621	18,756	7,945	45,465	11,226	18,933	17,418	10,495	19,132	431
1989	39,266	19,819	8,196	49,227	11,335	19,896	20,275	11,132	21,373	676
1990	41,836	21,729	8,835	50,311	12,214	20,708	19,528	11,997	24,242	117

Note: The entry for travel is consumption by the British abroad less consumption by foreigners in the United Kingdom.

Table A.8 *Consumers' expenditure (ii) (£m): 1920–1990*

	Furniture and floor coverings	TV, radio, electrical goods	Textiles and hardware	Matches and cleaning materials	Books and recreat-ional goods	Chemists' goods	Post and telecomm-unications	Catering	Other services	Total A.7 + A.8
1920	142		170	71	98	151	116	501		4,929
1921	118		102	60	94	130	113	432		4,129
1922	108		93	53	87	109	88	367		3,710
1923	106		89	52	82	94	82	351		3,588
1924	107		87	53	82	89	85	367		3,681
1925	113		90	53	84	91	87	383		3,752
1926	113		87	52	85	99	89	401		3,746
1927	120		94	53	87	99	90	424		3,817
1928	125		96	54	88	102	90	438		3,852
1929	130		98	55	90	97	91	454		3,905
1930	133		96	52	91	98	92	462		3,844
1931	133		90	51	89	98	93	472		3,734
1932	130		84	48	87	91	92	486		3,615
1933	136		88	48	87	100	93	514		3,673
1934	151		95	49	89	109	94	525		3,765
1935	160		98	47	94	113	96	544		3,898
1936	169		99	49	95	122	100	570		4,074
1937	178		107	53	99	142	105	584		4,262
1938	174		98	54	101	158	110	580		4,310
1939	529						663			4,426

Table A.8 (*cont.*)

	Furniture and floor coverings	TV, radio, electrical goods	Textiles and hardware	Matches and cleaning materials	Books and recreational goods	Chemists' goods	Post and telecommunications	Catering	Other services	Total A.7 + A.8
1940				473				663		4,515
1941				475				729		4,872
1942				461				766		5,221
1943				447				800		5,355
1944				463				862		5,704
1945				563				989		6,309
1946				796				1,182		7,138
1947				958				1,269		7,946
1948	176	134	175	84	263	267	58	491	875	8,680
1949	218	143	186	104	274	274	59	468	878	9,093
1950	255	171	201	114	286	273	62	499	892	9,594
1951	279	203	219	121	315	299	68	541	950	10,323
1952	259	205	215	127	336	304	72	576	1,021	10,831
1953	294	236	225	126	358	314	77	602	1,060	11,503
1954	331	275	246	128	382	330	81	639	1,112	12,210
1955	295	335	275	129	423	362	84	720	1,159	13,176
1956	303	317	286	139	467	380	103	774	1,194	13,866
1957	333	356	305	149	484	411	115	840	1,232	14,627

Table A.8 (*cont.*)

	Furniture and floor coverings	TV, radio, electrical goods	Textiles and hardware	Matches and cleaning materials	Books and recreat-ional goods	Chemists' goods	Post and telecomm-unications	Catering	Other services	Total A.7 + A.8
1958	365	391	307	151	523	427	129	882	1,277	15,442
1959	415	467	324	160	539	452	133	938	1,356	16,290
1960	414	446	333	159	590	481	140	974	1,441	17,136
1961	433	446	351	165	630	516	147	1,028	1,551	18,007
1962	454	459	358	174	654	530	156	1,104	1,674	19,096
1963	511	519	388	176	653	541	169	1,164	1,881	20,337
1964	573	526	425	180	704	590	183	1,230	2,002	21,725
1965	620	526	452	190	758	619	204	1,301	2,134	23,164
1966	625	515	477	194	813	650	215	1,361	2,309	24,502
1967	646	565	500	196	856	688	235	1,392	2,512	25,715
1968	723	632	556	203	958	778	252	1,469	2,760	27,688
1969	732	638	577	207	1,027	828	288	1,559	2,990	29,464
1970	795	731	627	218	1,161	908	342	1,700	3,300	32,105
1971	911	876	700	237	1,314	1,024	395	1,871	3,741	35,912
1972	1,104	1,159	808	249	1,525	1,183	460	2,156	4,252	40,715
1973	1,282	1,376	902	275	1,709	1,387	553	2,538	4,837	46,426
1974	1,440	1,495	1,034	337	2,123	1,653	652	2,930	5,495	53,298
1975	1,772	1,772	1,174	414	2,563	1,959	927	3,599	6,811	65,542
1976	2,072	2,041	1,360	467	2,906	2,239	1,222	4,270	7,893	75,966

Table A.8 (*cont.*)

	Furniture and floor coverings	TV, radio, electrical goods	Textiles and hardware	Matches and cleaning materials	Books and recreational goods	Chemists' goods	Post and telecommunications	Catering	Other services	Total A.7 + A.8
1977	2,250	2,303	1,547	533	3,356	2,639	1,244	5,106	9,185	87,140
1978	2,608	2,745	1,938	584	3,886	3,119	1,470	5,838	10,574	100,541
1979	3,248	3,344	2,154	666	4,663	3,788	1,688	6,874	12,329	119,483
1980	3,394	3,590	2,316	798	5,530	4,358	2,247	8,288	14,963	139,029
1981	3,487	3,895	2,468	886	5,988	4,649	2,792	8,814	17,099	154,642
1982	3,615	4,416	2,524	970	6,570	5,217	3,101	9,458	19,250	170,088
1983	3,883	5,253	2,682	1,050	7,021	5,773	3,291	10,922	21,710	186,517
1984	3,968	5,684	2,859	1,138	7,617	6,506	3,582	12,513	24,001	199,455
1985	4,193	6,138	3,277	1,237	8,439	7,156	3,983	13,876	27,037	217,679
1986	4,514	6,839	3,867	1,323	9,485	8,075	4,497	16,194	31,398	241,241
1987	5,058	7,752	4,198	1,394	10,603	9,036	4,863	18,309	36,080	265,070
1988	5,951	8,570	4,780	1,499	11,657	10,441	5,309	22,947	41,600	299,178
1989	6,349	9,222	5,075	1,739	12,878	11,184	5,584	26,019	47,662	326,906
1990	6,286	9,330	5,380	1,906	13,870	11,986	6,243	29,081	54,169	349,770

Note: Between 1939 and 1947 the figure listed under 'Furniture and floor coverings' includes purchases of textiles and hardware, matches and cleaning materials, books and recreational goods and chemists' goods. The figure listed under post and telecommunications also includes purchases of catering and other services.

Table A.9 *Consumers' expenditure (i) (£m constant prices): 1920–1990*

	Food	Drink	Tobacco	Housing	Fuel and light	Clothing	Motor vehicles	Public transport	Running costs of motor vehicles	Travel adjustment
					1920–1948 in 1938 prices					
1920	834	426	118	335	138	371	13	158	19	24
1921	861	356	115	337	118	302	7	145	21	−25
1922	921	318	111	339	134	343	11	154	23	−11
1923	983	319	109	342	138	350	15	159	26	−20
1924	998	336	112	345	147	361	21	164	30	−9
1925	1,001	338	117	349	149	367	27	171	35	−22
1926	1,010	323	118	356	130	370	26	170	39	−10
1927	1,027	321	123	364	162	393	28	173	43	−11
1928	1,045	310	128	372	156	395	28	176	49	−20
1929	1,053	310	133	377	163	404	28	178	52	−14
1930	1,080	300	136	385	162	399	27	177	56	−19
1931	1,118	273	137	391	162	407	23	166	56	−7
1932	1,117	238	134	397	158	391	25	164	57	−10
1933	1,121	250	139	403	161	407	29	171	59	11
1934	1,133	262	143	411	166	411	36	178	64	−1
1935	1,130	273	150	422	172	426	43	184	72	−4
1936	1,148	283	159	433	180	441	48	193	78	13
1937	1,156	296	168	444	186	438	49	200	84	3
1938	1,155	294	176	454	188	439	43	208	88	−10
1939	1,162	297	182	503	197	444	39	190	78	39

Table A.9 (*cont.*)

	Food	Drink	Tobacco	Housing	Fuel and light	Clothing	Motor vehicles	Public transport	Running costs of motor vehicles	Travel adjustment
1940	976	278	178	505	200	367	5	168	34	60
1941	922	291	196	503	202	275	1	189	31	113
1942	951	270	206	505	195	275	1	221	16	133
1943	911	273	204	512	182	251	0	241	17	163
1944	964	279	204	525	188	282	0	249	8	164
1945	986	304	224	539	191	289	1	278	25	212
1946	1,197	283	236	588	210	343	16	306	54	102
1947	1,294	290	206	610	224	388	20	297	60	75
1948	1,332	278	198	629	227	431	18	323	34	49
					1948–1990 in 1985 prices					
1948	20,471	5,953	6,621	14,922	5,113	4,555	269	5,797	777	358
1949	21,648	5,761	6,465	15,173	5,107	4,947	343	5,817	1,058	288
1950	22,763	5,847	6,562	15,599	5,369	5,165	357	5,679	1,301	215
1951	22,197	6,049	6,812	15,382	5,558	4,698	353	5,801	1,397	230
1952	20,941	5,783	6,686	14,755	5,309	4,463	477	5,991	1,397	158
1953	22,106	5,936	6,880	15,143	5,416	4,627	857	5,997	1,559	127
1954	22,806	5,936	7,136	15,739	5,704	5,016	1,106	6,076	1,733	177
1955	23,982	6,261	7,439	16,430	5,936	5,470	1,498	6,099	2,173	170

Table A.9 (*cont.*)

	Food	Drink	Tobacco	Housing	Fuel and light	Clothing	Motor vehicles	Public transport	Running costs of motor vehicles	Travel adjustment
1956	24,316	6,378	7,552	16,592	6,125	5,680	1,181	6,154	2,374	163
1957	24,894	6,531	7,819	16,901	6,035	5,884	1,360	6,327	2,381	152
1958	25,357	6,504	8,042	17,427	6,476	5,943	1,792	5,979	2,860	146
1959	26,061	6,991	8,289	18,200	6,474	6,320	2,229	6,057	3,209	152
1960	26,793	7,407	8,663	18,940	7,104	6,858	2,558	6,022	3,655	175
1961	27,045	7,897	8,766	19,167	7,226	6,967	2,290	5,901	4,039	194
1962	27,183	7,914	8,417	19,601	7,940	6,905	2,564	5,897	4,520	217
1963	27,364	8,318	8,741	20,243	8,607	7,230	3,562	5,376	4,843	274
1964	27,807	8,876	8,681	20,728	8,264	7,559	4,056	5,461	5,688	448
1965	27,712	8,798	8,321	21,252	8,540	7,823	3,914	5,472	6,366	628
1966	27,942	9,115	8,579	21,641	8,621	7,796	3,886	5,495	7,110	578
1967	28,310	9,460	8,616	22,041	8,642	7,895	4,261	5,496	7,753	220
1968	28,535	9,980	8,640	22,879	8,922	8,350	4,559	5,453	8,522	−365
1969	28,613	10,218	8,486	23,494	9,241	8,481	4,106	5,619	8,846	−625
1970	29,057	10,917	8,533	24,068	9,324	8,863	4,694	5,627	9,274	−894
1971	29,214	11,667	8,285	24,473	9,254	9,039	6,153	5,670	9,768	−811
1972	29,378	12,554	8,823	25,474	9,629	9,561	7,481	5,962	10,598	−804
1973	29,739	13,875	9,458	25,798	9,910	10,010	7,373	6,321	12,062	−1,072
1974	29,022	14,166	9,318	25,465	10,014	9,820	5,718	6,184	11,805	−1,682

Table A.9 (*cont.*)

	Food	Drink	Tobacco	Housing	Fuel and light	Clothing	Motor vehicles	Public transport	Running costs of motor vehicles	Travel adjustment
1975	28,999	13,979	8,832	25,271	9,777	9,961	6,032	6,099	11,741	−2,025
1976	29,316	14,161	8,551	25,125	9,712	10,052	6,285	5,940	12,401	−3,300
1977	29,041	14,282	8,194	25,932	9,938	10,183	5,638	5,979	12,572	−4,092
1978	29,738	15,078	8,939	26,866	10,164	11,187	6,992	6,241	13,230	−3,278
1979	30,483	15,871	8,961	28,024	10,686	12,012	7,940	6,633	13,431	−2,420
1980	30,364	15,154	8,675	28,470	10,217	11,828	7,499	6,738	13,670	−1,086
1981	30,110	14,664	8,065	28,730	10,170	11,697	7,641	6,777	13,870	−370
1982	30,291	14,381	7,487	29,547	10,003	12,171	7,944	6,645	14,323	−332
1983	30,879	15,042	7,459	30,663	9,915	13,066	9,948	6,855	14,788	−984
1984	30,399	15,364	7,204	31,571	9,824	13,761	9,357	7,182	15,166	−1,374
1985	30,726	15,648	7,007	32,416	10,512	14,912	9,916	7,487	15,558	−1,842
1986	31,630	15,692	6,815	33,651	10,795	16,222	10,646	8,075	16,608	−990
1987	32,472	16,017	6,765	34,853	10,781	16,935	11,045	8,981	17,655	−545
1988	33,268	16,397	6,783	36,485	10,971	17,529	12,776	9,746	18,911	859
1989	33,869	16,380	6,800	37,164	10,458	17,525	14,144	10,036	19,965	1,009
1990	33,481	16,353	6,863	37,790	10,497	17,475	12,988	10,146	20,859	584

Table A.10 *Consumers' expenditure (ii) (£m constant prices): 1920–1990*

	Furniture and floor coverings	TV, radio, electrical goods	Textiles and hardware	Matches and cleaning materials	Books and recreat-ional goods	Chemists' goods	Post and telecomm-unications	Catering	Other services	Total A.9 + A.10
	1920–1948 in 1938 prices									
1920	89		96	40	77	94	82	359		3,271
1921	81		70	41	74	83	83	332		3,002
1922	94		82	41	77	86	85	329		3,136
1923	101		88	43	77	85	86	329		3,232
1924	103		89	45	79	84	88	347		3,339
1925	109		93	45	81	90	89	359		3,397
1926	114		91	45	80	86	91	378		3,416
1927	124		101	46	83	91	92	405		3,564
1928	130		103	48	84	94	94	417		3,609
1929	137		107	49	88	97	95	435		3,692
1930	141		106	48	90	100	97	454		3,738
1931	147		104	47	89	103	99	478		3,793
1932	159		102	46	90	102	100	503		3,771
1933	164		108	47	89	112	102	539		3,913
1934	179		115	49	91	120	104	552		4,013
1935	190		119	49	97	128	105	569		4,126
1936	195		118	51	99	138	107	592		4,278
1937	187		112	53	101	151	108	592		4,330
1938	174		98	54	101	158	110	580		4,310
1939	521						646			4,299

Table A.10 (*cont.*)

	Furniture and floor coverings	TV, radio, electrical goods	Textiles and hardware	Matches and cleaning materials	Books and recreat-ional goods	Chemists' goods	Post and telecomm-unications	Catering	Other services	Total A.9 + A.10
1940				399				577		3,748
1941				331				595		3,649
1942				283				593		3,649
1943				276				590		3,620
1944				283				610		3,756
1945				329				671		4,050
1946				445				652		4,433
1947				497				661		4,622
1948				523				668		4,709
					1948–1990 in 1985 prices					
1948	1,333	447	1,016	585	2,766	1,499	867	7,197	11,722	92,268
1949	1,629	486	1,079	698	2,929	1,628	852	6,602	11,129	93,638
1950	1,850	559	1,132	775	3,062	1,633	865	6,733	10,747	96,211
1951	1,760	633	1,013	762	3,135	1,591	898	6,663	10,529	95,462
1952	1,522	577	1,028	735	3,027	1,513	937	6,681	10,941	92,922
1953	1,782	732	1,152	747	3,264	1,741	975	6,762	10,998	96,800
1954	2,046	912	1,268	779	3,503	1,937	989	7,078	11,384	101,324

Table A.10 (*cont.*)

	Furniture and floor coverings	TV, radio, electrical goods	Textiles and hardware	Matches and cleaning materials	Books and recreat-ional goods	Chemists' goods	Post and telecomm-unications	Catering	Other services	Total A.9 + A10
1955	2,039	1,009	1,425	834	3,829	2,098	1,023	7,640	11,421	106,777
1956	1,926	901	1,409	857	3,983	2,085	1,076	7,946	11,091	107,790
1957	2,199	964	1,507	874	3,936	2,232	1,102	8,488	10,826	110,412
1958	2,404	1,090	1,573	885	4,159	2,461	1,097	8,651	10,553	113,399
1959	2,755	1,356	1,713	916	4,416	2,735	1,129	9,217	10,671	118,891
1960	2,697	1,314	1,779	929	4,893	2,936	1,196	9,621	10,831	124,371
1961	2,699	1,297	1,866	974	5,040	3,071	1,220	9,805	10,992	126,459
1962	2,657	1,334	1,900	1,006	5,141	3,131	1,210	10,031	11,472	129,043
1963	2,643	1,449	1,986	1,031	5,351	3,399	1,317	10,703	12,510	134,946
1964	2,828	1,423	2,159	1,054	5,451	3,614	1,388	10,983	12,985	139,453
1965	2,938	1,397	2,245	1,051	5,520	3,722	1,470	11,055	13,314	141,540
1966	2,866	1,350	2,340	1,054	5,666	3,789	1,495	10,952	13,658	143,932
1967	2,881	1,452	2,410	1,077	5,810	3,922	1,542	10,675	14,313	146,777
1968	3,115	1,538	2,594	1,091	5,805	4,063	1,581	10,778	15,080	151,121
1969	3,038	1,488	2,547	1,093	5,834	4,069	1,663	10,842	15,564	152,619
1970	3,055	1,616	2,560	1,095	5,951	4,170	1,818	11,208	16,119	157,055
1971	3,186	1,797	2,685	1,109	6,059	4,374	1,773	11,152	16,847	161,694
1972	3,708	2,396	2,953	1,130	6,548	5,075	2,003	11,922	17,639	172,030
1973	3,958	3,017	3,039	1,164	7,038	5,933	2,223	12,162	18,540	180,547

Table A.10 (*cont.*)

	Furniture and floor coverings	TV, radio, electrical goods	Textiles and hardware	Matches and cleaning materials	Books and recreat-ional goods	Chemists' goods	Post and telecomm-unications	Catering	Other services	Total A.9 + A.10
1974	3,729	3,033	2,925	1,157	7,239	6,127	2,289	11,796	18,607	176,734
1975	3,855	2,808	2,770	1,118	7,113	5,892	2,265	12,144	18,732	175,362
1976	4,049	3,016	2,818	1,072	7,001	5,966	2,404	12,257	18,838	175,663
1977	3,781	2,984	2,789	1,052	6,914	6,076	2,541	12,470	19,359	175,631
1978	3,957	3,300	3,194	1,055	7,134	6,551	2,824	12,644	20,747	186,560
1979	4,397	3,771	3,114	1,065	7,564	6,617	3,190	12,749	21,251	195,340
1980	4,049	3,756	2,856	1,093	7,751	6,051	3,317	12,773	21,712	194,887
1981	3,978	3,954	2,865	1,121	7,675	6,093	3,367	12,136	22,089	194,634
1982	4,026	4,447	2,850	1,153	7,771	6,492	3,390	11,936	22,664	197,187
1983	4,221	5,259	2,963	1,180	7,867	6,627	3,619	12,702	24,272	206,343
1984	4,104	5,787	3,036	1,207	8,063	7,023	3,815	13,313	25,575	210,378
1985	4,193	6,138	3,277	1,237	8,439	7,156	3,983	13,876	27,037	217,678
1986	4,335	7,032	3,704	1,294	9,165	7,693	4,296	15,204	29,285	231,153
1987	4,735	8,105	3,927	1,325	9,884	8,334	4,569	16,089	31,555	243,482
1988	5,374	8,957	4,309	1,351	10,564	9,266	4,929	18,679	34,573	261,726
1989	5,478	9,733	4,377	1,470	11,167	9,521	5,103	19,910	36,888	270,996
1990	5,131	9,759	4,383	1,479	11,381	9,672	5,383	20,517	38,980	273,720

Note: See note to table A.8.

Table A.11 *Public authorities' current expenditure (£m): 1920–1990*

	Education	National health service	Defence	Other	Total public consumption
1920	77	0	186	226	489
1921	83	0	166	239	488
1922	81	0	121	233	435
1923	78	0	104	212	395
1924	79	0	104	215	398
1925	81	0	111	220	412
1926	82	0	116	222	420
1927	83	0	114	226	423
1928	86	0	111	227	425
1929	90	0	110	235	435
1930	93	0	107	243	443
1931	92	0	106	245	443
1932	89	0	102	240	431
1933	89	0	102	239	430
1934	93	0	110	243	446
1935	99	0	130	254	483
1936	103	0	172	262	537
1937	106	0	242	269	618
1938	109	0	352	287	748
1939			1,181		
1940			2,923		
1941			4,089		
1942			4,580		
1943			4,971		
1944			5,045		
1945			4,205		
1946			2,345		
1947			1,810		
1948	228	190	769	644	1,831
1949	246	384	801	626	2,056
1950	244	428	814	657	2,144
1951	281	445	1,081	708	2,516
1952	307	455	1,448	781	2,992
1953	334	474	1,536	783	3,127
1954	370	488	1,535	812	3,204

Table A.11 (*cont.*)

	Education	National health service	Defence	Other	Total public consumption
1955	402	523	1,485	855	3,265
1956	459	572	1,561	930	3,522
1957	524	616	1,540	991	3,671
1958	560	647	1,476	1,058	3,740
1959	613	696	1,518	1,163	3,989
1960	666	759	1,587	1,215	4,227
1961	723	812	1,685	1,339	4,559
1962	849	829	1,797	1,410	4,885
1963	926	882	1,842	1,494	5,144
1964	993	954	1,920	1,602	5,469
1965	1,114	1,070	2,055	1,760	5,998
1966	1,244	1,170	2,142	1,968	6,525
1967	1,377	1,279	2,325	2,232	7,213
1968	1,500	1,383	2,359	2,420	7,663
1969	1,641	1,500	2,246	2,617	8,004
1970	1,856	1,734	2,412	3,021	9,024
1971	2,108	1,965	2,704	3,510	10,288
1972	2,476	2,264	2,989	4,011	11,739
1973	2,863	2,533	3,398	4,604	13,398
1974	3,560	3,596	4,009	5,540	16,706
1975	5,321	4,916	5,091	7,769	23,097
1976	5,868	5,853	6,132	9,158	27,011
1977	6,254	6,547	6,758	9,879	29,438
1978	7,081	7,541	7,496	11,248	33,366
1979	8,035	8,726	8,845	13,179	38,785
1980	9,859	11,276	11,314	16,439	48,888
1981	11,111	12,975	12,524	18,705	55,314
1982	11,921	13,562	14,273	20,543	60,299
1983	12,643	15,371	15,580	22,129	65,723
1984	13,054	16,142	16,837	23,656	69,689
1985	13,308	17,205	17,847	25,376	73,736
1986	14,938	18,440	18,594	27,335	79,307
1987	16,229	20,294	18,653	30,095	85,271
1988	17,709	22,355	19,270	32,311	91,645
1989	18,574	24,243	20,426	35,694	98,937
1990	19,868	26,578	22,117	40,824	109,386

Note: Before 1948 central government education expenditure and all health expenditure is included in 'other'.

Table A.12 *Public authorities' current expenditure (£m constant prices): 1920–1990*

	Education	National health service	Defence	Other	Total public consumption
			1920–1948 in 1938 prices		
1920	79	0	163	205	447
1921	81	0	149	221	451
1922	82	0	116	226	424
1923	79	0	101	219	399
1924	80	0	102	221	403
1925	82	0	111	223	416
1926	83	0	116	226	425
1927	84	0	114	232	430
1928	88	0	112	234	435
1929	91	0	110	243	444
1930	94	0	109	252	455
1931	97	0	111	258	465
1932	98	0	109	259	465
1933	99	0	113	259	472
1934	101	0	118	262	482
1935	104	0	139	272	515
1936	105	0	181	276	563
1937	107	0	244	276	627
1938	109	0	352	287	748
1939			1,135		
1940			2,619		
1941			3,308		
1942			3,474		
1943			3,582		
1944			3,352		
1945			2,739		
1946			1,495		
1947			1,056		
1948			1,015		
			1948–1990 in 1985 prices		
1948	4,220	3,944	16,586	12,593	37,344
1949	4,431	6,075	16,423	12,260	39,188

Table A.12 (*cont.*)

	Education	National health service	Defence	Other	Total public consumption
1950	4,547	6,700	16,113	11,750	39,111
1951	4,750	6,815	19,141	11,661	42,367
1952	4,682	6,408	23,230	11,213	45,533
1953	4,952	6,635	23,715	11,545	46,848
1954	5,200	6,794	22,990	11,872	46,856
1955	5,484	7,092	21,585	11,938	46,098
1956	5,906	7,263	20,718	11,777	45,664
1957	6,110	7,439	19,412	12,107	45,068
1958	6,314	7,584	17,629	12,406	43,933
1959	6,681	7,873	17,574	12,745	44,875
1960	6,863	8,163	17,898	13,097	46,021
1961	7,223	8,158	18,303	13,729	47,413
1962	7,325	8,294	19,054	14,088	48,760
1963	7,718	8,519	18,998	14,361	49,595
1964	8,059	8,824	18,839	14,754	50,477
1965	8,395	9,230	18,984	15,119	51,729
1966	8,793	9,678	18,549	16,026	53,045
1967	9,195	10,059	19,380	17,201	55,836
1968	9,619	10,412	18,442	17,660	56,133
1969	9,897	10,646	16,635	17,990	55,168
1970	10,374	11,169	15,698	18,821	56,062
1971	10,793	11,446	15,673	19,763	57,675
1972	11,604	11,878	15,633	21,008	60,123
1973	12,460	12,299	15,857	22,067	62,683
1974	13,017	13,456	15,379	21,710	63,561
1975	13,440	14,558	15,660	23,301	66,959
1976	13,524	14,965	15,708	23,560	67,756
1977	13,250	15,062	15,566	22,832	66,710
1978	13,776	15,621	15,471	23,644	68,512
1979	13,901	16,109	15,670	24,231	69,911
1980	13,630	16,227	16,751	24,118	70,727
1981	13,428	16,539	16,759	24,067	70,793
1982	13,468	16,446	17,148	24,451	71,513
1983	13,655	16,865	17,614	24,833	72,968

Table A.12 (*cont.*)

	Education	National health service	Defence	Other	Total public consumption
1984	13,489	17,046	18,031	25,225	73,791
1985	13,308	17,205	17,847	25,376	73,736
1986	13,494	17,433	17,861	26,222	75,011
1987	13,826	17,651	17,227	27,249	75,953
1988	14,005	17,995	16,846	27,595	76,441
1989	13,936	18,013	16,722	28,480	77,151
1990	13,938	18,356	17,028	30,052	79,374

Note: See note to table A.11.

Table A.13 *Gross fixed capital formation (£m): 1920–1990*

<table>
<tr><th></th><th>Vehicles, ships and aircraft</th><th>Plant and machinery</th><th>Dwellings</th><th>Other buildings and works</th><th>Transfer costs of land</th><th>Total</th></tr>
<tr><td>1920</td><td>109</td><td>131</td><td>62</td><td>180</td><td>n.a.</td><td>482</td></tr>
<tr><td>1921</td><td>91</td><td>135</td><td>104</td><td>128</td><td>n.a.</td><td>457</td></tr>
<tr><td>1922</td><td>132</td><td>80</td><td>75</td><td>94</td><td>n.a.</td><td>381</td></tr>
<tr><td>1923</td><td>83</td><td>83</td><td>64</td><td>104</td><td>n.a.</td><td>334</td></tr>
<tr><td>1924</td><td>80</td><td>89</td><td>94</td><td>111</td><td>n.a.</td><td>374</td></tr>
<tr><td>1925</td><td>75</td><td>102</td><td>119</td><td>124</td><td>n.a.</td><td>419</td></tr>
<tr><td>1926</td><td>58</td><td>93</td><td>144</td><td>106</td><td>n.a.</td><td>401</td></tr>
<tr><td>1927</td><td>59</td><td>108</td><td>156</td><td>103</td><td>n.a.</td><td>427</td></tr>
<tr><td>1928</td><td>79</td><td>122</td><td>117</td><td>102</td><td>n.a.</td><td>420</td></tr>
<tr><td>1929</td><td>74</td><td>117</td><td>133</td><td>118</td><td>n.a.</td><td>442</td></tr>
<tr><td>1930</td><td>65</td><td>110</td><td>122</td><td>138</td><td>n.a.</td><td>435</td></tr>
<tr><td>1931</td><td>48</td><td>124</td><td>122</td><td>114</td><td>n.a.</td><td>408</td></tr>
<tr><td>1932</td><td>32</td><td>108</td><td>118</td><td>89</td><td>n.a.</td><td>347</td></tr>
<tr><td>1933</td><td>30</td><td>91</td><td>152</td><td>85</td><td>n.a.</td><td>358</td></tr>
<tr><td>1934</td><td>41</td><td>119</td><td>170</td><td>97</td><td>n.a.</td><td>427</td></tr>
<tr><td>1935</td><td>56</td><td>126</td><td>165</td><td>109</td><td>n.a.</td><td>456</td></tr>
<tr><td>1936</td><td>76</td><td>143</td><td>171</td><td>128</td><td>n.a.</td><td>518</td></tr>
<tr><td>1937</td><td>78</td><td>166</td><td>168</td><td>162</td><td>n.a.</td><td>575</td></tr>
<tr><td>1938</td><td>79</td><td>184</td><td>168</td><td>160</td><td>n.a.</td><td>591</td></tr>
<tr><td>1939</td><td>70</td><td>190</td><td colspan="2">280</td><td>n.a.</td><td>540</td></tr>
<tr><td>1940</td><td>50</td><td>300</td><td colspan="2">170</td><td>n.a.</td><td>519</td></tr>
<tr><td>1941</td><td>70</td><td>270</td><td colspan="2">140</td><td>n.a.</td><td>480</td></tr>
<tr><td>1942</td><td>100</td><td>240</td><td colspan="2">110</td><td>n.a.</td><td>450</td></tr>
<tr><td>1943</td><td>100</td><td>180</td><td colspan="2">80</td><td>n.a.</td><td>360</td></tr>
<tr><td>1944</td><td>90</td><td>130</td><td colspan="2">80</td><td>n.a.</td><td>300</td></tr>
<tr><td>1945</td><td>90</td><td>120</td><td colspan="2">140</td><td>n.a.</td><td>350</td></tr>
<tr><td>1946</td><td>172</td><td>202</td><td colspan="2">555</td><td>n.a.</td><td>929</td></tr>
<tr><td>1947</td><td>231</td><td>361</td><td colspan="2">612</td><td>n.a.</td><td>1,203</td></tr>
<tr><td>1948</td><td>249</td><td>502</td><td>344</td><td>293</td><td>46</td><td>1,435</td></tr>
<tr><td>1949</td><td>273</td><td>565</td><td>340</td><td>367</td><td>49</td><td>1,594</td></tr>
<tr><td>1950</td><td>263</td><td>645</td><td>339</td><td>420</td><td>59</td><td>1,725</td></tr>
<tr><td>1951</td><td>256</td><td>752</td><td>386</td><td>458</td><td>70</td><td>1,923</td></tr>
<tr><td>1952</td><td>260</td><td>792</td><td>513</td><td>519</td><td>69</td><td>2,154</td></tr>
<tr><td>1953</td><td>308</td><td>827</td><td>658</td><td>557</td><td>72</td><td>2,421</td></tr>
<tr><td>1954</td><td>332</td><td>924</td><td>674</td><td>612</td><td>82</td><td>2,624</td></tr>
<tr><td>1955</td><td>369</td><td>1,050</td><td>667</td><td>731</td><td>94</td><td>2,912</td></tr>
</table>

Table A.13 (*cont.*)

	Vehicles, ships and aircraft	Plant and machinery	Dwellings	Other buildings and works	Transfer costs of land	Total
1956	426	1,150	661	851	99	3,187
1957	497	1,291	643	936	105	3,472
1958	529	1,333	616	1,003	115	3,596
1959	571	1,418	684	1,053	128	3,854
1960	637	1,535	762	1,166	140	4,240
1961	598	1,806	835	1,359	149	4,747
1962	516	1,820	925	1,492	151	4,904
1963	515	1,922	1,019	1,512	168	5,136
1964	621	2,220	1,283	1,806	190	6,121
1965	613	2,499	1,386	1,949	188	6,635
1966	563	2,770	1,489	2,050	191	7,063
1967	632	2,890	1,673	2,277	212	7,684
1968	800	3,041	1,903	2,495	235	8,473
1969	843	3,179	1,916	2,653	241	8,832
1970	968	3,678	1,870	2,946	274	9,736
1971	1,091	3,940	2,212	3,269	323	10,834
1972	1,321	4,038	2,567	3,558	453	11,937
1973	1,618	4,859	3,140	4,469	564	14,650
1974	1,779	5,623	3,764	5,653	493	17,311
1975	1,980	6,623	4,653	6,927	623	20,806
1976	2,268	8,130	5,391	7,542	711	24,043
1977	3,139	9,581	5,666	7,556	829	26,770
1978	3,987	11,288	6,291	8,089	1,099	30,754
1979	4,676	13,454	7,631	9,585	1,414	36,761
1980	4,558	14,857	8,652	11,742	1,558	41,366
1981	3,838	14,941	8,113	12,393	1,778	41,063
1982	4,281	16,232	8,906	13,348	1,935	44,702
1983	4,524	17,844	10,425	13,258	2,393	48,445
1984	5,667	20,295	11,723	14,662	2,675	55,022
1985	6,440	23,872	11,854	15,221	2,972	60,359
1986	6,221	24,669	13,618	16,507	3,465	64,481
1987	7,808	27,097	15,279	19,890	4,053	74,125
1988	8,850	31,490	18,869	24,410	5,460	89,079
1989	10,221	36,327	20,088	30,958	4,384	101,977
1990	9,908	37,101	18,457	35,676	4,180	105,322

Note: Between 1939 and 1947 dwellings are included with other buildings and works.

Table A.14 *Gross fixed capital formation (£m constant prices): 1920–1990*

	Vehicles, ships and aircraft	Plant and machinery	Dwellings	Other buildings and works	Transfer costs of land	Total
			1920–1948 in 1938 prices			
1920	63	76	37	108	n.a.	284
1921	48	111	76	91	n.a.	325
1922	60	87	68	85	n.a.	300
1923	53	95	61	99	n.a.	308
1924	68	100	87	104	n.a.	359
1925	67	115	109	119	n.a.	409
1926	50	107	137	103	n.a.	397
1927	66	122	150	104	n.a.	443
1928	82	136	117	103	n.a.	438
1929	79	127	133	122	n.a.	461
1930	62	131	124	146	n.a.	463
1931	44	158	130	122	n.a.	454
1932	26	138	131	101	n.a.	396
1933	22	121	173	94	n.a.	410
1934	46	149	193	110	n.a.	498
1935	59	154	184	121	n.a.	518
1936	82	164	184	136	n.a.	566
1937	81	166	172	166	n.a.	585
1938	80	184	168	160	n.a.	592
1939	60	180	290		n.a.	530
1940	40	260	160		n.a.	460
1941	50	200	120		n.a.	370
1942	60	170	90		n.a.	320
1943	60	100	60		n.a.	220
1944	60	70	40		n.a.	170
1945	50	70	70		n.a.	190
1946	90	130	260		n.a.	480
1947	110	180	270		n.a.	560
1948	110	220	270		n.a.	600
			1948–1990 in 1985 prices			
1948	2,384	5,009	4,440	3,183	551	15,566
1949	2,539	5,491	4,356	3,974	551	16,911

Table A.14 (*cont.*)

	Vehicles, ships and aircraft	Plant and machinery	Dwellings	Other buildings and works	Transfer costs of land	Total
1950	2,280	6,131	4,272	4,542	653	17,879
1951	2,077	6,682	4,243	4,433	748	18,183
1952	1,796	6,078	4,920	4,453	720	17,968
1953	2,086	6,107	6,358	4,700	775	20,026
1954	2,380	6,442	6,726	5,393	943	21,883
1955	2,686	7,130	6,397	6,117	1,097	23,427
1956	2,877	7,757	5,971	6,739	1,184	24,527
1957	3,273	8,041	5,937	7,395	1,293	25,939
1958	3,373	8,106	5,685	7,626	1,452	26,242
1959	3,670	8,457	6,461	8,202	1,620	28,410
1960	4,162	9,100	7,217	9,092	1,663	31,233
1961	3,898	10,350	7,760	10,387	1,687	34,081
1962	3,426	10,171	8,332	10,825	1,519	34,272
1963	3,500	10,683	8,420	10,493	1,661	34,756
1964	4,183	12,043	10,394	12,173	1,837	40,631
1965	4,163	12,898	11,138	12,812	1,727	42,738
1966	3,851	13,773	11,517	12,992	1,644	43,777
1967	4,182	14,189	12,905	14,316	1,746	47,338
1968	5,039	14,487	13,930	15,041	1,881	50,378
1969	5,059	14,563	13,519	15,410	1,811	50,362
1970	5,404	15,770	12,391	16,112	1,964	51,641
1971	5,507	15,282	13,397	16,117	2,016	52,319
1972	6,161	14,722	13,751	15,557	2,245	52,436
1973	6,946	16,620	13,583	16,316	2,216	55,680
1974	6,687	16,963	12,737	15,664	1,791	53,842
1975	5,810	16,162	13,030	15,544	2,160	52,708
1976	5,687	16,558	13,377	15,430	2,182	53,234
1977	6,465	16,906	12,740	14,365	2,274	52,749
1978	7,127	18,052	12,838	13,977	2,495	54,489
1979	7,485	19,562	13,299	13,681	2,293	56,321
1980	6,275	19,442	12,295	12,962	2,157	53,130
1981	4,883	18,094	10,204	12,433	2,286	47,901
1982	5,030	18,448	10,908	13,806	2,524	50,716
1983	5,170	19,299	12,220	13,826	2,768	53,283
1984	6,105	21,257	12,555	15,197	2,977	58,091
1985	6,440	23,872	11,854	15,221	2,972	60,359

Table A.14 (*cont.*)

	Vehicles, ships and aircraft	Plant and machinery	Dwellings	Other buildings and works	Transfer costs of land	Total
1986	5,768	24,229	12,897	15,818	3,067	61,780
1987	6,650	25,966	13,479	18,415	3,288	67,799
1988	7,134	29,823	15,127	21,077	3,598	76,760
1989	7,680	33,552	14,574	23,569	2,590	81,965
1990	7,006	32,732	12,466	25,460	2,341	80,005

Note: See note to table A.13.

Table A.15 *Exports and imports (£m constant prices): 1920–1990*

	Exports			Imports		
	Goods	Services	Total	Goods	Services	Total
			1920–1948 in 1938 prices			
1920	647	162	810	649	82	731
1921	490	152	643	551	94	645
1922	665	147	811	639	103	741
1923	725	164	890	693	102	794
1924	764	155	920	771	102	872
1925	776	138	914	796	100	896
1926	683	157	840	819	111	930
1927	765	181	946	837	108	945
1928	781	171	952	811	105	916
1929	803	181	984	846	116	962
1930	664	182	846	822	128	950
1931	506	177	682	835	150	985
1932	493	175	667	737	142	879
1933	505	173	678	735	143	878
1934	537	166	704	785	133	918
1935	625	169	794	822	141	963
1936	585	187	772	840	145	985
1937	596	214	811	887	135	1,022
1938	563	193	756	850	152	1,002
1939	500	202	702	792	293	1,086
1940	320	156	476	718	419	1,138
1941	273	137	409	689	284	973
1942	185	185	370	486	334	821
1943	133	275	408	432	382	815
1944	145	371	516	476	429	906
1945	236	186	422	354	491	845
1946	477	232	709	501	361	862
1947	507	203	710	598	266	865
1948	646	219	865	621	224	846
			1948–1990 in 1985 prices			
1948	16,363	4,764	21,127	15,966	6,337	22,303
1949	18,024	5,277	23,300	17,468	6,386	23,855

Table A.15 (*cont.*)

	Exports			Imports		
	Goods	Services	Total	Goods	Services	Total
1950	20,628	5,994	26,622	17,681	6,390	24,071
1951	20,807	5,794	26,601	20,010	6,031	26,041
1952	19,615	5,895	25,510	17,935	5,694	23,629
1953	19,430	7,170	26,601	19,370	6,204	25,574
1954	20,488	7,762	28,250	19,886	6,755	26,642
1955	22,353	8,002	30,355	22,179	7,501	29,680
1956	23,820	7,889	31,709	22,154	7,726	29,880
1957	24,251	8,374	32,624	23,225	7,533	30,757
1958	23,536	8,641	32,177	23,364	7,778	31,142
1959	24,236	8,971	33,207	25,296	8,018	33,314
1960	25,590	9,783	35,373	28,485	9,011	37,496
1961	26,239	10,073	36,312	27,991	9,153	37,145
1962	26,705	10,135	36,840	28,589	9,281	37,870
1963	28,479	10,156	38,635	30,228	9,336	39,564
1964	29,495	10,523	40,018	33,880	9,921	43,801
1965	31,088	10,593	41,681	33,944	10,205	44,150
1966	32,337	11,484	43,821	34,740	10,500	45,241
1967	31,764	12,121	43,885	37,712	10,589	48,301
1968	36,166	13,281	49,447	41,627	10,507	52,134
1969	39,839	14,660	54,499	42,116	11,833	53,949
1970	41,406	15,958	57,363	44,491	12,120	56,612
1971	43,763	17,348	61,111	46,568	13,147	59,715
1972	43,740	18,230	61,970	51,944	13,568	65,512
1973	49,586	19,648	69,234	59,376	13,912	73,288
1974	52,885	20,953	73,838	59,481	14,428	73,909
1975	50,712	21,014	71,726	54,312	14,674	68,986
1976	55,599	22,252	77,850	57,984	14,581	72,565
1977	60,478	23,314	83,792	59,158	14,374	73,532
1978	62,002	23,431	85,433	62,019	14,835	76,854
1979	64,963	24,031	88,994	67,982	16,171	84,153
1980	65,456	22,997	88,454	64,154	16,761	80,915
1981	64,650	22,889	87,538	61,506	17,038	78,544
1982	66,712	21,904	88,616	64,993	17,388	82,381
1983	68,185	22,139	90,324	70,878	16,972	87,850
1984	73,981	21,641	95,622	78,833	17,544	96,377
1985	77,989	24,207	102,196	81,335	17,530	98,865

Table A.15 (*cont.*)

	Exports			Imports		
	Goods	Services	Total	Goods	Services	Total
1986	81,246	25,738	106,983	87,336	18,345	105,681
1987	85,528	27,585	113,113	93,767	20,125	113,892
1988	87,069	26,150	113,219	105,976	21,915	127,891
1989	91,199	26,794	117,993	114,319	22,979	137,298
1990	97,276	26,463	123,739	115,659	23,348	139,007

Table A.16 *Value added by industry (i) (£m): 1920–1990*

	Agriculture			Mining and quarrying			Oil and gas extraction		
	Employment income	Operating surplus	Total	Employment income	Operating surplus	Total	Employment income	Operating surplus	Total
1920	129	275	404	314	50	364	n.a.	n.a.	n.a.
1921	123	254	377	203	23	225	n.a.	n.a.	n.a.
1922	89	156	245	170	20	191	n.a.	n.a.	n.a.
1923	78	101	178	192	30	223	n.a.	n.a.	n.a.
1924	81	96	177	200	26	226	n.a.	n.a.	n.a.
1925	86	136	222	176	15	191	n.a.	n.a.	n.a.
1926	87	110	197	98	18	116	n.a.	n.a.	n.a.
1927	85	81	167	156	4	160	n.a.	n.a.	n.a.
1928	86	86	172	134	0	135	n.a.	n.a.	n.a.
1929	86	104	189	141	17	157	n.a.	n.a.	n.a.
1930	82	149	232	133	16	150	n.a.	n.a.	n.a.
1931	79	95	174	122	14	136	n.a.	n.a.	n.a.
1932	77	84	161	113	9	122	n.a.	n.a.	n.a.
1933	75	84	159	109	10	119	n.a.	n.a.	n.a.
1934	75	107	182	114	13	127	n.a.	n.a.	n.a.
1935	75	95	170	114	16	130	n.a.	n.a.	n.a.
1936	76	87	164	126	21	147	n.a.	n.a.	n.a.
1937	77	73	150	140	27	168	n.a.	n.a.	n.a.
1938	77	133	210	142	29	171	n.a.	n.a.	n.a.
1939	n.a.	n.a.	n.a.	n.a.	n.a.	n.a.	n.a.	n.a.	n.a.

Table A.16 (*cont.*)

	Agriculture			Mining and quarrying			Oil and gas extraction		
	Employment income	Operating surplus	Total	Employment income	Operating surplus	Total	Employment income	Operating surplus	Total
1940	n.a.	n.a.	n.a.	n.a.	n.a.	n.a.	n.a.	n.a.	n.a.
1941	n.a.	n.a.	n.a.	n.a.	n.a.	n.a.	n.a.	n.a.	n.a.
1942	n.a.	n.a.	n.a.	n.a.	n.a.	n.a.	n.a.	n.a.	n.a.
1943	n.a.	n.a.	n.a.	n.a.	n.a.	n.a.	n.a.	n.a.	n.a.
1944	n.a.	n.a.	n.a.	n.a.	n.a.	n.a.	n.a.	n.a.	n.a.
1945	n.a.	n.a.	n.a.	n.a.	n.a.	n.a.	n.a.	n.a.	n.a.
1946	n.a.	n.a.	n.a.	n.a.	n.a.	n.a.	n.a.	n.a.	n.a.
1947	n.a.	n.a.	n.a.	n.a.	n.a.	n.a.	n.a.	n.a.	n.a.
1948	259	367	626	354	45	399	0	0	0
1949	269	418	687	368	61	429	0	0	0
1950	265	357	622	372	57	429	0	0	0
1951	276	336	612	406	44	450	0	0	0
1952	286	480	766	472	52	524	0	0	0
1953	298	516	814	487	79	567	0	0	0
1954	297	508	805	519	78	597	0	0	0
1955	304	488	792	546	69	615	0	0	0
1956	317	514	831	596	119	716	0	0	0
1957	327	548	875	644	105	749	0	0	0
1958	338	553	891	644	107	751	0	0	0
1959	340	558	898	609	106	715	0	0	0

Table A.16 (*cont.*)

	Agriculture			Mining and quarrying			Oil and gas extraction		
	Employment income	Operating surplus	Total	Employment income	Operating surplus	Total	Employment income	Operating surplus	Total
1960	342	564	906	589	121	710	0	0	0
1961	338	609	947	596	132	728	0	0	0
1962	341	661	1,002	614	157	771	0	0	0
1963	351	641	992	613	159	772	0	0	0
1964	354	709	1,063	618	159	777	0	0	0
1965	359	723	1,082	619	125	744	0	0	0
1966	367	790	1,157	615	126	741	0	0	0
1967	371	814	1,185	623	123	746	0	0	0
1968	373	837	1,210	602	135	737	0	0	0
1969	380	814	1,194	576	100	676	0	0	0
1970	385	856	1,241	544	−85	459	56	111	167
1971	436	971	1,407	597	345	942	66	106	172
1972	488	1,047	1,535	710	56	766	79	168	247
1973	565	1,394	1,959	740	94	834	89	90	179
1974	679	1,383	2,062	975	118	1,093	116	−112	4
1975	826	1,661	2,487	1,413	151	1,564	158	139	297
1976	961	2,224	3,185	1,535	152	1,687	193	787	980
1977	934	2,260	3,194	1,635	167	1,802	236	2,472	2,708
1978	1,017	2,415	3,431	1,974	113	2,087	281	3,241	3,522
1979	1,153	2,594	3,747	2,295	247	2,542	380	6,158	6,538

Table A.16 (*cont.*)

	Agriculture			Mining and quarrying			Oil and gas extraction		
	Employment income	Operating surplus	Total	Employment income	Operating surplus	Total	Employment income	Operating surplus	Total
1980	1,452	2,806	4,258	2,917	428	3,346	505	9,135	9,640
1981	1,564	3,289	4,853	3,108	573	3,681	595	12,002	12,597
1982	1,691	3,824	5,515	3,290	654	3,944	651	13,640	14,291
1983	1,828	3,514	5,342	3,162	894	4,055	726	16,316	17,042
1984	1,889	4,555	6,444	1,327	928	2,256	777	19,442	20,219
1985	2,023	3,689	5,711	2,766	1,004	3,770	851	19,795	20,646
1986	2,028	4,153	6,181	2,785	794	3,578	879	10,001	10,880
1987	2,042	4,243	6,286	2,549	589	3,138	893	10,383	11,276
1988	2,151	3,989	6,140	2,469	723	3,191	991	7,499	8,490
1989	2,269	4,688	6,957	2,491	455	2,945	1,141	6,969	8,110
1990	2,467	4,635	7,101	2,635	269	2,904	1,232	7,282	8,514

Note: See notes to table A.19.

Table A.17 *Value added by industry (ii) (£m): 1920–1990*

	Manufacturing			Construction			Utilities		
	Employment income	Operating surplus	Total	Employment income	Operating surplus	Total	Employment income	Operating surplus	Total
1920	1,372	537	1,909	199	38	238	46	39	85
1921	997	344	1,341	178	34	212	45	36	81
1922	864	362	1,225	129	34	163	41	40	80
1923	825	326	1,151	122	30	152	39	43	82
1924	846	364	1,210	128	32	161	39	43	82
1925	846	398	1,244	142	38	180	41	48	89
1926	814	359	1,173	147	36	183	43	44	87
1927	859	371	1,230	157	42	200	44	51	95
1928	852	364	1,217	155	40	195	45	52	97
1929	862	390	1,252	155	40	195	46	55	101
1930	788	389	1,177	158	37	196	47	61	108
1931	730	286	1,016	151	33	184	47	59	106
1932	717	269	986	137	33	170	47	61	107
1933	747	268	1,015	143	34	177	48	61	109
1934	785	329	1,114	156	36	192	49	60	109
1935	820	361	1,181	168	39	207	52	62	114
1936	882	397	1,278	181	45	226	55	64	119
1937	956	468	1,424	191	45	236	57	68	125
1938	966	512	1,477	195	48	243	60	72	132
1939	n.a.	n.a.	n.a.	n.a.	n.a.	n.a.	n.a.	n.a.	n.a.

Table A.17 (*cont.*)

	Manufacturing			Construction			Utilities		
	Employment income	Operating surplus	Total	Employment income	Operating surplus	Total	Employment income	Operating surplus	Total
1940	n.a.	n.a.	n.a.	n.a.	n.a.	n.a.	n.a.	n.a.	n.a.
1941	n.a.	n.a.	n.a.	n.a.	n.a.	n.a.	n.a.	n.a.	n.a.
1942	n.a.	n.a.	n.a.	n.a.	n.a.	n.a.	n.a.	n.a.	n.a.
1943	n.a.	n.a.	n.a.	n.a.	n.a.	n.a.	n.a.	n.a.	n.a.
1944	n.a.	n.a.	n.a.	n.a.	n.a.	n.a.	n.a.	n.a.	n.a.
1945	n.a.	n.a.	n.a.	n.a.	n.a.	n.a.	n.a.	n.a.	n.a.
1946	n.a.	n.a.	n.a.	n.a.	n.a.	n.a.	n.a.	n.a.	n.a.
1947	n.a.	n.a.	n.a.	n.a.	n.a.	n.a.	n.a.	n.a.	n.a.
1948	2,300	1,245	3,545	455	34	489	121	88	209
1949	2,459	1,353	3,812	485	81	566	133	95	228
1950	2,665	1,418	4,083	513	−47	466	146	100	246
1951	2,923	1,794	4,717	558	−140	418	160	100	260
1952	3,209	1,912	5,121	606	112	718	176	136	312
1953	3,496	2,026	5,522	661	201	862	188	156	345
1954	3,759	2,090	5,849	705	210	915	200	175	375
1955	4,179	2,186	6,365	768	172	940	220	283	503
1956	4,546	2,226	6,772	871	212	1,082	239	211	451
1957	4,834	2,425	7,259	894	213	1,107	252	228	480
1958	5,001	2,534	7,535	923	245	1,169	264	269	533
1959	5,268	2,658	7,927	970	271	1,242	276	306	582

Table A.17 (*cont.*)

	Manufacturing			Construction			Utilities		
	Employment income	Operating surplus	Total	Employment income	Operating surplus	Total	Employment income	Operating surplus	Total
1960	5,728	2,850	8,578	1,049	307	1,356	296	329	625
1961	6,178	2,748	8,926	1,147	335	1,481	320	366	686
1962	6,290	2,697	8,986	1,272	356	1,628	344	412	756
1963	6,461	2,957	9,418	1,296	414	1,710	373	479	852
1964	7,069	3,288	10,357	1,439	504	1,943	402	529	931
1965	7,687	3,404	11,091	1,535	560	2,095	438	584	1,022
1966	8,221	3,324	11,545	1,583	641	2,223	489	602	1,091
1967	8,352	3,462	11,813	1,603	755	2,357	502	659	1,161
1968	8,949	3,651	12,600	1,667	884	2,551	516	790	1,306
1969	9,686	3,654	13,340	1,697	1,025	2,722	531	843	1,374
1970	11,059	3,658	14,717	1,762	1,133	2,895	590	768	1,358
1971	11,994	3,769	15,763	1,896	1,306	3,202	655	888	1,543
1972	13,303	4,581	17,884	2,191	1,757	3,947	751	975	1,726
1973	15,404	5,407	20,811	2,677	2,191	4,868	836	1,096	1,932
1974	18,362	4,855	23,217	3,172	1,964	5,136	987	1,104	2,091
1975	23,348	4,758	28,106	4,127	2,205	6,333	1,400	1,412	2,812
1976	26,619	6,108	32,727	4,620	2,673	7,293	1,623	2,061	3,684
1977	29,454	9,201	38,656	4,951	2,933	7,884	1,778	2,381	4,160
1978	33,592	11,113	44,705	5,666	3,551	9,217	2,074	2,511	4,585
1979	39,086	10,772	49,858	6,571	4,119	10,690	2,496	2,380	4,875

Table A.17 (*cont.*)

	Manufacturing			Construction			Utilities		
	Employment income	Operating surplus	Total	Employment income	Operating surplus	Total	Employment income	Operating surplus	Total
1980	43,509	10,486	53,995	7,634	4,652	12,286	3,148	3,326	6,474
1981	44,901	10,416	55,317	7,837	5,214	13,051	3,590	3,808	7,398
1982	46,309	13,421	59,730	8,105	5,994	14,099	3,769	4,241	8,010
1983	47,063	14,998	62,061	8,673	7,013	15,686	3,805	5,247	9,052
1984	50,061	17,228	67,289	9,133	7,814	16,947	3,960	3,697	7,657
1985	53,383	19,796	73,178	9,428	8,348	17,776	4,162	4,532	8,694
1986	56,237	22,403	78,640	9,948	10,215	20,163	4,351	5,395	9,746
1987	59,420	24,594	84,014	10,908	12,724	23,632	4,487	6,024	10,511
1988	63,659	29,336	92,995	12,455	15,943	28,398	4,604	6,258	10,862
1989	69,316	31,226	100,542	14,361	17,908	32,269	5,005	6,407	11,412
1990	76,531	30,376	106,907	16,198	19,900	36,097	5,491	7,440	12,931

Note: See notes to table A.19.

Table A.18 *Value added by industry (iii) (£m): 1920–1990*

	Transport and communication			Distribution			Education and health		
	Employment income	Operating surplus	Total	Employment income	Operating surplus	Total	Employment income	Operating surplus	Total
1920	347	183	530	292	422	714	n.a.	n.a.	n.a.
1921	317	165	482	258	315	574	n.a.	n.a.	n.a.
1922	285	136	421	228	323	550	n.a.	n.a.	n.a.
1923	271	110	381	218	301	518	n.a.	n.a.	n.a.
1924	278	114	392	217	321	538	n.a.	n.a.	n.a.
1925	278	121	399	231	351	582	n.a.	n.a.	n.a.
1926	266	103	368	243	330	573	n.a.	n.a.	n.a.
1927	287	132	419	258	344	602	n.a.	n.a.	n.a.
1928	283	128	412	264	345	609	n.a.	n.a.	n.a.
1929	285	134	419	271	348	619	n.a.	n.a.	n.a.
1930	278	118	396	276	344	620	n.a.	n.a.	n.a.
1931	273	108	381	286	290	576	n.a.	n.a.	n.a.
1932	255	94	349	293	252	545	n.a.	n.a.	n.a.
1933	256	103	359	303	257	559	n.a.	n.a.	n.a.
1934	258	121	379	305	260	566	n.a.	n.a.	n.a.
1935	271	124	395	312	282	594	n.a.	n.a.	n.a.
1936	281	136	417	323	294	617	n.a.	n.a.	n.a.
1937	301	157	458	339	316	656	n.a.	n.a.	n.a.
1938	299	150	449	341	322	663	n.a.	n.a.	n.a.
1939	n.a.	n.a.	n.a.	n.a.	n.a.	n.a.	n.a.	n.a.	n.a.

Table A.18 (*cont.*)

	Transport and communication			Distribution			Education and health		
	Employment income	Operating surplus	Total	Employment income	Operating surplus	Total	Employment income	Operating surplus	Total
1940	n.a.	n.a.	n.a.	n.a.	n.a.	n.a.	n.a.	n.a.	n.a.
1941	n.a.	n.a.	n.a.	n.a.	n.a.	n.a.	n.a.	n.a.	n.a.
1942	n.a.	n.a.	n.a.	n.a.	n.a.	n.a.	n.a.	n.a.	n.a.
1943	n.a.	n.a.	n.a.	n.a.	n.a.	n.a.	n.a.	n.a.	n.a.
1944	n.a.	n.a.	n.a.	n.a.	n.a.	n.a.	n.a.	n.a.	n.a.
1945	n.a.	n.a.	n.a.	n.a.	n.a.	n.a.	n.a.	n.a.	n.a.
1946	n.a.	n.a.	n.a.	n.a.	n.a.	n.a.	n.a.	n.a.	n.a.
1947	n.a.	n.a.	n.a.	n.a.	n.a.	n.a.	n.a.	n.a.	n.a.
1948	629	257	886	815	889	1,704	350	27	377
1949	661	268	929	882	919	1,801	422	30	452
1950	684	302	986	910	970	1,880	455	35	490
1951	760	393	1,153	1,022	991	2,013	515	41	556
1952	820	399	1,219	1,071	912	1,983	553	48	601
1953	853	364	1,217	1,165	1,038	2,203	583	53	636
1954	924	372	1,296	1,250	1,112	2,362	641	58	699
1955	1,008	417	1,425	1,353	1,151	2,505	697	64	761
1956	1,109	470	1,579	1,509	1,220	2,730	768	72	840
1957	1,190	479	1,669	1,656	1,250	2,907	844	78	922
1958	1,205	413	1,619	1,794	1,285	3,079	898	86	984
1959	1,246	461	1,708	1,923	1,330	3,253	978	90	1,068

Table A.18 (*cont.*)

	Transport and communication			Distribution			Education and health		
	Employment income	Operating surplus	Total	Employment income	Operating surplus	Total	Employment income	Operating surplus	Total
1960	1,353	620	1,972	1,978	1,402	3,380	1,072	95	1,167
1961	1,445	603	2,048	2,142	1,411	3,553	1,173	104	1,277
1962	1,507	628	2,135	2,297	1,458	3,755	1,298	113	1,411
1963	1,600	707	2,307	2,433	1,575	4,007	1,420	120	1,540
1964	1,710	756	2,466	2,565	1,669	4,234	1,535	129	1,664
1965	1,857	794	2,651	2,727	1,884	4,611	1,704	157	1,861
1966	1,959	850	2,809	2,966	1,869	4,836	1,874	218	2,092
1967	2,023	848	2,871	3,043	1,947	4,990	2,034	279	2,313
1968	2,174	1,002	3,176	3,211	1,931	5,142	2,216	348	2,564
1969	2,267	1,096	3,363	3,288	2,022	5,309	2,471	429	2,901
1970	2,586	1,097	3,683	3,788	2,177	5,965	2,757	517	3,273
1971	2,792	1,135	3,927	4,121	2,797	6,919	3,235	601	3,836
1972	3,084	1,253	4,337	4,647	3,101	7,748	3,912	680	4,592
1973	3,513	1,485	4,998	5,454	3,389	8,844	4,437	813	5,250
1974	4,290	1,772	6,062	6,538	3,737	10,275	5,564	983	6,547
1975	5,683	2,209	7,892	8,380	4,082	12,463	7,906	1,248	9,154
1976	6,374	3,139	9,513	9,890	4,576	14,466	9,020	1,481	10,501
1977	6,789	3,477	10,266	11,139	5,847	16,985	9,614	1,592	11,206
1978	7,780	4,190	11,969	12,765	7,433	20,198	10,609	1,776	12,385
1979	9,347	4,092	13,439	15,268	7,790	23,058	12,070	2,079	14,149

Table A.18 (*cont.*)

	Transport and communication			Distribution			Education and health		
	Employment income	Operating surplus	Total	Employment income	Operating surplus	Total	Employment income	Operating surplus	Total
1980	10,634	3,978	14,611	18,207	7,747	25,954	15,367	2,656	18,024
1981	11,493	4,724	16,217	20,175	7,337	27,512	17,751	2,868	20,619
1982	11,958	5,542	17,500	21,462	8,886	30,349	18,301	2,996	21,297
1983	12,737	5,786	18,523	23,093	10,211	33,304	19,952	3,383	23,335
1984	13,749	6,421	20,170	25,048	11,373	36,420	21,109	3,539	24,648
1985	14,355	7,355	21,710	26,845	13,737	40,582	22,616	3,949	26,565
1986	15,011	8,474	23,485	28,903	16,350	45,253	25,735	4,297	30,032
1987	15,947	9,795	25,742	31,228	18,116	49,344	28,505	4,626	33,132
1988	17,498	11,146	28,643	36,300	20,865	57,165	32,239	4,927	37,166
1989	19,315	11,911	31,226	40,933	22,324	63,257	35,478	5,612	41,090
1990	22,005	12,033	34,038	46,104	24,062	70,167	39,125	6,016	45,141

Note: See note to table A.19.

Table A.19 *Value added by industry (iv) (£m): 1920–1990*

	Financial services					Ownership	Public administration and defence		
	Employment income	Operating profit	Rent	Adjustment	Total	of dwellings, Rent	Employment income	Imputed income	Total
1920	139	−7	55	174	361	142	324	n.a.	324
1921	122	−36	61	166	313	165	266	n.a.	266
1922	109	−9	69	136	305	175	226	n.a.	226
1923	111	−8	63	137	303	177	202	n.a.	202
1924	115	−6	71	142	322	180	200	n.a.	200
1925	119	−13	79	155	340	184	204	n.a.	204
1926	123	−10	83	160	357	190	204	n.a.	204
1927	125	−2	90	158	371	196	205	n.a.	205
1928	126	−1	103	174	402	203	204	n.a.	204
1929	127	−16	112	201	425	211	208	n.a.	208
1930	127	−33	120	165	379	220	213	n.a.	213
1931	124	−28	126	153	375	226	213	n.a.	213
1932	124	−19	133	151	389	233	209	n.a.	209
1933	128	−13	130	146	391	237	206	n.a.	206
1934	133	−19	130	157	401	242	212	n.a.	212
1935	135	−17	140	167	425	249	222	n.a.	222
1936	138	−18	143	180	443	256	232	n.a.	232
1937	143	−28	159	190	464	264	246	n.a.	246
1938	143	−33	159	190	459	272	269	n.a.	269
1939	n.a.	n.a.	n.a.	n.a.	n.a.	n.a.	n.a.	n.a.	n.a.

Table A.19 (*cont.*)

	Financial services					Ownership of dwellings,	Public administration and defence		
	Employment income	Operating profit	Rent	Adjustment	Total	Rent	Employment income	Imputed income	Total
1940	n.a.	n.a.	n.a.	n.a.	n.a.	n.a.	n.a.	n.a.	n.a.
1941	n.a.	n.a.	n.a.	n.a.	n.a.	n.a.	n.a.	n.a.	n.a.
1942	n.a.	n.a.	n.a.	n.a.	n.a.	n.a.	n.a.	n.a.	n.a.
1943	n.a.	n.a.	n.a.	n.a.	n.a.	n.a.	n.a.	n.a.	n.a.
1944	n.a.	n.a.	n.a.	n.a.	n.a.	n.a.	n.a.	n.a.	n.a.
1945	n.a.	n.a.	n.a.	n.a.	n.a.	n.a.	n.a.	n.a.	n.a.
1946	n.a.	n.a.	n.a.	n.a.	n.a.	n.a.	n.a.	n.a.	n.a.
1947	n.a.	n.a.	n.a.	n.a.	n.a.	n.a.	n.a.	n.a.	n.a.
1948	361	78	35	259	733	296	648	29	677
1949	387	78	36	270	771	297	660	30	690
1950	415	91	38	286	830	367	685	32	717
1951	457	114	39	326	936	367	790	37	827
1952	494	99	41	359	994	406	885	41	926
1953	528	96	52	387	1,063	462	919	42	961
1954	548	156	48	428	1,180	517	951	43	994
1955	595	163	36	503	1,297	557	969	43	1,012
1956	647	153	38	587	1,425	593	1,072	49	1,121
1957	698	167	32	662	1,559	636	1,108	51	1,159
1958	754	169	46	683	1,652	763	1,166	53	1,219
1959	824	181	63	698	1,766	833	1,205	55	1,260

Table A.19 (*cont.*)

	Financial services					Ownership of dwellings,	Public administration and defence		
	Employment income	Operating profit	Rent	Adjustment	Total	Rent	Employment income	Imputed income	Total
1960	926	217	49	817	2,010	902	1,262	57	1,319
1961	1,015	260	60	883	2,218	967	1,316	60	1,376
1962	1,118	181	175	693	2,167	1,052	1,381	63	1,444
1963	1,236	174	178	722	2,311	1,123	1,527	67	1,594
1964	1,357	121	166	831	2,475	1,247	1,590	73	1,663
1965	1,508	151	166	942	2,767	1,411	1,709	78	1,787
1966	1,588	106	197	970	2,861	1,535	1,870	85	1,955
1967	1,724	154	223	1,024	3,125	1,672	2,004	91	2,095
1968	1,915	190	240	1,143	3,488	1,849	2,132	95	2,227
1969	2,117	218	317	1,210	3,862	2,080	2,404	103	2,507
1970	2,327	249	407	1,299	4,283	2,368	2,834	123	2,957
1971	2,633	582	462	1,507	5,184	2,627	3,338	144	3,482
1972	2,975	573	532	1,918	5,998	3,011	3,799	166	3,965
1973	3,483	730	623	2,740	7,575	3,525	4,276	167	4,443
1974	4,055	141	810	3,519	8,525	4,556	5,277	214	5,491
1975	5,288	654	912	3,451	10,304	5,589	6,957	284	7,241
1976	6,013	703	1,040	4,742	12,499	6,735	8,114	343	8,457
1977	6,878	1,238	1,198	5,172	14,486	7,516	8,568	396	8,964
1978	8,180	778	1,443	5,232	15,634	8,598	9,494	463	9,957
1979	9,776	1,314	1,648	6,436	19,174	10,306	10,906	556	11,462

Table A.19 (*cont.*)

	Financial services					Ownership of dwellings,	Public administration and defence		
	Employment income	Operating profit	Rent	Adjustment	Total	Rent	Employment income	Imputed income	Total
1980	12,639	49	2,098	8,464	23,250	12,147	13,866	679	14,545
1981	14,494	−1,638	2,477	9,705	25,037	13,895	15,522	763	16,285
1982	16,651	−1,718	2,659	11,147	28,740	15,044	16,610	805	17,415
1983	19,089	718	2,911	11,893	34,611	15,945	18,016	854	18,870
1984	21,644	−663	3,040	13,671	37,693	16,769	19,306	900	20,206
1985	24,554	1,568	3,623	15,010	44,755	18,175	20,471	985	21,456
1986	27,918	2,659	4,325	17,131	52,033	19,501	21,974	1,087	23,061
1987	31,900	5,145	4,752	17,533	59,330	21,013	23,778	1,199	24,977
1988	36,893	4,403	6,030	19,643	66,969	23,255	25,705	1,347	27,052
1989	43,491	4,711	6,930	25,369	80,500	25,154	27,134	1,482	28,616
1990	49,941	2,877	7,720	26,706	87,244	30,719	29,885	1,634	31,519

Note: The profit of the financial services industry is net of the adjustment for interest flows. The latter is shown in the table but does not enter into aggregate value added. Before 1938, the imputed income from consumption of non-trading capital is included in rent earned by the financial services industry. After 1948 it is shown as part of the operating surplus of the industry concerned (see tables A.16–A.20). In the case of public administration and defence, no profit is earned; the whole of the surplus is imputed income.

Table A.20 *Value added by industry (v) (£m): 1920–1990*

	Other services			All industries		
	Employment income	Operating surplus	Total	Employment income	Operating surplus	Total
1920	439	218	657	3,603	1,951	5,554
1921	423	170	593	2,931	1,530	4,462
1922	362	171	533	2,502	1,477	3,980
1923	347	184	531	2,404	1,358	3,762
1924	356	197	553	2,461	1,438	3,899
1925	363	196	559	2,486	1,554	4,040
1926	372	203	575	2,397	1,466	3,862
1927	380	214	593	2,556	1,524	4,080
1928	377	217	594	2,527	1,539	4,066
1929	380	219	599	2,562	1,614	4,175
1930	382	212	594	2,486	1,632	4,118
1931	384	203	587	2,409	1,411	3,820
1932	385	192	576	2,356	1,340	3,695
1933	394	195	589	2,410	1,365	3,775
1934	403	201	604	2,491	1,480	3,971
1935	422	213	635	2,592	1,565	4,157
1936	441	227	668	2,736	1,652	4,388
1937	471	234	705	2,923	1,784	4,706
1938	482	228	710	2,976	1,891	4,867
1939	n.a.	n.a.	n.a.	3,294	1,930	5,225
1940	n.a.	n.a.	n.a.	4,167	2,143	6,310
1941	n.a.	n.a.	n.a.	4,848	2,671	7,519
1942	n.a.	n.a.	n.a.	5,303	2,938	8,241
1943	n.a.	n.a.	n.a.	5,704	3,076	8,780
1944	n.a.	n.a.	n.a.	5,875	3,001	8,876
1945	n.a.	n.a.	n.a.	5,798	2,869	8,667
1946	n.a.	n.a.	n.a.	5,625	3,075	8,700
1947	n.a.	n.a.	n.a.	6,150	3,188	9,338
1948	498	267	765	6,790	3,657	10,447
1949	510	256	766	7,236	3,922	11,158
1950	525	250	775	7,637	3,971	11,608
1951	648	237	885	8,515	4,354	12,869
1952	542	233	775	9,114	4,872	13,986
1953	514	232	745	9,692	5,318	15,010
1954	527	214	741	10,321	5,582	15,903

Table A.20 (*cont.*)

	Other services			All industries		
	Employment income	Operating surplus	Total	Employment income	Operating surplus	Total
1955	626	205	831	11,266	5,833	17,099
1956	648	203	851	12,322	6,082	18,403
1957	600	227	828	13,047	6,440	19,487
1958	575	242	816	13,562	6,766	20,328
1959	563	312	874	14,203	7,225	21,428
1960	569	318	887	15,164	7,831	22,995
1961	753	317	1,070	16,422	7,972	24,393
1962	868	264	1,131	17,329	8,215	25,544
1963	906	330	1,235	18,215	8,924	27,138
1964	1,142	335	1,477	19,781	9,685	29,467
1965	1,175	258	1,433	21,317	10,296	31,613
1966	1,359	255	1,614	22,891	10,598	33,490
1967	1,614	283	1,898	23,893	11,311	35,204
1968	1,783	345	2,127	25,538	12,295	37,833
1969	1,753	385	2,138	27,170	13,086	40,256
1970	1,828	424	2,252	30,516	13,803	44,319
1971	1,876	508	2,384	33,640	16,240	49,880
1972	2,014	563	2,577	37,953	18,463	56,416
1973	2,459	656	3,116	43,934	21,661	65,595
1974	3,040	861	3,902	53,055	22,386	75,441
1975	3,876	1,126	5,002	69,362	26,431	95,793
1976	4,360	1,472	5,832	79,324	33,495	112,819
1977	5,078	1,822	6,900	87,053	42,500	129,553
1978	5,881	2,209	8,090	99,312	49,835	149,146
1979	6,972	2,302	9,274	116,320	56,356	172,676
1980	8,208	2,520	10,728	138,087	62,706	200,793
1981	9,127	2,944	12,071	150,157	68,671	218,828
1982	10,260	3,097	13,358	159,059	79,086	238,145
1983	11,653	3,520	15,173	169,796	91,310	261,106
1984	12,944	3,815	16,759	180,947	98,858	279,804
1985	14,115	4,431	18,546	195,569	110,987	306,556
1986	15,719	4,992	20,711	211,488	114,645	326,134
1987	17,479	5,811	23,291	229,138	129,016	358,153
1988	20,037	6,459	26,496	255,000	142,180	397,180
1989	22,297	6,905	29,202	283,231	152,682	435,912
1990	24,680	6,283	30,963	316,294	161,246	477,540

Note: See note to table A.19.

Table A.21 *Manufacturing output (i) (£m constant prices): 1920–1990*

	Metal manu-facture	Other mineral products	Chemicals and fibres	Mechanical engineering	Electrical and instrumental engineering	Motor vehicles	Other transport equipment
				1920–1948 in 1938 prices			
1920	123	42	72	74	53	48	36
1921	69	42	52	49	46	43	29
1922	89	37	63	61	38	50	21
1923	114	41	68	75	48	59	17
1924	123	50	73	79	57	69	24
1925	122	57	70	90	64	75	17
1926	104	58	65	79	60	79	13
1927	136	64	74	87	65	87	25
1928	133	59	77	92	67	85	22
1929	140	63	81	95	69	92	26
1930	130	60	77	84	69	88	23
1931	109	57	74	69	66	75	9
1932	111	55	79	61	71	74	3
1933	124	63	83	63	72	83	3
1934	149	72	89	73	86	96	11
1935	164	78	97	86	100	114	14
1936	184	85	101	94	111	137	21
1937	203	88	107	100	120	152	28
1938	185	83	102	102	119	155	23
1939	n.a.	n.a.	n.a.	n.a.	n.a.	n.a.	n.a.

Table A.21 (*cont.*)

	Metal manu-facture	Other mineral products	Chemicals and fibres	Mechanical engineering	Electrical and instrumental engineering	Motor vehicles	Other transport equipment
1940	n.a.	n.a.	n.a.	n.a.	n.a.	n.a.	n.a.
1941	n.a.	n.a.	n.a.	n.a.	n.a.	n.a.	n.a.
1942	n.a.	n.a.	n.a.	n.a.	n.a.	n.a.	n.a.
1943	n.a.	n.a.	n.a.	n.a.	n.a.	n.a.	n.a.
1944	n.a.	n.a.	n.a.	n.a.	n.a.	n.a.	n.a.
1945	n.a.	n.a.	n.a.	n.a.	n.a.	n.a.	n.a.
1946	231	86	161	330		179	
1947	246	98	160	361		183	
1948	264	108	175	390		200	
			1948–1990 in 1985 prices				
1948	4,996	1,651	897	4,047	1,512	1,205	4,319
1949	5,068	1,753	948	4,530	1,683	1,439	4,268
1950	5,313	1,858	1,005	5,007	1,922	1,725	4,463
1951	5,708	1,984	1,068	5,430	2,046	1,738	4,552
1952	5,788	1,945	1,134	5,429	2,040	1,769	4,085
1953	5,715	2,047	1,201	5,483	2,213	2,042	4,234
1954	5,976	2,045	1,273	5,705	2,393	2,282	4,851

Table A.21 (*cont.*)

	Metal manu-facture	Other mineral products	Chemicals and fibres	Mechanical engineering	Electrical and instrumental engineering	Motor vehicles	Other transport equipment
1955	6,658	2,152	1,350	6,104	2,658	2,675	5,044
1956	6,716	2,156	1,432	6,248	2,677	2,361	5,018
1957	6,800	2,102	1,517	6,500	2,866	2,598	5,009
1958	6,410	2,061	1,607	6,203	3,034	2,896	4,915
1959	6,581	2,233	1,700	6,378	3,371	3,432	4,848
1960	7,592	2,483	1,802	7,016	3,611	4,104	4,724
1961	7,283	2,635	1,913	7,695	3,805	3,735	4,422
1962	6,994	2,666	2,028	7,657	3,987	3,971	4,270
1963	7,329	2,773	2,154	7,732	4,250	4,662	4,019
1964	8,474	3,245	2,279	8,501	4,649	5,244	3,808
1965	8,793	3,280	2,416	8,956	4,634	5,256	4,035
1966	8,339	3,293	2,560	9,546	5,038	5,210	4,027
1967	8,009	3,444	2,719	9,702	5,384	4,974	3,999
1968	8,829	3,741	2,884	10,346	5,868	5,630	4,062
1969	9,207	3,879	3,059	10,991	6,395	5,996	4,067
1970	9,091	3,809	3,242	11,342	6,658	6,057	3,770
1971	8,367	4,088	3,441	10,857	6,702	5,941	4,041
1972	8,416	4,331	3,633	10,245	6,962	6,058	3,947
1973	9,250	4,820	3,872	11,485	8,018	6,399	4,162
1974	8,709	4,592	4,117	12,316	8,412	5,920	4,290

Table A.21 (*cont.*)

	Metal manu-facture	Other mineral products	Chemicals and fibres	Mechanical engineering	Electrical and instrumental engineering	Motor vehicles	Other transport equipment
1975	7,731	4,244	4,387	12,240	8,008	5,397	4,126
1976	8,119	4,270	4,681	11,949	7,986	5,489	3,975
1977	8,109	4,225	4,930	11,725	8,271	5,896	3,784
1978	7,760	4,285	5,186	11,135	8,506	5,498	3,923
1979	7,862	4,240	5,489	10,692	8,438	5,327	3,779
1980	6,222	3,829	5,852	9,913	8,326	4,625	4,113
1981	6,235	3,397	6,208	8,822	7,785	3,823	4,245
1982	6,111	3,471	6,545	8,907	8,121	3,693	4,130
1983	6,238	3,590	6,945	8,572	8,987	3,876	3,893
1984	6,382	3,712	7,264	8,623	9,857	3,787	3,722
1985	6,569	3,699	7,723	9,023	10,508	4,054	3,775
1986	6,568	3,748	8,202	8,724	10,595	3,930	4,230
1987	6,994	3,949	8,679	8,735	11,168	4,209	4,251
1988	7,724	4,331	9,167	9,464	12,322	4,815	4,058
1989	7,857	4,431	9,702	9,839	13,158	5,059	4,800
1990	7,644	4,181	10,250	10,001	13,006	4,880	4,882

Note: From 1946 to 1948 the mechanical engineering data include electrical and instrumental engineering. The motor vehicles data include other transport equipment.

Table A.22 *Manufacturing output (ii) (£m constant prices): 1920–1990*

	Food	Drink and tobacco	Textiles	Clothing and footwear	Paper and printing	Other manufacturing	Total all manufacturing
			1920–1948 in 1938 prices				
1920	180		126	62	83	31	928
1921	169		85	65	50	29	727
1922	172		124	74	80	35	843
1923	177		103	74	88	39	904
1924	183		120	79	94	44	995
1925	188		119	81	97	47	1,027
1926	189		115	82	100	49	994
1927	194		120	87	104	55	1,098
1928	199		113	88	104	56	1,097
1929	205		114	87	109	62	1,143
1930	206		100	88	110	62	1,096
1931	200		105	87	109	57	1,018
1932	201		114	88	115	52	1,024
1933	208		125	93	119	61	1,097
1934	219		128	93	121	64	1,202
1935	233		133	96	124	70	1,308
1936	243		145	101	131	78	1,429
1937	256		146	102	134	80	1,515
1938	265		133	99	133	77	1,477
1939	n.a.		n.a.	n.a.	n.a.	n.a.	n.a.

Table A.22 (*cont.*)

	Food	Drink and tobacco	Textiles	Clothing and footwear	Paper and printing	Other manufacturing	Total all manufacturing
1940	n.a.		n.a.	n.a.	n.a.	n.a.	n.a.
1941	n.a.		n.a.	n.a.	n.a.	n.a.	n.a.
1942	n.a.		n.a.	n.a.	n.a.	n.a.	n.a.
1943	n.a.		n.a.	n.a.	n.a.	n.a.	n.a.
1944	n.a.		n.a.	n.a.	n.a.	n.a.	n.a.
1945	n.a.		n.a.	n.a.	n.a.	n.a.	n.a.
1946	325		112	69	132	109	1,735
1947	313		120	75	138	97	1,792
1948	324		139	84	144	92	1,920
	1948–1990 in 1985 prices						
1948	3,156	1,027	1,961	1,731	2,771	1,781	31,054
1949	3,384	1,053	2,154	1,891	3,211	1,946	33,328
1950	3,579	1,028	2,353	1,990	3,647	2,147	36,037
1951	3,493	1,043	2,375	1,924	3,820	2,275	37,457
1952	3,667	1,029	1,929	1,819	3,144	2,064	35,842
1953	4,107	1,067	2,364	2,038	3,643	2,315	38,468
1954	4,010	1,074	2,415	2,013	4,172	2,591	40,800

Table A.22 (*cont.*)

	Food	Drink and tobacco	Textiles	Clothing and footwear	Paper and printing	Other manufacturing	Total all manufacturing
1955	4,100	1,144	2,382	2,062	4,558	2,791	43,678
1956	4,280	1,173	2,388	2,075	4,557	2,708	43,789
1957	4,303	1,233	2,405	2,046	4,683	2,857	44,920
1958	4,451	1,245	2,164	1,915	4,827	2,795	44,524
1959	4,577	1,346	2,311	2,107	5,102	3,179	47,165
1960	4,719	1,418	2,441	2,231	5,647	3,506	51,295
1961	4,900	1,483	2,377	2,256	5,614	3,592	51,710
1962	5,057	1,479	2,338	2,154	5,612	3,650	51,862
1963	5,162	1,576	2,471	2,167	5,829	3,885	54,008
1964	5,201	1,706	2,644	2,307	6,422	4,537	59,017
1965	5,283	1,752	2,713	2,384	6,534	4,695	60,729
1966	5,445	1,827	2,718	2,391	6,738	4,773	61,904
1967	5,537	1,891	2,676	2,308	6,763	4,994	62,402
1968	5,845	1,999	3,128	2,471	7,155	5,490	67,448
1969	6,016	2,110	3,247	2,441	7,486	5,482	70,378
1970	6,101	2,194	3,221	2,425	7,534	5,534	70,978
1971	6,130	2,257	3,215	2,590	7,263	5,678	70,569
1972	6,384	2,348	3,267	2,640	7,594	6,029	71,854
1973	6,568	2,585	3,434	2,802	8,322	7,045	78,761
1974	6,473	2,643	3,151	2,746	8,339	6,473	78,182

Table A.22 (*cont.*)

	Food	Drink and tobacco	Textiles	Clothing and footwear	Paper and printing	Other manufacturing	Total all manufacturing
1975	6,241	2,651	2,910	2,756	7,246	6,112	74,049
1976	6,477	2,738	3,014	2,700	7,532	6,631	75,561
1977	6,601	2,724	3,032	2,843	7,822	6,670	76,632
1978	6,558	2,862	2,895	2,848	7,858	6,719	76,032
1979	6,638	2,915	2,769	2,886	8,135	6,719	75,888
1980	6,642	2,888	2,294	2,509	7,549	5,841	70,604
1981	6,563	2,777	2,099	2,340	7,144	5,301	66,742
1982	6,790	2,710	2,052	2,323	6,893	5,216	66,962
1983	6,876	2,739	2,100	2,440	6,946	5,552	68,753
1984	6,902	2,756	2,163	2,542	7,233	5,797	70,741
1985	6,948	2,685	2,254	2,656	7,417	5,866	73,177
1986	7,046	2,675	2,258	2,683	7,735	6,169	74,564
1987	7,172	2,773	2,357	2,735	8,481	6,786	78,287
1988	7,286	2,777	2,290	2,708	9,255	7,505	83,702
1989	7,276	2,862	2,179	2,636	9,742	7,728	87,271
1990	7,275	2,907	2,069	2,612	9,857	7,695	87,259

Note: The food data include drink and tobacco for 1920–48.

Table A.23 *Industrial output* (*i*) (*£m constant prices*): *1920–1990*

	Agriculture	Mining and quarrying	Oil and gas extraction	Manufact-uring	Construction	Utilities	Transport and communication
				1920–1948 in 1938 prices			
1920	165	162	n.a.	928	94	55	303
1921	182	116	n.a.	727	130	51	282
1922	177	173	n.a.	843	107	52	327
1923	181	193	n.a.	904	89	56	358
1924	171	189	n.a.	995	142	61	366
1925	192	174	n.a.	1,027	181	64	375
1926	192	97	n.a.	994	210	67	353
1927	188	181	n.a.	1,098	231	72	385
1928	207	172	n.a.	1,097	186	75	397
1929	206	187	n.a.	1,143	201	80	417
1930	217	178	n.a.	1,096	186	81	418
1931	186	160	n.a.	1,018	175	84	388
1932	206	152	n.a.	1,024	166	86	377
1933	208	152	n.a.	1,097	192	91	377
1934	222	164	n.a.	1,202	217	100	393
1935	212	165	n.a.	1,308	222	106	400
1936	208	171	n.a.	1,429	243	117	416
1937	200	180	n.a.	1,515	253	127	431
1938	210	171	n.a.	1,477	243	132	449
1939	n.a.	n.a.	n.a.	n.a.	n.a.	n.a.	n.a.

Table A.23 (*cont.*)

	Agriculture	Mining and quarrying	Oil and gas extraction	Manufact-uring	Construct-ion	Utilities	Transport and communication
1940	n.a.	n.a.	n.a.	n.a.	n.a.	n.a.	n.a.
1941	n.a.	n.a.	n.a.	n.a.	n.a.	n.a.	n.a.
1942	n.a.	n.a.	n.a.	n.a.	n.a.	n.a.	n.a.
1943	n.a.	n.a.	n.a.	n.a.	n.a.	n.a.	n.a.
1944	n.a.	n.a.	n.a.	n.a.	n.a.	n.a.	n.a.
1945	n.a.	n.a.	n.a.	n.a.	n.a.	n.a.	n.a.
1946	248	134	n.a.	1,735	191	177	580
1947	232	137	n.a.	1,792	197	184	595
1948	249	145	n.a.	1,920	215	209	635
1948–1990 in 1985 prices							
1948	1,962	10,524	0	31,054	8,763	1,739	7,417
1949	2,117	10,947	0	33,328	9,239	1,875	7,864
1950	2,171	11,151	0	36,037	9,334	2,065	8,201
1951	2,232	11,503	0	37,457	9,017	2,206	8,605
1952	2,279	11,586	0	35,842	9,269	2,259	8,841
1953	2,337	11,655	0	38,468	9,993	2,388	9,177
1954	2,379	11,856	0	40,800	10,524	2,609	9,445

Table A.23 (*cont.*)

	Agriculture	Mining and quarrying	Oil and gas extraction	Manufact-uring	Construct-ion	Utilities	Transport and communication
1955	2,381	11,680	0	43,678	10,643	2,768	9,763
1956	2,517	11,748	0	43,789	11,265	2,899	9,961
1957	2,584	11,758	0	44,920	11,303	3,029	9,990
1958	2,536	11,282	0	44,524	11,278	3,165	9,918
1959	2,656	10,916	0	47,165	11,984	3,274	10,426
1960	2,855	10,499	0	51,295	12,754	3,560	11,077
1961	2,871	10,199	0	51,710	13,763	3,722	11,346
1962	2,966	10,554	0	51,862	13,913	4,019	11,440
1963	3,094	10,550	0	54,008	13,960	4,237	11,878
1964	3,238	10,358	0	59,017	15,471	4,478	12,713
1965	3,328	9,897	0	60,729	16,259	4,796	13,046
1966	3,348	9,186	0	61,904	16,599	5,004	13,443
1967	3,458	8,981	0	62,402	17,306	5,184	13,632
1968	3,475	8,355	0	67,448	17,870	5,163	14,285
1969	3,485	7,667	0	70,378	17,838	5,527	14,948
1970	3,723	7,140	91	70,978	17,650	5,847	15,699
1971	3,929	6,951	96	70,569	18,006	6,138	16,156
1972	4,072	5,439	82	71,854	18,393	6,644	16,988
1973	4,191	5,967	1,199	78,761	18,874	7,056	18,301
1974	4,252	4,961	1,059	78,182	16,977	7,117	18,412

Table A.23 (*cont.*)

	Agriculture	Mining and quarrying	Oil and gas extraction	Manufact-uring	Construct-ion	Utilities	Transport and communication
1975	3,916	5,773	846	74,049	16,116	7,250	18,230
1976	3,600	5,376	2,571	75,561	15,950	7,387	18,181
1977	4,070	5,220	5,767	76,632	15,868	7,688	18,665
1978	4,354	5,118	9,920	76,032	16,799	7,807	19,170
1979	4,282	5,120	13,845	75,888	16,908	8,114	19,909
1980	4,748	5,242	13,804	70,604	16,002	8,067	19,566
1981	4,870	5,105	15,016	66,742	14,754	8,252	19,603
1982	5,277	4,894	17,005	66,962	15,898	8,186	19,376
1983	4,985	4,699	18,913	68,753	16,907	8,465	19,931
1984	5,974	2,101	20,190	70,741	17,661	7,162	20,823
1985	5,711	3,770	20,646	73,177	17,776	8,694	21,710
1986	5,546	4,305	20,896	74,564	18,586	9,558	22,661
1987	5,592	4,177	20,396	78,287	20,036	9,818	24,428
1988	5,563	4,144	18,815	83,702	21,829	9,893	25,704
1989	5,779	3,990	15,630	87,271	23,152	9,997	27,167
1990	5,960	3,668	15,600	87,259	23,375	10,079	27,717

Table A.24 *Industrial output (ii) (£m constant prices): 1920–1990*

	Distribution	Business and financial services	Ownership of dwellings	Public administ-ration and defence	Education and health	Other services	Total GDP factor cost
				1920–1948 in 1938 prices			
1920	513	226	201	312	599		3,559
1921	467	199	204	254	585		3,198
1922	515	208	204	225	567		3,398
1923	522	217	206	213	564		3,504
1924	531	226	207	211	576		3,676
1925	550	235	210	212	590		3,811
1926	525	242	213	211	584		3,687
1927	553	258	218	211	594		3,988
1928	565	274	223	210	613		4,021
1929	581	257	226	213	628		4,140
1930	581	256	232	217	642		4,103
1931	575	229	234	220	630		3,899
1932	578	237	238	220	633		3,916
1933	586	246	240	220	635		4,045
1934	617	256	245	223	656		4,296
1935	631	264	252	229	664		4,454
1936	649	273	257	237	674		4,673
1937	655	276	265	250	683		4,835

Table A.24 (*cont.*)

	Distribution	Business and financial services	Ownership of dwellings	Public administ-ration and defence	Education and health	Other services	Total GDP factor cost
1938	663	269	272	269	710		4,867
1939	n.a.	n.a.	n.a.	n.a.	n.a.		5,093
1940	n.a.	n.a.	n.a.	n.a.	n.a.		5,668
1941	n.a.	n.a.	n.a.	n.a.	n.a.		6,192
1942	n.a.	n.a.	n.a.	n.a.	n.a.		6,318
1943	n.a.	n.a.	n.a.	n.a.	n.a.		6,431
1944	n.a.	n.a.	n.a.	n.a.	n.a.		6,119
1945	n.a.	n.a.	n.a.	n.a.	n.a.		5,794
1946	611	288	294	694	671		5,624
1947	650	302	294	499	668		5,550
1948	671	303	296	434	675		5,753
				1948–1990 in 1985 prices			
1948	15,239	5,554	8,518	18,511	8,982	8,745	127,007
1949	15,538	5.449	8,698	18,079	9,810	8,430	131,373
1950	16,077	5,793	8,792	17,682	10,166	8,328	135,799
1951	16,436	5,952	8,791	18,709	10,419	8,404	139,730
1952	16,974	5,982	8,744	19,042	10,366	8,311	139,494

Table A.24 (*cont.*)

	Distribution	Business and financial services	Ownership of dwellings	Public administ-ration and defence	Education and health	Other services	Total GDP factor cost
1953	18,026	5,852	8,901	19,364	10,684	8,386	145,231
1954	19,080	6,150	9,271	19,106	11,008	8,665	150,894
1955	20,483	6,481	9,683	19,054	11,341	8,718	156,673
1956	21,376	6,549	9,876	18,717	11,622	8,584	158,903
1957	21,844	7,252	9,924	18,406	11,933	8,767	161,709
1958	21,796	7,511	10,107	17,816	12,450	8,746	161,128
1959	22,896	8,131	10,369	17,554	12,812	8,810	166,993
1960	24,536	8,428	10,824	17,532	13,198	9,269	175,825
1961	25,846	9,289	10,996	17,547	13,711	9,676	180,677
1962	26,007	9,745	11,175	17,560	13,973	9,862	183,076
1963	28,009	10,288	11,384	18,049	14,536	10,145	190,139
1964	28,804	10,924	11,638	18,170	14,893	10,716	200,421
1965	29,457	11,122	12,021	18,428	15,710	10,930	205,724
1966	29,732	11,899	12,404	18,895	16,269	11,130	209,814
1967	30,700	12,421	12,751	19,529	17,044	11,175	214,583
1968	32,021	13,431	13,184	19,656	17,669	11,257	223,813
1969	32,466	13,695	13,606	19,544	17,750	11,512	228,416
1970	33,515	14,869	14,070	19,697	18,149	11,786	233,214
1971	34,789	15,417	14,268	20,164	18,971	12,031	237,484

Table A.24 (*cont.*)

	Distribution	Business and financial services	Ownership of dwellings	Public administ-ration and defence	Education and health	Other services	Total GDP factor cost
1972	35,686	15,937	14,701	20,892	19,857	12,202	242,747
1973	39,612	16,751	15,022	21,519	20,613	12,659	260,524
1974	37,774	17,165	15,416	21,361	21,726	12,868	257,269
1975	36,947	18,197	15,765	21,795	23,046	13,276	255,205
1976	38,497	19,147	16,121	22,029	23,841	13,929	262,190
1977	37,211	19,644	16,697	21,836	24,146	14,442	267,887
1978	38,004	20,719	16,781	21,477	24,531	14,858	275,570
1979	38,231	21,953	16,952	21,682	25,050	15,197	283,129
1980	36,775	22,340	17,109	21,888	25,294	16,192	277,632
1981	36,470	23,176	17,458	21,880	25,543	16,007	274,877
1982	36,523	24,592	17,646	21,453	25,812	15,943	279,567
1983	38,819	26,368	17,807	21,438	26,320	16,557	289,963
1984	38,495	27,967	17,991	21,429	26,291	17,504	294,328
1985	40,582	29,745	18,175	21,457	26,565	18,546	306,556
1986	42,839	32,739	18,176	21,463	26,837	19,477	317,645
1987	45,449	35,683	18,178	21,462	27,634	20,942	332,082
1988	47,543	38,939	18,363	21,245	28,429	21,826	345,995
1989	48,991	40,671	18,547	21,245	28,695	22,383	353,519
1990	48,754	42,405	18,727	21,666	28,685	22,700	356,596

Note: For 1920–48 education and health output is included with other services.

Table A.25 *Personal sector income (£m): 1920–1990*

	Income from employment	Self-employment income	Rent, dividends and interest	Transfers from government	Other transfers	Capital consump-tion	Total income	Income excluding stock appreciation
1920	3,603	809	926	162	1	n.a.	5,501	n.a.
1921	2,931	590	928	208	3	n.a.	4,661	n.a.
1922	2,502	642	885	197	4	n.a.	4,231	n.a.
1923	2,404	623	901	179	0	n.a.	4,107	n.a.
1924	2,461	653	948	176	6	n.a.	4,244	n.a.
1925	2,486	636	985	183	5	n.a.	4,296	n.a.
1926	2,397	646	1,009	205	3	n.a.	4,259	n.a.
1927	2,556	662	1,006	198	5	n.a.	4,427	n.a.
1928	2,527	668	1,035	203	6	n.a.	4,438	n.a.
1929	2,562	658	1,052	211	5	n.a.	4,487	n.a.
1930	2,486	601	1,076	241	10	n.a.	4,414	n.a.
1931	2,409	556	1,032	284	10	n.a.	4,292	n.a.
1932	2,356	543	975	284	10	n.a.	4,167	n.a.
1933	2,410	584	948	274	7	n.a.	4,224	n.a.
1934	2,491	576	944	270	4	n.a.	4,285	n.a.
1935	2,592	613	990	275	3	n.a.	4,472	n.a.
1936	2,736	648	1,051	268	4	n.a.	4,706	n.a.
1937	2,923	625	1,102	266	3	n.a.	4,918	n.a.
1938	2,976	590	1,155	282	2	n.a.	5,005	n.a.
1939	3,294	701	1,141	267	0	n.a.	5,403	n.a.

Table A.25 (*cont.*)

	Income from employment	Self-employment income	Rent, dividends and interest	Transfers from government	Other transfers	Capital consumption	Total income	Income excluding stock appreciation
1940	4,167	822	1,174	269	0	n.a.	6,432	n.a.
1941	4,848	921	1,158	284	0	n.a.	7,211	n.a.
1942	5,303	972	1,207	304	0	n.a.	7,786	n.a.
1943	5,704	996	1,235	331	0	n.a.	8,266	n.a.
1944	5,875	1,001	1,289	361	0	n.a.	8,526	n.a.
1945	5,798	1,066	1,331	419	0	n.a.	8,614	n.a.
1946	5,625	1,166	1,227	628	53	n.a.	8,699	n.a.
1947	6,150	1,266	1,277	629	55	n.a.	9,376	n.a.
1948	6,790	1,458	1,129	648	57	8	10,090	10,031
1949	7,236	1,518	1,107	683	52	9	10,605	10,566
1950	7,637	1,558	1,232	695	64	10	11,196	11,133
1951	8,515	1,614	1,225	720	62	12	12,148	12,036
1952	9,114	1,659	1,255	836	63	13	12,940	12,930
1953	9,692	1,753	1,373	926	72	13	13,829	13,822
1954	10,321	1,782	1,381	944	85	13	14,526	14,506
1955	11,266	1,857	1,464	1,035	89	14	15,725	15,681
1956	12,322	1,940	1,480	1,106	102	15	16,965	16,926
1957	13,047	2,035	1,562	1,169	102	16	17,931	17,899
1958	13,562	2,061	1,773	1,407	126	17	18,946	18,930
1959	14,203	2,163	1,976	1,555	127	18	20,042	20,020

Table A.25 (*cont.*)

	Income from employment	Self-employment income	Rent, dividends and interest	Transfers from government	Other transfers	Capital consumption	Total income	Income excluding stock appreciation
1960	15,164	2,259	2,319	1,569	134	20	21,465	21,434
1961	16,422	2,409	2,546	1,708	141	21	23,246	23,208
1962	17,329	2,485	2,693	1,881	146	26	24,560	24,521
1963	18,215	2,599	2,914	2,128	151	30	26,037	26,024
1964	19,781	2,749	3,290	2,250	166	32	28,269	28,223
1965	21,317	2,982	3,587	2,596	178	34	30,693	30,643
1966	22,891	3,193	3,756	2,825	186	38	32,889	32,839
1967	23,893	3,376	3,924	3,188	193	45	34,618	34,575
1968	25,538	3,691	4,141	3,678	219	53	37,320	37,227
1969	27,170	3,857	4,497	3,937	241	61	39,763	39,656
1970	30,516	4,136	4,661	4,330	266	73	43,982	43,887
1971	33,640	4,933	4,990	4,780	284	94	48,720	48,588
1972	37,953	5,852	5,254	5,837	305	98	55,298	55,146
1973	43,934	7,452	5,721	6,411	362	116	63,996	63,602
1974	53,055	8,255	7,211	7,870	399	151	76,941	76,236
1975	69,362	9,376	8,647	10,278	435	188	98,285	97,674
1976	79,324	11,582	9,978	12,749	579	217	114,428	113,732
1977	87,053	12,118	10,622	15,031	657	242	125,723	125,140
1978	99,312	13,920	12,763	17,871	819	266	144,951	144,504
1979	116,320	16,121	16,691	20,917	901	308	171,259	170,483

Table A.25 (*cont.*)

	Income from employment	Self-employment income	Rent, dividends and interest	Transfers from government	Other transfers	Capital consumption	Total income	Income excluding stock appreciation
1980	138,087	18,221	19,164	25,524	987	368	202,351	201,632
1981	150,157	20,092	21,283	31,242	1,179	403	224,356	223,730
1982	159,059	22,164	23,816	36,584	1,317	409	243,349	242,987
1983	169,796	24,613	25,816	39,856	1,614	417	262,113	261,563
1984	180,947	27,695	27,483	43,020	1,757	432	281,333	281,008
1985	195,569	29,761	30,056	46,813	1,894	458	304,551	304,076
1986	211,488	34,431	32,629	50,984	1,877	485	331,895	331,729
1987	229,138	38,981	35,020	52,494	1,826	503	357,962	357,472
1988	255,000	44,521	42,004	54,087	1,915	524	398,052	397,293
1989	283,231	51,339	46,460	56,793	2,034	557	440,413	439,604
1990	316,294	57,680	54,386	61,983	2,071	585	493,000	492,317

Note: Capital consumption relates only to non-profit-making bodies and does not include depreciation of dwellings or of the capital of unincorporated businesses.

Table A.26 *Personal sector outlay (£m): 1920–1990*

	Consumers' expend-iture	Social security contri-butions	Income taxes	Transfers paid abroad	Community charge	Other transfers paid	Saving	Total outgoings	Disposable income	Savings ratio
1920	4,929	28	335	n.a.	0	n.a.	209	5,501	5,138	4.1
1921	4,129	47	303	n.a.	0	n.a.	181	4,661	4,311	4.2
1922	3,710	59	308	n.a.	0	n.a.	154	4,231	3,864	4.0
1923	3,588	62	264	n.a.	0	n.a.	193	4,107	3,781	5.1
1924	3,681	64	260	n.a.	0	n.a.	239	4,244	3,920	6.1
1925	3,752	65	256	n.a.	0	n.a.	222	4,296	3,975	5.6
1926	3,746	75	229	n.a.	0	n.a.	209	4,259	3,955	5.3
1927	3,817	80	221	n.a.	0	n.a.	310	4,427	4,126	7.5
1928	3,852	82	228	n.a.	0	n.a.	276	4,438	4,128	6.7
1929	3,905	82	228	n.a.	0	n.a.	272	4,487	4,177	6.5
1930	3,844	81	233	n.a.	0	n.a.	256	4,414	4,100	6.2
1931	3,734	82	264	n.a.	0	n.a.	211	4,292	3,946	5.4
1932	3,615	89	288	n.a.	0	n.a.	175	4,167	3,790	4.6
1933	3,673	90	254	n.a.	0	n.a.	207	4,224	3,880	5.3
1934	3,765	94	245	n.a.	0	n.a.	181	4,285	3,946	4.6
1935	3,898	98	231	n.a.	0	n.a.	245	4,472	4,143	5.9
1936	4,074	104	231	n.a.	0	n.a.	297	4,706	4,371	6.8
1937	4,262	107	264	n.a.	0	n.a.	285	4,918	4,547	6.3
1938	4,310	109	295	n.a.	0	n.a.	292	5,005	4,601	6.3
1939	4,426	110	382	n.a.	0	n.a.	485	5,403	4,911	9.9

Table A.26 (*cont.*)

	Consumers' expend-iture	Social security contri-butions	Income taxes	Transfers paid abroad	Community charge	Other transfers paid	Saving	Total outgoings	Disposable income	Savings ratio
1940	4,515	120	565	n.a.	0	n.a.	1,232	6,432	5,747	21.4
1941	4,872	125	730	n.a.	0	n.a.	1,484	7,211	6,356	23.3
1942	5,221	143	875	n.a.	0	n.a.	1,547	7,786	6,768	22.9
1943	5,355	144	1,108	n.a.	0	n.a.	1,659	8,266	7,014	23.6
1944	5,704	141	1,254	n.a.	0	n.a.	1,427	8,526	7,131	20.0
1945	6,309	137	1,301	n.a.	0	n.a.	867	8,614	7,176	12.1
1946	7,138	170	1,053	33	0	n.a.	305	8,699	7,443	4.1
1947	7,946	232	968	84	0	n.a.	147	9,376	8,092	1.8
1948	8,680	335	956	83	0	n.a.	36	10,090	8,716	0.4
1949	9,093	436	981	65	0	n.a.	31	10,605	9,123	0.3
1950	9,594	440	1,001	48	0	n.a.	113	11,196	9,707	1.2
1951	10,323	452	1,140	64	0	n.a.	169	12,148	10,492	1.6
1952	10,831	476	1,156	65	0	n.a.	412	12,940	11,243	3.7
1953	11,503	525	1,113	61	0	n.a.	627	13,829	12,130	5.2
1954	12,210	532	1,213	66	0	n.a.	505	14,526	12,715	4.0
1955	13,176	594	1,305	82	0	5	563	15,725	13,739	4.1
1956	13,866	642	1,428	109	0	6	915	16,965	14,780	6.2
1957	14,627	657	1,577	110	0	7	953	17,931	15,580	6.1
1958	15,442	859	1,668	99	0	8	870	18,946	16,312	5.3
1959	16,290	897	1,746	91	0	10	1,007	20,042	17,298	5.8

Table A.26 (*cont.*)

	Consumers' expend-iture	Social security contri-butions	Income taxes	Transfers paid abroad	Community charge	Other transfers paid	Saving	Total outgoings	Disposable income	Savings ratio
1960	17,136	913	1,961	91	0	10	1,354	21,465	18,490	7.3
1961	18,007	1,072	2,214	92	0	12	1,849	23,246	19,856	9.3
1962	19,096	1,197	2,430	101	0	13	1,723	24,560	20,819	8.3
1963	20,337	1,303	2,480	118	0	15	1,784	26,037	22,121	8.1
1964	21,725	1,444	2,751	135	0	17	2,197	28,269	23,922	9.2
1965	23,164	1,685	3,297	142	0	18	2,387	30,693	25,551	9.3
1966	24,502	1,804	3,689	157	0	20	2,717	32,889	27,219	10.0
1967	25,715	1,924	4,069	189	0	22	2,699	34,618	28,414	9.5
1968	27,688	2,161	4,615	229	0	27	2,599	37,320	30,288	8.6
1969	29,464	2,242	5,223	235	0	33	2,567	39,763	32,030	8.0
1970	32,105	2,655	5,783	243	0	37	3,158	43,982	35,264	9.0
1971	35,912	2,826	6,515	247	0	41	3,179	48,720	39,091	8.1
1972	40,715	3,337	6,629	316	0	46	4,256	55,298	44,970	9.5
1973	46,426	3,937	7,726	419	0	55	5,433	63,996	51,859	10.5
1974	53,298	5,000	10,418	477	0	57	7,691	76,941	60,989	12.6
1975	65,542	6,848	15,042	531	0	73	10,249	98,285	75,791	13.5
1976	75,966	8,423	17,422	547	0	118	11,952	114,428	87,918	13.6
1977	87,140	9,503	18,149	659	0	136	10,136	125,723	97,276	10.4
1978	100,541	10,101	19,460	901	0	151	13,797	144,951	114,338	12.1
1979	119,483	11,526	21,586	1,044	0	134	17,486	171,259	136,969	12.8

Table A.26 (*cont.*)

	Consumers' expend-iture	Social security contri-butions	Income taxes	Transfers paid abroad	Community charge	Other transfers paid	Saving	Total outgoings	Disposable income	Savings ratio
1980	139,029	13,939	25,683	1,139	0	169	22,392	202,351	161,421	13.9
1981	154,642	15,916	28,949	1,057	0	177	23,614	224,356	178,257	13.2
1982	170,088	18,095	31,366	1,200	0	187	22,413	243,349	192,501	11.6
1983	186,517	20,780	33,180	1,191	0	222	20,223	262,113	206,740	9.8
1984	199,455	22,322	34,736	1,283	0	215	23,322	281,333	222,777	10.5
1985	217,679	24,210	37,774	1,459	0	225	23,204	304,551	240,883	9.6
1986	241,241	26,165	40,805	1,656	0	253	21,774	331,895	263,016	8.3
1987	265,070	28,642	43,386	1,789	0	339	18,736	357,962	283,806	6.6
1988	299,178	32,108	48,290	1,985	0	362	16,129	398,052	315,307	5.1
1989	326,906	33,025	53,517	2,050	619	391	23,906	440,413	350,811	6.8
1990	349,770	34,775	62,120	2,100	8,811	469	34,955	493,000	384,725	9.1

Table A.27 *Company sector income (£m): 1920–1990*

	Gross trading profits (GTP)	Rent, dividends and interest	Income from abroad	Total
1920	698	128	184	1,010
1921	313	125	127	565
1922	458	109	142	710
1923	468	113	151	732
1924	506	116	168	790
1925	446	121	188	755
1926	425	125	188	738
1927	485	122	184	791
1928	472	133	179	784
1929	478	157	181	815
1930	402	125	157	684
1931	363	127	108	598
1932	318	140	88	546
1933	378	134	106	618
1934	455	144	116	715
1935	508	153	126	787
1936	622	170	144	935
1937	718	197	166	1,081
1938	673	190	148	1,011
1939				898
1940				1,201
1941				1,328
1942				1,462
1943				1,483
1944				1,449
1945				1,382
1946	1,484	265	270	2,019
1947	1,713	326	336	2,375
1948	1,810	356	468	2,634
1949	1,842	360	472	2,674
1950	2,146	318	670	3,134
1951	2,509	341	535	3,385
1952	2,188	374	476	3,038

Table A.27 (*cont.*)

	Gross trading profits (GTP)	Rent, dividends and interest	Income from abroad	Total
1953	2,379	402	453	3,234
1954	2,627	472	498	3,597
1955	2,908	551	470	3,929
1956	2,983	653	519	4,155
1957	3,181	732	522	4,435
1958	3,112	764	607	4,483
1959	3,422	747	578	4,747
1960	3,712	839	580	5,131
1961	3,637	904	581	5,122
1962	3,587	904	651	5,142
1963	4,003	925	738	5,666
1964	4,464	1,057	693	6,214
1965	4,621	1,218	884	6,723
1966	4,513	1,332	848	6,694
1967	4,597	1,476	865	6,939
1968	5,212	1,724	1,008	7,945
1969	5,577	1,903	1,240	8,721
1970	5,949	2,128	1,332	9,409
1971	7,094	2,450	1,339	10,882
1972	7,999	2,958	1,544	12,501
1973	10,085	4,272	2,593	16,950
1974	11,426	5,351	2,990	19,768
1975	11,871	5,617	2,554	20,043
1976	14,975	6,801	3,742	25,518
1977	20,174	8,035	3,660	31,869
1978	22,930	8,333	4,456	35,719
1979	29,492	11,662	7,025	48,179
1980	28,013	16,215	7,145	51,373
1981	27,600	17,730	8,893	54,223
1982	31,339	19,331	9,201	59,872
1983	39,495	19,348	11,118	69,961
1984	44,977	22,604	14,067	81,647
1985	51,941	28,159	14,899	94,999
1986	46,889	30,054	15,324	92,267
1987	58,964	32,578	17,806	109,348

Table A.27 (*cont.*)

	Gross trading profits (GTP)	Rent, dividends and interest	Income from abroad	Total
1988	63,633	36,338	21,743	121,714
1989	65,931	48,436	26,829	141,196
1990	62,958	57,626	30,058	150,642

Note: Between 1939 and 1945 information on rent, dividends and interest and property income from abroad is not available. The total shown is gross trading profits only.

Table A.28 *Company sector outlay (£m): 1920–1990*

	Dividends	Other interest payments	Profits due abroad	Taxes on profits	Advance corporation tax	Miscellaneous transfers	Royalties	Transfers to charities	Undistributed profits	Total outgoings
1920	345	98	26	274	n.a.	0	n.a.	n.a.	267	1,010
1921	354	99	17	200	n.a.	0	n.a.	n.a.	−105	565
1922	309	74	20	123	n.a.	0	n.a.	n.a.	184	710
1923	329	79	24	113	n.a.	0	n.a.	n.a.	187	732
1924	354	88	27	91	n.a.	0	n.a.	n.a.	230	790
1925	363	96	30	88	n.a.	0	n.a.	n.a.	178	755
1926	365	101	30	79	n.a.	0	n.a.	n.a.	163	738
1927	365	104	30	75	n.a.	0	n.a.	n.a.	217	791
1928	367	111	30	58	n.a.	0	n.a.	n.a.	218	784
1929	373	128	31	67	n.a.	0	n.a.	n.a.	216	815
1930	373	128	27	70	n.a.	0	n.a.	n.a.	86	684
1931	337	132	19	64	n.a.	0	n.a.	n.a.	46	598
1932	301	124	15	64	n.a.	0	n.a.	n.a.	42	546
1933	298	114	20	56	n.a.	0	n.a.	n.a.	130	618
1934	305	120	23	46	n.a.	0	n.a.	n.a.	221	715
1935	341	117	26	53	n.a.	0	n.a.	n.a.	250	787
1936	409	123	30	57	n.a.	0	n.a.	n.a.	316	935
1937	461	126	36	62	n.a.	0	n.a.	n.a.	396	1,081
1938	481	137	33	88	n.a.	0	n.a.	n.a.	272	1,011
1939		301		56	n.a.	0	n.a.	n.a.	541	898

Table A.28 (*cont.*)

	Dividends	Other interest payments	Profits due abroad	Taxes on profits	Advance corporat-ion tax	Miscell-aneous transfers	Royalties	Transfers to charities	Undistrib-uted profits	Total outgoings
1940		313		62	n.a.	0	n.a.	n.a.	826	1,201
1941		314		325	n.a.	0	n.a.	n.a.	689	1,328
1942		362		457	n.a.	0	n.a.	n.a.	643	1,462
1943		336		614	n.a.	0	n.a.	n.a.	533	1,483
1944		384		662	n.a.	0	n.a.	n.a.	403	1,449
1945		417		634	n.a.	0	n.a.	n.a.	331	1,382
1946	321	443		673	n.a.	0	n.a.	n.a.	582	2,019
1947	348	450		536	n.a.	0	n.a.	n.a.	1,041	2,375
1948	356	464		651	n.a.	0	n.a.	n.a.	1,163	2,634
1949	351	465		812	n.a.	0	n.a.	n.a.	1,046	2,674
1950	362	487		807	n.a.	0	n.a.	n.a.	1,478	3,134
1951	395	241	119	782	n.a.	0	n.a.	n.a.	1,848	3,385
1952	386	284	100	1,014	n.a.	0	n.a.	n.a.	1,254	3,038
1953	428	300	100	979	n.a.	0	n.a.	n.a.	1,427	3,234
1954	471	310	105	897	n.a.	0	n.a.	8	1,806	3,597

Table A.28 (*cont.*)

	Dividends	Other interest payments	Profits due abroad	Taxes on 1profits	Advance corporat-ion tax	Miscell-aneous transfers	Royalties	Transfers to charities	Undistrib-uted profits	Total outgoings
1955	520	361	121	982	n.a.	0	n.a.	8	1,937	3,929
1956	545	418	112	906	n.a.	0	n.a.	11	2,163	4,155
1957	587	457	124	993	n.a.	0	n.a.	12	2,262	4,435
1958	625	492	139	1,036	n.a.	0	n.a.	13	2,178	4,483
1959	734	478	173	1,001	n.a.	0	n.a.	15	2,346	4,747
1960	1,068	460	160	752	n.a.	0	n.a.	17	2,674	5,131
1961	1,207	512	127	852	n.a.	0	n.a.	19	2,405	5,122
1962	1,223	553	143	1,017	n.a.	0	n.a.	21	2,185	5,142
1963	1,360	564	172	899	n.a.	0	n.a.	24	2,647	5,666
1964	1,516	676	209	838	n.a.	0	n.a.	26	2,949	6,214
1965	1,741	846	226	799	n.a.	0	n.a.	28	3,083	6,723
1966	1,661	1,076	199	867	n.a.	0	n.a.	30	2,861	6,694
1967	1,607	1,184	217	1,208	n.a.	0	n.a.	32	2,691	6,939
1968	1,588	1,402	331	1,240	n.a.	0	n.a.	34	3,350	7,945
1969	1,693	1,642	286	1,284	n.a.	0	n.a.	35	3,781	8,721
1970	1,531	1,826	356	1,617	n.a.	0	n.a.	36	4,043	9,409
1971	1,704	2,013	451	1,497	n.a.	0	n.a.	38	5,179	10,882
1972	1,690	2,275	627	1,480	n.a.	0	n.a.	41	6,388	12,501
1973	1,496	3,363	744	1,613	253	0	n.a.	42	9,439	16,950
1974	1,352	4,481	649	1,885	987	0	n.a.	42	10,372	19,768

Table A.28 (*cont.*)

	Dividends	Other interest payments	Profits due abroad	Taxes on profits	Advance corporation tax	Miscell-aneous transfers	Royalties	Transfers to charities	Undistrib-uted profits	Total outgoings
1975	1,421	4,784	602	1,488	899	0	n.a.	42	10,807	20,043
1976	1,637	5,251	964	1,346	966	0	n.a.	42	15,312	25,518
1977	1,880	5,394	1,997	2,087	1,165	0	n.a.	43	19,303	31,869
1978	2,058	6,104	2,229	2,748	1,323	0	n.a.	45	21,212	35,719
1979	3,516	9,293	3,992	3,552	1,444	0	n.a.	51	26,331	48,179
1980	3,508	13,072	4,769	4,582	2,031	0	1,079	52	22,280	51,373
1981	3,648	13,514	4,695	6,520	1,872	0	1,258	62	22,654	54,223
1982	4,259	14,946	4,659	7,940	2,114	0	1,488	69	24,397	59,872
1983	5,152	13,934	5,258	9,935	1,849	0	1,867	86	31,880	69,961
1984	5,510	16,352	6,271	10,958	2,862	2	2,445	105	37,142	81,647
1985	6,895	21,830	7,499	12,585	3,865	4	2,361	119	39,841	94,999
1986	8,673	22,345	5,185	9,998	4,217	13	935	145	40,756	92,267
1987	10,954	23,899	6,821	10,876	4,869	24	1,151	160	50,594	109,348
1988	14,968	28,152	8,280	12,205	5,693	32	823	200	51,361	121,714
1989	18,449	43,408	8,799	15,218	6,782	40	556	284	47,660	141,196
1990	21,678	55,300	7,122	13,634	7,661	35	654	271	44,287	150,642

Note: The entry shown as dividend payments for 1939–45 is calculated as a residual and includes all payments of net property income. See note to table A.27.

Table A.29 *Public corporations' income (£m): 1946–1990*

	Rent, dividends and interest	Gross trading surplus (GTS)	Income from abroad	Total income
1946	6	20	0	26
1947	9	36	1	46
1948	20	117	0	137
1949	21	155	−1	175
1950	24	196	1	221
1951	22	259	0	281
1952	27	276	1	304
1953	31	319	2	352
1954	36	351	2	389
1955	44	311	3	358
1956	44	342	4	390
1957	52	321	4	377
1958	52	337	5	394
1959	57	388	6	451
1960	69	534	6	609
1961	74	640	8	722
1962	77	746	8	831
1963	69	841	7	917
1964	76	925	8	1,009
1965	89	988	8	1,085
1966	98	1,043	9	1,150
1967	102	1,135	10	1,247
1968	122	1,368	13	1,503
1969	144	1,449	15	1,608
1970	164	1,446	14	1,624
1971	172	1,529	14	1,715
1972	215	1,685	17	1,917
1973	325	2,067	20	2,412
1974	402	2,575	30	3,007
1975	455	3,112	40	3,607
1976	696	4,549	56	5,301
1977	743	5,120	52	5,915
1978	825	5,434	66	6,325
1979	884	5,615	71	6,570

Table A.29 (*cont.*)

	Rent, dividends and interest	Gross trading surplus (GTS)	Income from abroad	Total income
1980	871	6,322	85	7,278
1981	1,148	7,994	70	9,212
1982	1,313	9,514	33	10,860
1983	1,435	10,002	45	11,482
1984	1,529	8,388	73	9,990
1985	1,986	7,131	64	9,181
1986	1,616	8,066	27	9,709
1987	1,477	6,798	52	8,327
1988	1,627	7,351	73	9,051
1989	1,890	6,416	68	8,374
1990	1,780	4,265	68	6,113

Note: Before 1946 the public corporations are included in the company sector.

Table A.30 *Public corporations' outlay (£m): 1946–1990*

	Royalties	Dividends and interest	Taxes on income	Balance	Total outlay
1946	0	9	2	15	26
1947	0	12	4	30	46
1948	0	57	3	77	137
1949	0	87	2	86	175
1950	0	91	3	127	221
1951	0	106	4	171	281
1952	0	118	3	183	304
1953	0	134	24	194	352
1954	0	148	37	204	389
1955	0	160	32	166	358
1956	0	155	30	205	390
1957	0	188	22	167	377
1958	0	223	21	150	394
1959	0	254	11	186	451
1960	0	288	12	309	609
1961	0	345	12	365	722
1962	0	420	8	403	831
1963	0	333	6	578	917
1964	0	394	6	609	1,009
1965	0	421	3	661	1,085
1966	0	473	31	646	1,150
1967	0	552	9	686	1,247
1968	0	636	17	850	1,503
1969	0	722	8	878	1,608
1970	0	796	10	818	1,624
1971	0	884	8	823	1,715
1972	0	943	7	967	1,917
1973	0	1,150	8	1,254	2,412
1974	0	1,604	11	1,392	3,007
1975	0	1,930	12	1,665	3,607
1976	0	2,459	2	2,840	5,301
1977	0	2,585	21	3,309	5,915
1978	0	2,468	28	3,829	6,325
1979	0	2,693	68	3,809	6,570

Table A.30 (*cont.*)

	Royalties	Dividends and interest	Taxes on income	Balance	Total outlay
1980	77	2,886	52	4,263	7,278
1981	104	3,355	172	5,581	9,212
1982	112	3,694	435	6,619	10,860
1983	20	3,705	244	7,513	11,482
1984	14	3,519	301	6,156	9,990
1985	5	3,711	106	5,359	9,181
1986	6	3,303	328	6,072	9,709
1987	0	3,127	77	5,123	8,327
1988	0	2,968	116	5,967	9,051
1989	0	3,207	120	5,047	8,374
1990	0	2,514	176	3,423	6,113

Note: Before 1946 the public corporations are included in the company sector.

Table A.31 *Central government income (£m): 1920–1990*

	Capital consumption	Income taxes	Gross trading surplus	Expenditure taxes	Rent, dividends and interest	Social security contributions	Miscellaneous transfers	Total income
1920	n.a.	609	−1	333	26	28	n.a.	995
1921	n.a.	503	2	344	30	47	n.a.	926
1922	n.a.	431	10	331	29	59	n.a.	860
1923	n.a.	377	8	313	31	62	n.a.	791
1924	n.a.	351	6	281	32	64	n.a.	734
1925	n.a.	344	7	289	36	65	n.a.	741
1926	n.a.	308	8	293	43	75	n.a.	727
1927	n.a.	296	9	309	47	80	n.a.	741
1928	n.a.	286	10	321	50	82	n.a.	749
1929	n.a.	295	11	317	55	82	n.a.	760
1930	n.a.	303	12	308	57	81	n.a.	761
1931	n.a.	328	13	312	46	82	n.a.	781
1932	n.a.	352	14	348	35	89	n.a.	838
1933	n.a.	310	14	346	33	90	n.a.	793
1934	n.a.	291	15	365	33	94	n.a.	798
1935	n.a.	284	14	373	33	98	n.a.	802
1936	n.a.	288	14	395	33	104	n.a.	834
1937	n.a.	326	15	413	33	107	n.a.	894
1938	n.a.	383	16	415	34	109	n.a.	957
1939	n.a.	438	19	466	34	110	n.a.	1,067

Table A.31 (*cont.*)

	Capital consumption	Income taxes	Gross trading surplus	Expenditure taxes	Rent, dividends and interest	Social security contributions	Miscellaneous transfers	Total income
1940	n.a.	627	20	681	30	120	n.a.	1,478
1941	n.a.	1,055	31	1,006	30	125	n.a.	2,247
1942	n.a.	1,332	76	1,139	31	143	n.a.	2,721
1943	n.a.	1,722	89	1,235	32	144	n.a.	3,222
1944	n.a.	1,916	73	1,238	31	141	n.a.	3,399
1945	n.a.	1,935	58	1,205	1	137	n.a.	3,336
1946	20	1,728	42	1,300	−8	170	n.a.	3,252
1947	20	1,508	75	1,505	−15	232	n.a.	3,325
1948	20	1,610	74	1,693	74	335	n.a.	3,806
1949	21	1,795	80	1,663	97	436	n.a.	4,092
1950	22	1,811	115	1,723	98	440	n.a.	4,209
1951	26	1,926	93	1,900	136	452	n.a.	4,533
1952	30	2,173	15	1,894	165	476	n.a.	4,753
1953	32	2,116	32	1,925	186	525	n.a.	4,816
1954	34	2,147	75	2,033	204	532	n.a.	5,025
1955	37	2,319	78	2,163	225	594	5	5,421
1956	41	2,364	86	2,255	254	642	6	5,648
1957	45	2,592	90	2,333	260	657	7	5,984
1958	49	2,725	113	2,370	301	859	8	6,425
1959	50	2,758	128	2,463	338	897	10	6,644

Table A.31 (*cont.*)

	Capital consumption	Income taxes	Gross trading surplus	Expenditure taxes	Rent, dividends and interest	Social security contributions	Miscellaneous transfers	Total income
1960	53	2,725	141	2,597	361	913	10	6,800
1961	56	3,078	59	2,784	433	1,072	12	7,494
1962	60	3,455	31	2,950	524	1,197	13	8,230
1963	64	3,385	33	2,998	479	1,303	15	8,277
1964	67	3,595	39	3,319	535	1,444	17	9,016
1965	71	4,099	41	3,694	592	1,685	18	10,200
1966	76	4,587	33	4,006	695	1,804	20	11,221
1967	80	5,286	33	4,484	758	1,924	22	12,587
1968	87	5,872	49	5,207	879	2,161	27	14,282
1969	93	6,515	62	6,043	1,017	2,242	33	16,005
1970	109	7,410	63	6,525	1,169	2,655	37	17,968
1971	125	8,020	66	6,567	1,401	2,826	41	19,046
1972	144	8,116	29	6,812	1,555	3,337	46	20,039
1973	173	9,257	17	7,411	1,791	3,937	55	22,641
1974	229	12,716	36	8,285	2,170	5,000	57	28,493
1975	299	16,758	38	10,058	2,591	6,848	73	36,665
1976	360	18,969	35	11,781	3,189	8,423	118	42,875
1977	413	20,490	35	14,757	3,704	9,503	136	49,038
1978	466	22,624	30	17,096	4,050	10,101	151	54,518
1979	552	25,239	−24	23,103	4,844	11,526	134	65,374

Table A.31 (*cont.*)

	Capital consumption	Income taxes	Gross trading surplus	Expenditure taxes	Rent, dividends and interest	Social security contributions	Miscellaneous transfers	Total income
1980	689	31,002	−74	28,213	6,092	13,939	169	80,030
1981	773	36,134	−26	32,271	6,970	15,916	177	92,215
1982	811	40,282	−134	34,735	7,920	18,095	187	101,896
1983	844	43,344	−304	37,281	8,345	20,780	222	110,512
1984	896	46,655	−489	39,809	9,343	22,322	217	118,753
1985	983	51,643	−175	42,954	10,656	24,210	229	130,500
1986	1,076	52,239	−279	47,696	9,296	26,165	266	136,459
1987	1,179	55,702	−485	52,297	10,035	28,642	363	147,733
1988	1,303	61,852	−459	57,785	10,129	32,108	394	163,112
1989	1,484	70,275	−323	61,012	10,664	33,025	431	176,568
1990	1,623	77,262	−545	73,941	10,451	34,775	504	198,011

Table A.32 *Central government outlay (£m): 1920–1990*

	Debt interest	Transfers to local authorities	Subsidies	Consumption of goods and services	Transfers to persons	Transfers abroad	Balance	Total outlay
1920	320	66	123	277	152	4	53	995
1921	303	77	126	259	188	−38	11	926
1922	307	77	72	214	172	−6	24	860
1923	315	77	25	181	156	−1	38	791
1924	315	79	13	180	155	2	−10	734
1925	313	82	26	186	160	−12	−14	741
1926	328	84	22	187	174	−15	−53	727
1927	303	87	17	185	172	−19	−4	741
1928	312	88	17	181	181	−19	−11	749
1929	316	104	20	182	190	−19	−33	760
1930	304	128	21	180	221	−25	−68	761
1931	283	132	19	181	264	−16	−82	781
1932	279	125	22	177	260	4	−29	838
1933	243	124	26	176	247	5	−28	793
1934	226	126	30	184	241	4	−13	798
1935	227	134	32	209	243	5	−48	802
1936	223	139	29	252	236	6	−51	834
1937	228	139	27	322	238	6	−66	894
1938	232	142	35	438	254	7	−151	957
1939	234	178	41	830	241	15	−472	1,067

Table A.32 (*cont.*)

	Debt interest	Transfers to local authorities	Subsidies	Consumption of goods and services	Transfers to persons	Transfers abroad	Balance	Total outlay
1940	243	225	93	2,529	247	13	−1,872	1,478
1941	265	278	166	3,643	265	12	−2,382	2,247
1942	313	269	200	4,142	285	18	−2,506	2,721
1943	361	245	232	4,555	309	16	−2,496	3,222
1944	405	240	248	4,627	336	11	−2,468	3,399
1945	450	247	289	3,773	390	60	−1,874	3,336
1946	485	255	375	1,858	608	−60	−270	3,252
1947	517	275	457	1,262	606	−74	282	3,325
1948	507	294	557	1,265	632	−55	606	3,806
1949	505	302	509	1,470	673	5	628	4,092
1950	505	313	460	1,531	682	24	694	4,209
1951	548	352	452	1,833	705	26	617	4,533
1952	607	389	399	2,243	819	−86	382	4,753
1953	637	416	343	2,341	907	−53	225	4,816
1954	635	441	399	2,366	924	20	240	5,025

Table A.32 (*cont.*)

	Debt interest	Transfers to local authorities	Subsidies	Consumption of goods and services	Transfers to persons	Transfers abroad	Balance	Total outlay
1955	705	490	322	2,357	1,013	24	510	5,421
1956	720	544	330	2,504	1,080	47	423	5,648
1957	702	621	377	2,555	1,140	54	535	5,984
1958	776	660	356	2,555	1,374	74	630	6,425
1959	770	711	341	2,722	1,518	82	500	6,644
1960	857	780	456	2,875	1,529	94	209	6,800
1961	893	828	544	3,070	1,665	118	376	7,494
1962	874	926	561	3,241	1,829	121	678	8,230
1963	930	1,031	522	3,350	2,065	132	247	8,277
1964	937	1,159	465	3,546	2,176	163	570	9,016
1965	968	1,249	495	3,860	2,507	177	944	10,200
1966	1,036	1,481	480	4,129	2,719	180	1,196	11,221
1967	1,105	1,706	720	4,525	3,068	188	1,275	12,587
1968	1,240	1,898	801	4,767	3,545	179	1,852	14,282
1969	1,280	2,099	726	4,887	3,789	177	3,047	16,005
1970	1,299	2,450	766	5,473	4,168	169	3,643	17,968
1971	1,390	2,858	838	6,217	4,608	195	2,940	19,046
1972	1,589	3,233	1,085	7,000	5,624	220	1,288	20,039
1973	1,773	3,988	1,395	7,901	6,147	344	1,093	22,641
1974	2,122	4,686	2,833	10,133	7,565	302	852	28,493

Table A.32 (*cont.*)

	Debt interest	Transfers to local authorities	Subsidies	Consumption of goods and services	Transfers to persons	Transfers abroad	Balance	Total outlay
1975	2,684	7,619	3,314	13,510	9,877	337	−676	36,665
1976	3,641	9,246	3,100	16,157	12,217	776	−2,262	42,875
1977	4,573	9,201	2,915	17,806	14,357	1,083	−898	49,038
1978	5,533	9,954	3,185	20,123	17,044	1,664	−2,985	54,518
1979	6,670	11,272	3,837	23,377	20,032	2,016	−1,830	65,374
1980	8,264	13,233	4,620	29,960	24,419	1,780	−2,246	80,030
1981	10,122	15,201	5,171	33,846	30,100	1,607	−3,831	92,215
1982	11,420	16,190	4,386	36,965	35,288	1,789	−4,142	101,896
1983	12,263	18,703	4,744	40,619	36,675	1,930	−4,423	110,512
1984	14,119	19,908	6,040	43,105	39,284	2,099	−5,802	118,753
1985	15,748	20,438	5,939	45,846	42,732	3,427	−3,630	130,500
1986	15,961	21,813	5,025	48,763	46,596	2,233	−3,932	136,459
1987	17,074	23,277	5,223	51,999	47,885	3,277	−1,003	147,733
1988	17,345	23,452	4,910	55,566	49,220	3,248	9,371	163,112
1989	17,976	24,043	4,684	60,476	51,435	4,278	13,676	176,568
1990	17,872	38,088	5,573	66,798	55,920	4,635	9,125	198,011

Table A.33 *Local authority income (£m): 1920–1990*

	Rates	Gross trading surplus	Grants from central government	Community charge	Rent, dividends and interest	Capital consumption	Total income
1920	160	21	66	0	21	n.a.	268
1921	187	23	77	0	27	n.a.	315
1922	181	34	77	0	32	n.a.	324
1923	167	36	77	0	36	n.a.	316
1924	163	34	79	0	37	n.a.	313
1925	168	35	82	0	39	n.a.	324
1926	180	32	84	0	44	n.a.	340
1927	190	39	87	0	47	n.a.	363
1928	192	41	88	0	52	n.a.	373
1929	182	41	104	0	55	n.a.	382
1930	173	42	128	0	59	n.a.	402
1931	169	42	132	0	61	n.a.	404
1932	167	44	125	0	64	n.a.	400
1933	169	45	124	0	64	n.a.	402
1934	175	45	126	0	65	n.a.	411
1935	185	46	134	0	66	n.a.	431
1936	194	46	139	0	68	n.a.	447
1937	200	47	139	0	70	n.a.	456
1938	212	46	142	0	73	n.a.	473
1939	223	47	178	0	79	n.a.	527

Table A.33 (*cont.*)

	Rates	Gross trading surplus	Grants from central government	Community charge	Rent, dividends and interest	Capital consumption	Total income
1940	229	47	225	0	86	n.a.	586
1941	225	48	278	0	85	n.a.	637
1942	225	48	269	0	84	n.a.	627
1943	228	49	245	0	83	n.a.	606
1944	232	48	240	0	82	n.a.	602
1945	247	45	247	0	76	n.a.	615
1946	269	48	255	0	42	32	646
1947	307	48	275	0	42	34	706
1948	317	33	294	0	64	36	744
1949	326	28	302	0	74	38	768
1950	337	28	313	0	84	41	803
1951	364	29	352	0	93	50	888
1952	392	31	389	0	107	56	975
1953	433	37	416	0	125	56	1,067
1954	460	40	441	0	143	59	1,143

Table A.33 (*cont.*)

	Rates	Gross trading surplus	Grants from central government	Community charge	Rent, dividends and interest	Capital consumption	Total income
1955	475	42	490	0	162	65	1,234
1956	556	44	544	0	184	71	1,399
1957	615	49	621	0	210	76	1,571
1958	650	53	660	0	226	80	1,669
1959	714	58	711	0	245	82	1,810
1960	771	60	780	0	265	87	1,963
1961	831	62	828	0	292	94	2,107
1962	916	67	926	0	318	101	2,328
1963	1,014	75	1,031	0	339	108	2,567
1964	1,096	80	1,159	0	376	117	2,828
1965	1,228	88	1,249	0	433	125	3,123
1966	1,374	91	1,481	0	488	136	3,570
1967	1,467	94	1,706	0	545	144	3,956
1968	1,548	102	1,898	0	616	159	4,324
1969	1,678	113	2,099	0	698	175	4,763
1970	1,827	116	2,450	0	779	197	5,369
1971	2,086	135	2,858	0	822	231	6,132
1972	2,379	134	3,233	0	862	269	6,877
1973	2,647	134	3,988	0	1,068	275	8,112
1974	3,089	97	4,686	0	1,559	360	9,791

Table A.33 (*cont.*)

	Rates	Gross trading surplus	Grants from central government	Community charge	Rent, dividends and interest	Capital consumption	Total income
1975	3,978	89	7,619	0	1,925	478	14,089
1976	4,503	117	9,246	0	2,350	565	16,781
1977	5,077	148	9,201	0	2,483	632	17,541
1978	5,660	186	9,954	0	2,668	716	19,184
1979	6,567	204	11,272	0	3,153	854	22,050
1980	8,261	254	13,233	0	3,738	1,059	26,545
1981	10,194	262	15,201	0	4,017	1,175	30,849
1982	11,732	350	16,190	0	3,995	1,206	33,473
1983	12,219	354	18,703	0	3,602	1,237	36,115
1984	12,767	372	19,908	0	3,533	1,291	37,871
1985	13,638	440	20,438	0	3,794	1,389	39,699
1986	15,251	434	21,813	0	3,907	1,507	42,912
1987	16,777	410	23,277	0	4,034	1,625	46,123
1988	18,726	427	23,452	0	4,202	1,807	48,614
1989	19,913	522	24,043	619	4,741	1,964	51,802
1990	5,126	562	38,088	8,811	4,872	2,070	59,529

Table A.34 *Local authority outlay (£m): 1920–1990*

	Debt interest	Transfers	Subsidies	Consumption of goods and services	Balance	Total
1920	26	8	1	211	21	268
1921	34	18	2	229	31	315
1922	40	23	1	221	40	324
1923	42	21	1	214	39	316
1924	43	19	1	218	32	313
1925	45	21	2	226	31	324
1926	49	29	2	233	27	340
1927	54	24	3	238	44	363
1928	59	20	3	244	47	373
1929	62	19	3	253	44	382
1930	65	18	3	263	53	402
1931	67	18	3	262	54	404
1932	69	22	3	254	52	400
1933	68	25	3	254	52	402
1934	67	27	3	262	52	411
1935	65	30	4	274	58	431
1936	65	30	4	284	64	447
1937	66	26	4	295	65	456
1938	68	26	5	310	64	473
1939	71	26	6	350	74	527
1940	72	22	6	394	92	586
1941	71	19	6	446	95	637
1942	69	19	6	438	95	627
1943	67	22	6	417	94	606
1944	66	25	6	418	87	602
1945	63	29	7	432	84	615
1946	61	20	11	487	67	646
1947	61	23	14	548	60	706
1948	66	16	16	567	79	744
1949	72	10	17	587	82	768
1950	81	13	16	613	81	803
1951	89	15	18	683	84	888
1952	104	17	22	748	84	975
1953	123	19	23	786	116	1,067
1954	142	20	24	838	119	1,143

Table A.34 (*cont.*)

	Debt interest	Transfers	Subsidies	Consumption of goods and services	Balance	Total
1955	161	22	30	908	113	1,234
1956	193	26	34	1,018	129	1,399
1957	221	29	35	1,115	170	1,571
1958	241	33	35	1,185	175	1,669
1959	262	37	33	1,267	211	1,810
1960	287	40	37	1,351	248	1,963
1961	335	43	49	1,490	191	2,107
1962	364	52	47	1,644	221	2,328
1963	392	63	47	1,794	271	2,567
1964	445	74	51	1,923	336	2,828
1965	522	89	76	2,138	298	3,123
1966	600	106	79	2,395	390	3,570
1967	671	120	81	2,688	396	3,956
1968	791	133	94	2,896	410	4,324
1969	930	148	116	3,117	452	4,763
1970	1,068	162	118	3,551	470	5,369
1971	1,104	172	101	4,071	685	6,132
1972	1,144	213	75	4,739	706	6,877
1973	1,444	264	108	5,497	799	8,112
1974	2,046	305	274	6,573	593	9,791
1975	2,333	401	457	9,588	1,310	14,089
1976	2,757	532	472	10,854	2,166	16,781
1977	2,959	674	471	11,631	1,806	17,541
1978	2,914	827	590	13,243	1,611	19,184
1979	3,481	885	806	15,409	1,470	22,050
1980	4,248	1,105	1,099	18,928	1,165	26,545
1981	4,413	1,142	1,198	21,468	2,628	30,849
1982	4,298	1,296	1,425	23,334	3,120	33,473
1983	3,959	3,181	1,525	25,103	2,347	36,115
1984	4,032	3,736	1,497	26,584	2,022	37,871
1985	4,433	4,081	1,286	27,890	2,009	39,699
1986	4,415	4,388	1,162	30,544	2,403	42,912
1987	4,627	4,609	950	33,272	2,665	46,123
1988	4,795	4,867	1,030	36,079	1,843	48,614
1989	5,160	5,358	1,008	38,460	1,816	51,802
1990	5,304	6,063	644	42,588	4,930	59,529

Table A.35 *Personal sector capital account (£m): 1948–1990*

	Savings	Depreciation	Net fixed capital formation	Stock appreciation	Physical increase in stocks	Net capital transfers paid	Net acquisition of financial assets
1948	36	228	0	59	35	99	−385
1949	31	239	9	39	31	160	−447
1950	113	259	2	63	42	106	−359
1951	169	305	−24	112	70	124	−418
1952	412	337	−17	10	−15	97	0
1953	627	343	48	7	23	116	90
1954	505	356	137	20	47	144	−199
1955	563	390	196	44	38	117	−222
1956	915	419	189	39	27	106	134
1957	953	441	153	32	29	125	174
1958	870	462	206	16	6	128	53
1959	1,007	476	158	22	41	155	156
1960	1,354	498	255	31	63	172	335
1961	1,849	529	293	38	45	185	760
1962	1,723	554	240	39	4	172	714
1963	1,784	595	275	13	26	204	672
1964	2,197	635	290	46	55	182	989
1965	2,387	664	510	50	32	133	998
1966	2,717	702	508	50	16	156	1,284
1967	2,699	742	623	43	40	170	1,081
1968	2,599	808	775	93	28	233	663
1969	2,567	866	669	107	52	397	476

Table A.35 (*cont.*)

	Savings	Depreciation	Net fixed capital formation	Stock appreciation	Physical increase in stocks	Net capital transfers paid	Net acquisition of financial assets
1970	3,158	975	628	95	21	359	1,081
1971	3,179	1,119	1,176	132	81	327	344
1972	4,256	1,354	1,525	152	66	376	783
1973	5,433	1,718	1,053	394	227	327	1,714
1974	7,691	2,034	740	705	−2	321	3,893
1975	10,249	2,534	1,238	611	−244	302	5,808
1976	11,952	2,980	1,325	696	93	63	6,795
1977	10,136	3,480	1,963	583	358	−75	3,827
1978	13,797	4,155	2,067	447	310	−301	7,119
1979	17,486	5,008	3,218	776	389	−196	8,291
1980	22,392	6,089	3,266	719	−240	−253	12,811
1981	23,614	6,920	2,865	626	−213	−88	13,505
1982	22,413	7,409	4,598	362	60	−367	10,351
1983	20,223	8,201	5,662	550	146	−1,019	6,682
1984	23,322	9,124	5,676	325	189	−1,266	9,274
1985	23,204	10,006	5,657	475	−45	−422	7,533
1986	21,774	11,052	7,130	166	354	150	2,922
1987	18,736	12,341	9,431	490	317	268	−4,111
1988	16,129	14,572	13,715	744	607	1,246	−14,756
1989	23,906	15,209	11,994	821	445	759	−5,322
1990	34,955	16,673	9,435	665	425	215	7,542

Table A.36 *Company sector capital account (£m): 1948–1990*

	Savings	Depreciation	Net fixed capital formation	Stock appreciation	Physical increase in stocks	Net capital transfers paid	Net acquisition of financial assets
1948	1,163	356	186	200	212	−64	273
1949	1,046	375	207	170	56	−55	293
1950	1,478	411	227	440	−12	−51	462
1951	1,848	477	161	465	431	−32	346
1952	1,254	550	96	−22	−65	−32	726
1953	1,427	577	111	−44	63	−42	763
1954	1,806	602	202	53	209	−23	763
1955	1,937	663	312	119	388	−26	482
1956	2,163	736	420	159	220	−18	646
1957	2,262	796	557	141	159	−11	620
1958	2,178	842	546	−18	45	−10	772
1959	2,346	870	698	77	95	−7	613
1960	2,674	919	865	77	638	−15	190
1961	2,405	994	1,047	121	188	−9	64
1962	2,185	1,057	1,007	110	0	−12	23
1963	2,647	1,111	911	133	162	−9	339
1964	2,949	1,188	1,291	182	623	−13	−321
1965	3,083	1,291	1,384	226	501	−14	−305
1966	2,861	1,405	1,302	240	268	−19	−336
1967	2,691	1,459	1,221	87	118	−228	34
1968	3,350	1,546	1,551	478	253	−422	−57
1969	3,781	1,715	1,844	580	689	−544	−503

Table A.36 (*cont.*)

	Savings	Depreciation	Net fixed capital formation	Stock appreciation	Physical increase in stocks	Net capital transfers paid	Net acquisition of financial assets
1970	4,043	1,955	2,059	864	523	−406	−952
1971	5,179	2,271	1,833	848	−289	−492	1,008
1972	6,388	2,590	1,952	1,082	67	−306	1,003
1973	9,439	3,050	3,089	2,261	1,400	−295	−65
1974	10,372	3,810	3,488	5,063	875	−248	−2,616
1975	10,807	4,919	3,205	4,504	−1,472	−420	71
1976	15,312	6,052	3,578	5,587	85	−301	311
1977	19,303	7,324	4,410	4,118	1,615	−217	2,053
1978	21,212	8,799	5,968	3,443	1,377	−412	2,037
1979	26,331	10,333	7,145	7,408	1,904	−246	−213
1980	22,280	12,716	6,815	5,394	−2,598	−287	240
1981	22,654	14,478	5,206	5,064	−2,609	−242	757
1982	24,397	15,659	5,285	3,511	−1,627	−343	1,912
1983	31,880	16,976	3,673	3,619	649	−261	7,224
1984	37,142	18,253	7,809	4,123	1,347	−153	5,764
1985	39,841	21,490	10,403	2,155	418	6	5,368
1986	40,756	23,143	10,099	1,510	1,039	111	4,854
1987	50,594	25,412	14,755	4,136	1,798	331	4,163
1988	51,361	26,943	22,723	5,226	4,512	−109	−7,934
1989	47,660	29,758	29,944	6,387	2,671	629	−21,730
1990	44,287	33,137	28,682	5,612	−1,107	535	−22,572

Table A.37 *Public corporations' capital account (£m): 1948–1990*

	Savings	Depreciation	Net fixed capital formation	Stock appreciation	Physical increase in stocks	Net capital transfers paid	Net acquisition of financial assets
1948	77	153	22	42	−10	−4	−126
1949	86	165	93	0	33	−42	−163
1950	127	178	105	29	−15	−3	−167
1951	171	205	151	80	4	−5	−264
1952	183	235	173	−6	50	−5	−264
1953	194	248	235	−6	−31	−7	−244
1954	204	260	267	7	−72	−7	−251
1955	166	287	279	18	21	−12	−427
1956	205	319	271	10	17	−16	−395
1957	167	348	326	14	53	−9	−565
1958	150	373	339	−3	26	−7	−578
1959	186	387	393	−1	11	−7	−597
1960	309	410	398	14	−24	−7	−482
1961	365	495	434	12	−4	−8	−564
1962	403	545	419	3	−2	−8	−554
1963	578	581	479	6	−48	−9	−431
1964	609	624	607	15	−4	−10	−623
1965	661	679	613	15	−11	−11	−624
1966	646	741	714	15	27	−11	−840
1967	686	815	850	7	65	−16	−1,035
1968	850	921	694	12	5	−69	−713
1969	878	995	487	46	−73	−70	−507

Table A.37 (*cont.*)

	Savings	Depreciation	Net fixed capital formation	Stock appreciation	Physical increase in stocks	Net capital transfers paid	Net acquisition of financial assets
1970	818	1,129	547	102	−39	−76	−846
1971	823	1,298	560	75	59	−83	−1,085
1972	967	1,441	330	56	14	−121	−752
1973	1,254	1,632	436	151	−30	−150	−785
1974	1,392	2,120	737	341	−52	−213	−1,540
1975	1,665	2,752	1,166	406	440	−289	−2,810
1976	2,840	3,287	1,402	398	362	−377	−2,232
1977	3,309	3,832	945	394	−95	−418	−1,350
1978	3,829	4,332	735	338	−56	−500	−1,020
1979	3,809	4,994	838	653	−43	−412	−2,221
1980	4,263	6,037	790	278	219	−472	−2,589
1981	5,581	6,728	195	284	58	−532	−1,152
1982	6,619	7,012	301	403	265	−473	−890
1983	7,513	7,296	768	35	335	−602	−320
1984	6,156	7,576	−135	65	−443	−568	−339
1985	5,359	6,300	−369	108	−4	−634	−42
1986	6,072	6,482	−934	114	−465	−456	1,332
1987	5,123	5,672	−1,063	99	−221	−714	1,350
1988	5,967	5,819	−1,200	242	16	−805	1,895
1989	5,047	5,751	−261	84	207	−1,305	571
1990	3,423	5,166	−311	114	−185	−5,645	4,284

Table A.38 *Central government capital account (£m): 1948–1990*

	Savings	Depreciation	Net fixed capital formation	Stock appreciation	Physical increase in stocks	Net capital transfers paid	Net acquisition of financial assets
1948	606	77	37	24	−62	−145	675
1949	628	79	37	−8	−48	−172	740
1950	694	82	46	118	−211	−176	835
1951	617	91	83	93	75	−117	392
1952	382	102	116	−32	75	−45	165
1953	225	104	118	−32	49	−37	24
1954	240	106	87	−5	−126	−87	264
1955	510	114	87	15	−114	−64	472
1956	423	123	106	0	−26	−58	278
1957	535	130	122	0	−36	−85	404
1958	630	134	119	0	−9	−85	470
1959	500	133	129	0	−10	−114	362
1960	209	135	131	0	−16	−119	78
1961	376	90	137	0	6	−137	280
1962	678	73	154	0	8	−113	556
1963	247	75	164	0	−8	−141	157
1964	570	76	224	0	−3	−106	379
1965	944	79	229	0	−1	−52	689
1966	1,196	80	263	0	0	−64	917
1967	1,275	85	318	0	−3	165	710
1968	1,852	91	372	0	3	380	1,006
1969	3,047	102	394	0	6	339	2,206

Table A.38 (*cont.*)

	Savings	Depreciation	Net fixed capital formation	Stock appreciation	Physical increase in stocks	Net capital transfers paid	Net acquisition of financial assets
1970	3,643	113	477	0	4	249	2,800
1971	2,940	130	485	0	7	371	1,947
1972	1,288	147	507	0	17	155	461
1973	1,093	179	606	0	21	256	31
1974	852	236	734	0	15	230	−363
1975	−676	311	950	0	−9	440	−2,367
1976	−2,262	370	1,037	0	2	609	−4,280
1977	−898	425	869	0	50	685	−2,926
1978	−2,985	483	809	0	31	1,246	−5,554
1979	−1,830	576	984	0	−35	946	−4,300
1980	−2,246	713	1,048	0	43	1,092	−5,142
1981	−3,831	806	1,062	0	−93	904	−6,510
1982	−4,142	848	1,382	0	155	1,009	−7,536
1983	−4,423	889	1,608	0	246	1,107	−8,272
1984	−5,802	933	1,795	0	280	1,373	−10,183
1985	−3,630	1,021	2,105	0	450	1,080	−8,286
1986	−3,932	1,117	2,234	0	−237	588	−7,634
1987	−1,003	1,224	2,134	0	−498	400	−4,263
1988	9,371	1,342	2,367	0	−322	−72	6,056
1989	13,676	1,543	3,408	0	−163	1,415	7,473
1990	9,125	1,737	4,661	0	155	6,186	−3,614

Table A.39 *Local authorities' capital account (£m): 1948–1990*

	Savings	Depreciation	Net fixed capital formation	Stock appreciation	Physical increase in stocks	Net capital transfers paid	Net acquisition of financial assets
1948	79	86	290	0	0	−24	−273
1949	82	92	296	0	0	−45	−261
1950	81	99	315	0	0	−16	−318
1951	84	120	354	0	0	−13	−378
1952	84	136	425	0	0	−15	−462
1953	116	139	498	0	0	−30	−491
1954	119	145	462	0	0	−27	−461
1955	113	161	424	0	0	−15	−457
1956	129	175	428	0	0	−14	−460
1957	170	186	413	0	0	−20	−409
1958	175	195	380	0	0	−26	−374
1959	211	197	413	0	0	−27	−372
1960	248	205	424	0	0	−31	−350
1961	191	218	511	0	0	−31	−507
1962	221	233	622	0	0	−39	−595
1963	271	253	693	0	0	−45	−630
1964	336	270	916	0	0	−53	−797
1965	298	287	899	0	0	−56	−832
1966	390	311	1,037	0	0	−62	−896
1967	396	330	1,242	0	0	−91	−1,084
1968	410	361	1,355	0	0	−122	−1,184
1969	452	399	1,360	0	0	−122	−1,185

Table A.39 (*cont.*)

	Savings	Depreciation	Net fixed capital formation	Stock appreciation	Physical increase in stocks	Net capital transfers paid	Net acquisition of financial assets
1970	470	446	1,407	0	0	−126	−1,257
1971	685	512	1,450	0	0	−123	−1,155
1972	706	599	1,492	0	0	−104	−1,281
1973	799	750	2,138	0	0	−79	−2,010
1974	593	888	2,525	0	0	−15	−2,805
1975	1,310	1,105	2,627	0	0	−33	−2,389
1976	2,166	1,287	2,725	0	0	6	−1,851
1977	1,806	1,440	2,082	0	0	25	−1,742
1978	1,611	1,609	1,797	0	0	−33	−1,762
1979	1,470	1,916	1,749	0	0	−92	−2,103
1980	1,165	2,397	1,494	0	0	−80	−2,646
1981	2,628	2,709	95	0	0	−42	−134
1982	3,120	2,725	−518	0	0	174	739
1983	2,347	2,788	584	0	0	775	−1,800
1984	2,022	2,873	1,118	0	0	614	−2,583
1985	2,009	3,066	680	0	0	−30	−1,707
1986	2,403	3,289	869	0	0	−393	−1,362
1987	2,665	3,501	718	0	0	−285	−1,269
1988	1,843	3,920	−1,123	0	0	−260	−694
1989	1,816	4,372	259	0	0	−1,498	−1,317
1990	4,930	4,413	1,730	0	0	−1,291	78

Table A.40 *Gross fixed capital formation by sector (£m): 1948–1990*

	Personal sector	Company sector	Public corpor- ations	Central govern- ment	Local author- ities	Total
1948	228	542	175	114	376	1,435
1949	248	582	258	116	388	1,594
1950	261	638	283	128	414	1,725
1951	281	638	356	174	474	1,923
1952	320	646	408	218	561	2,154
1953	391	688	483	222	637	2,421
1954	493	804	527	193	607	2,624
1955	586	975	566	201	585	2,912
1956	608	1,157	590	229	603	3,187
1957	594	1,353	674	252	599	3,472
1958	668	1,388	712	253	575	3,596
1959	634	1,568	780	262	610	3,854
1960	753	1,784	808	266	629	4,240
1961	822	2,041	929	227	729	4,747
1962	794	2,064	964	227	855	4,904
1963	870	2,022	1,060	239	946	5,136
1964	925	2,479	1,231	300	1,186	6,121
1965	1,174	2,675	1,292	308	1,186	6,635
1966	1,210	2,707	1,455	343	1,348	7,063
1967	1,365	2,680	1,665	403	1,572	7,684
1968	1,583	3,097	1,615	463	1,716	8,473
1969	1,535	3,559	1,482	496	1,759	8,832
1970	1,603	4,014	1,676	590	1,853	9,736
1971	2,295	4,104	1,858	615	1,962	10,834
1972	2,879	4,542	1,771	654	2,091	11,937
1973	2,771	6,139	2,068	785	2,888	14,650
1974	2,774	7,298	2,857	970	3,413	17,311
1975	3,772	8,124	3,918	1,261	3,732	20,806
1976	4,305	9,630	4,689	1,407	4,012	24,043
1977	5,443	11,734	4,777	1,294	3,522	26,770
1978	6,222	14,767	5,067	1,292	3,406	30,754
1979	8,226	17,478	5,832	1,560	3,665	36,761
1980	9,355	19,531	6,827	1,761	3,891	41,366
1981	9,785	19,684	6,923	1,868	2,804	41,063

Table A.40 (*cont.*)

	Personal sector	Company sector	Public corpor-ations	Central govern-ment	Local author-ities	Total
1982	12,007	20,944	7,313	2,230	2,207	44,702
1983	13,863	20,649	8,064	2,497	3,372	48,445
1984	14,800	26,062	7,441	2,728	3,991	55,022
1985	15,663	31,893	5,931	3,126	3,746	60,359
1986	18,182	33,242	5,548	3,351	4,158	64,481
1987	21,772	40,167	4,609	3,358	4,219	74,125
1988	28,287	49,666	4,619	3,709	2,797	89,079
1989	27,203	59,702	5,490	4,951	4,631	101,977
1990	26,108	61,819	4,855	6,398	6,143	105,322

Table A.41 *Increase in value of stocks held by sector (£m): 1948–1990*

	Personal sector	Company sector	Public corpor-ations	Central govern-ment	Local author-ities	Total
1948	94	412	32	−38	0	500
1949	70	226	33	−56	0	274
1950	105	428	14	−93	0	454
1951	182	896	84	168	0	1,330
1952	−5	−87	44	43	0	−4
1953	30	19	−37	17	0	28
1954	67	262	−65	−131	0	133
1955	82	507	39	−99	0	529
1956	66	379	27	−26	0	446
1957	61	300	67	−36	0	391
1958	22	27	23	−9	0	63
1959	63	172	10	−10	0	235
1960	94	715	−10	−16	0	783
1961	83	309	8	6	0	406
1962	43	110	1	8	0	161
1963	39	295	−42	−8	0	283
1964	101	805	11	−3	0	913
1965	82	727	4	−1	0	812
1966	66	508	42	0	0	617
1967	83	205	72	−3	0	357
1968	121	731	17	3	0	872
1969	159	1,269	−27	6	0	1,407
1970	116	1,387	63	4	0	1,570
1971	213	559	134	7	0	913
1972	218	1,149	70	17	0	1,453
1973	621	3,661	121	21	0	4,423
1974	703	5,938	289	15	0	6,944
1975	367	3,032	846	−9	0	4,236
1976	789	5,672	760	2	0	7,223
1977	941	5,733	299	50	0	7,023
1978	757	4,820	282	31	0	5,889
1979	1,165	9,312	610	−35	0	11,052
1980	479	2,796	497	43	0	3,815
1981	413	2,455	342	−93	0	3,117

Table A.41 (*cont.*)

	Personal sector	Company sector	Public corpor-ations	Central govern-ment	Local author-ities	Total
1982	422	1,884	668	155	0	3,129
1983	696	4,268	370	246	0	5,580
1984	514	5,470	−378	280	0	5,886
1985	430	2,573	104	450	0	3,557
1986	520	2,549	−351	−237	0	2,481
1987	807	5,934	−122	−498	0	6,121
1988	1,351	9,738	258	−322	0	11,025
1989	1,266	9,058	291	−163	0	10,452
1990	1,090	4,505	−71	155	0	5,680

Table A.42 *Capital transfers and taxes (£m): 1920–1990*

	Personal sector	Company sector	Public corporations	Central government	Local authorities	Rest of world	Total
1948	99	−64	−4	−145	−24	138	0
1949	160	−55	−42	−172	−45	154	0
1950	106	−51	−3	−176	−16	140	0
1951	124	−32	−5	−117	−13	43	0
1952	97	−32	−5	−45	−15	0	0
1953	116	−42	−7	−37	−30	0	0
1954	144	−23	−7	−87	−27	0	0
1955	117	−26	−12	−64	−15	0	0
1956	106	−18	−16	−58	−14	0	0
1957	125	−11	−9	−85	−20	0	0
1958	128	−10	−7	−85	−26	0	0
1959	155	−7	−7	−114	−27	0	0
1960	172	−15	−7	−119	−31	0	0
1961	185	−9	−8	−137	−31	0	0
1962	172	−12	−8	−113	−39	0	0
1963	204	−9	−9	−141	−45	0	0
1964	182	−13	−10	−106	−53	0	0
1965	133	−14	−11	−52	−56	0	0
1966	156	−19	−11	−64	−62	0	0
1967	170	−228	−16	165	−91	0	0
1968	233	−422	−69	380	−122	0	0
1969	397	−544	−70	339	−122	0	0

Table A.42 (*cont.*)

	Personal sector	Company sector	Public corporations	Central government	Local authorities	Rest of world	Total
1970	359	−406	−76	249	−126	0	0
1971	327	−492	−83	371	−123	0	0
1972	376	−306	−121	155	−104	0	0
1973	327	−295	−150	256	−79	−59	0
1974	321	−248	−213	230	−15	−75	0
1975	302	−420	−289	440	−33	0	0
1976	63	−301	−377	609	6	0	0
1977	−75	−217	−418	685	25	0	0
1978	−301	−412	−500	1,246	−33	0	0
1979	−196	−246	−412	946	−92	0	0
1980	−253	−287	−472	1,092	−80	0	0
1981	−88	−242	−532	904	−42	0	0
1982	−367	−343	−473	1,009	174	0	0
1983	−1,019	−261	−602	1,107	775	0	0
1984	−1,266	−153	−568	1,373	614	0	0
1985	−422	6	−634	1,080	−30	0	0
1986	150	111	−456	588	−393	0	0
1987	268	331	−714	400	−285	0	0
1988	1,246	−109	−805	−72	−260	0	0
1989	759	629	−1,305	1,415	−1,498	0	0
1990	215	535	−5,645	6,186	−1,291	0	0

Table A.43 *Financial reconciliation accounts (£m): 1948–1990*

	Net acquisition of financial assets						
	Personal sector	Company sector	Public corporations	Central government	Local authorities	Rest of world	Total
1948	−385	273	−126	675	−273	−165	0
1949	−447	293	−163	740	−261	−160	0
1950	−359	462	−167	835	−318	−454	0
1951	−418	346	−264	392	−378	322	0
1952	0	726	−264	165	−462	−164	0
1953	90	763	−244	24	−491	−141	0
1954	−199	763	−251	264	−461	−117	0
1955	−222	482	−427	472	−457	152	0
1956	134	646	−395	278	−460	−202	0
1957	174	620	−565	404	−409	−225	0
1958	53	772	−578	470	−374	−343	0
1959	156	613	−597	362	−372	−162	0
1960	335	190	−482	78	−350	229	0
1961	760	64	−564	280	−507	−32	0
1962	714	23	−554	556	−595	−145	0
1963	672	339	−431	157	−630	−108	0
1964	989	−321	−623	379	−797	373	0
1965	998	−305	−624	689	−832	74	0
1966	1,284	−336	−840	917	−896	−130	0
1967	1,081	34	−1,035	710	−1,084	293	0
1968	663	−57	−713	1,006	−1,184	285	0
1969	476	−503	−507	2,206	−1,185	−486	0

Table A.43 (*cont.*)

	Net acquisition of financial assets						
	Personal sector	Company sector	Public corporations	Central government	Local authorities	Rest of world	Total
1970	1,081	−952	−846	2,800	−1,257	−827	0
1971	344	1,008	−1,085	1,947	−1,155	−1,060	0
1972	783	1,003	−752	461	−1,281	−214	0
1973	1,714	−65	−785	31	−2,010	1,115	0
1974	3,893	−2,616	−1,540	−363	−2,805	3,431	0
1975	5,808	71	−2,810	−2,367	−2,389	1,687	0
1976	6,795	311	−2,232	−4,280	−1,851	1,257	0
1977	3,827	2,053	−1,350	−2,926	−1,742	137	0
1978	7,119	2,037	−1,020	−5,554	−1,762	−821	0
1979	8,291	−213	−2,221	−4,300	−2,103	547	0
1980	12,811	240	−2,589	−5,142	−2,646	−2,674	0
1981	13,505	757	−1,152	−6,510	−134	−6,466	0
1982	10,351	1,912	−890	−7,536	739	−4,577	0
1983	6,682	7,224	−320	−8,272	−1,800	−3,514	0
1984	9,274	5,764	−339	−10,183	−2,583	−1,933	0
1985	7,533	5,368	−42	−8,286	−1,707	−2,866	0
1986	2,922	4,854	1,332	−7,634	−1,362	−112	0
1987	−4,111	4,163	1,350	−4,263	−1,269	4,130	0
1988	−14,756	−7,934	1,895	6,056	−694	15,433	0
1989	−5,322	−21,730	571	7,473	−1,317	20,325	0
1990	7,542	−22,572	4,284	−3,614	78	14,283	0

Bibliography

Antonello, P. (1990), 'Simultaneous Balancing of Input–Output Tables at Current and Constant Prices with First-order Vector Autocorrelated Errors', *Economic Systems Research*, Vol. 2, 157–71

Arkhipoff, O. (1969), 'Essai de mese sur ordinateur des comptes nationaux', *Compatibilité Nationale 1966/7*, étude speciale No. 1, Direction de la statistique et de la compatibilité nationale

Bacharach, M. (1971), *Biproportional Matrices and Input–Output Change*, Cambridge University Press

Barker, T. S., F. van der Ploeg and M. R. Weale (1984), 'A Balanced System of National Accounts for the United Kingdom', *Review of Income and Wealth*, Series 30, 461–86

Baxter, M. A. (1992), 'The Production of Fully Reconciled UK National and Sector Accounts for 1988–91', *Economic Trends*, No. 469, 80–98

Begg, I. G. and M. R. Weale (1992), 'Trade Credit', *Economic Trends*, No. 467, 130–6

Britton, A. and D. Savage (1984), 'The Three Measures of GDP', *National Institute Economic Review*, No. 107, 54–60

Byron, R. P. (1978), 'The Estimation of Large Social Account Matrices', *Journal of the Royal Statistical Society*, Series A, Vol. 141, 359–67

Campbell, J. Y. and N. G. Mankiw (1987), 'Are Output Fluctuations Temporary?', *Quarterly Journal of Economics*, Vol. 52, 857–80

Central Statistical Office (CSO) (1968), *UK National Accounts: Sources and Methods*, H.M.S.O.

(1985), *UK National Accounts: Sources and Methods*, H.M.S.O.

(1988), *Economic Trends*, No. 420

(1993a), *Blue Book*, CSO

(1993b), 'UK National and Sector Accounts for 1989–1992', *Economic Trends*, No. 482

Chapman, A. L. (1953), *Wages and Salaries in the United Kingdom, 1920–38*, Cambridge University Press

Cramer, H. (1946), *Mathematical Methods of Statistics*, Princeton University Press

Dunn, G. and D. M. Egginton (1990), 'Balancing the National Accounts: An Asymptotically Maximum-likelihood Approach using Trends', Bank of England Technical Paper No. 35

Durbin, J. and H. Fischer (1953), 'The Adjustment of Observations with Applications to National Income Statistics', Mimeo, Department of Applied Economics, Cambridge

Engle, R. F. and M. Watson. (1981), 'A One-factor Multivariate Time Series Model of Metropolitan Wage Rates', *Journal of the American Statistical Association*, Vol. 76, 774–8

Evans, G. B. A. and N. E. Savin (1982), 'Conflict among the Criteria Revisited: the W. l and LM Tests', *Econometrica*, Vol. 50, 737–48

Feinstein, C. H. (1965), *Domestic Capital Formation in the United Kingdom, 1920–38*, Cambridge University Press

(1972), *National Income, Expenditure and Output of the United Kingdom: 1855–1965*, Cambridge University Press

Godley, W. A. H. and C. Gillion (1964), 'Measuring National Product', *National Institute Economic Review*, No. 27, 61–7

Harvey, A. C. (1989), *Forecasting, Structural Time Series Models and the Kalman Filter*, Cambridge University Press

de Jong, J., J. C. Nankveris, N. E. Savin and C. M. Whiteman (1992), 'Integration versus Trend Stationarity in Time Series', *Econometrica*, Vol. 60, 423–35

Kendall, M. (1980), *Multivariate Analysis*, 2nd Edition, Charles Griffin

Kendall, M. and A. Stuart (1993), *The Advanced Theory of Statistics*, Charles Griffin

Kenny, P. (1989), 'An Investigation into Balancing the U.K. National Accounts, 1985–1987', *Economic Trends*, No. 424, 74–103

Kenny, P. (1991), 'Work on Balanced Accounts in the CSO: History and Prospects', *National Institute Economic Review*, No. 135, 79–85

Lawley, D. N. and A. E. Mitchell (1971) *Factor Analysis as a Statistical Method*, Butterworth

Lomax, K. S. (1959), 'Production and Productivity Movements in the United Kingdom since 1900', *Journal of the Royal Statistical Society*, Series A, Vol. 122, 185–210

Mahalanobis, P. C. (1936), 'On Generalized Distance in Statistics', National Institute of Science, *Proceedings*, Vol. 2, 49–55

Mood, A. M. and F. A. Graybill (1963), *An Introduction to the Theory of Statistics*, McGraw-Hill

Ploeg, F. van der (1982) 'Reliability and Adjustment of Sequences of Large Economic Accounting Matrices', *Journal of the Royal Statistical Society* Series A, Vol. 145, 169–94

Rao, C. R. (1945), 'Information and the Accuracy Attainable in the Estimation of Statistical Parameters', *Bulletin of the Calcutta Mathematical Society*, Vol. 37, 81

Satchell, S. E., R. J. Smith and M. R. Weale (1992), 'Measurement Error with

Accounting Constraints', paper presented to the Royal Economic Society Conference, London

Solomou, S. and M. R. Weale (1991), 'Balanced Estimates of UK GDP: 1870–1913', *Explorations in Economic History*, Vol. 28, 54–63

(1993), 'Balanced Estimates of National Accounts when Measurement Errors are Autocorrelated: the UK 1920–38', *Journal of the Royal Statistical Society*, Series A, Vol. 156, 89–102

Statistical Digest of the War (1951), HMSO and Longmans, Green and Co.

Stock J. H. and M. W. Watson (1989), 'New Indices of Coincident and Leading Economic Indicators', in *NBER Macroeconomics Annual*, MIT Press, 351–93

Stone, J. R. N. (1954), *The Measurement of Consumers' Expenditure and Behaviour in the United Kingdom: 1920–38*, Vol. 1, Cambridge University Press

Stone, J. R. N., J. Bates and M. Bacharach (1963), *Input-Output Relationships, 1954–1966, A Programme for Growth*, Vol 3, Chapman and Hall

Stone, J. R. N., D. G. Champernowne and J. E. Meade (1942), 'The Precision of National Income Estimates', *Review of Economic Studies*, Vol. 9, 111–35

Stone, J. R. N. and D. A. Rowe (1966), *The Measurement of Consumers' Expenditure and Behaviour in the United Kingdom: 1920–38*, Vol. 2, Cambridge University Press

(1980), 'The Adjustment of Observations', mimeo, Department of Applied Economics, Cambridge

(1987), 'How Accurate are the British National Accounts', in *Specification Analysis in the Linear Model*, ed. M. L. King and D. E. A. Giles, Routledge & Kegan Paul, 253–67

US Bureau of Economic Analysis (1989), *National Income and Product Accounts of the United States*, Vol. 2

Weale, M. R. (1985), 'Testing Linear Hypotheses on National Account Data'. *Review of Economics and Statistics*, Vol. 90, 685–9

(1986), 'The Structure of Personal Sector Short-term Asset Holdings', *Manchester School*, Vol. 54, 141–61

(1988), 'The Reconciliation of Values, Volumes and Prices in the National Accounts, *Journal of the Royal Statistical Society*, Series A, Vol. 151, 211–21

(1992), 'Estimation of Data Measured with Error and Subject to Linear Restrictions', *Journal of Applied Econometrics*, Vol. 7, 167–74

White, H. (1980), 'A Heteroscedasticity-consistent Covariance Matrix Estimator and a Direct Test for Heteroscedasticity', *Econometrica*, Vol. 48, 817–38.

Index

Note: References preceded by 'A' indicate table numbers in part three (pp. 180–315)

For EU product safety concerns, contact us at Calle de José Abascal, 56–1°, 28003 Madrid, Spain or eugpsr@cambridge.org.

www.ingramcontent.com/pod-product-compliance
Ingram Content Group UK Ltd.
Pitfield, Milton Keynes, MK11 3LW, UK
UKHW042211180425
457623UK00011B/156

* 9 7 8 0 5 2 1 1 2 0 0 7 4 *